MASTERING
TECHNICAL
ANALYSIS

OTHER BOOKS IN THE MCGRAW-HILL TRADER'S EDGE SERIES

MASTERING
TECHNICAL
ANALYSIS

USING THE TOOLS OF TECHNICAL ANALYSIS FOR PROFITABLE TRADING

JOHN C. BROOKS

McGraw-Hill

New York   Chicago   San Francisco   Lisbon   London
Madrid   Mexico City   Milan   New Delhi   San Juan
Seoul   Singapore   Sydney   Toronto

1 2 3 4 5 6 7 8 9 0 DOC/DOC 0 9 8 7 6 5

ISBN 0-07-144882-9

This publication is designed to provide accurate and authoritative information in regard to the subject matter covered. It is sold with the understanding that neither the author nor the publisher is engaged in rendering legal, accounting, or other professional service. If legal advice or other expert assistance is required, the services of a competent professional person should be sought.

—From a Declaration of Principles jointly adopted by Committee of the American Bar Association and a Committee of Publishers

McGraw-Hill books are available at special quantity discounts to use as premiums and sales promotions, or for use in corporate training programs. For more information, please write to the Director of Special Sales, Professional Publishing, McGraw-Hill, Two Penn Plaza, New York, NY 10121-2298. Or contact your local bookstore.

Library of Congress Cataloging-in-Publication Data

Brooks, John C.
    Mastering technical analysis : using the tools of technical analysis for profitable trading / by John C. Brooks.
        p. cm.
    Includes index.
    ISBN 0-07-144882-9 (hardcover : alk. paper)
  1. Investment analysis. 2. Stocks. I. Title.
    HG4529.B74 2005
    332.63'2042—dc22

                                                            2005009357

Contents

MASTERING
TECHNICAL
ANALYSIS

Chapter 1

Technical Analysis from My Perspective

I began my career as a technical analyst on Wall Street in October of 1964 working for the brokerage house F.I. Dupont & Co. The job itself was as a posting clerk in the technical Research Department, and my duties included updating a 4000 Point and Figure chart library every morning before the opening bell. Every chart was to be ready before the opening and done neatly in pencil. It was about as far down on the Wall Street food chain as you could go in those days, but at least it got me into the game. Make no mistake about it, being given that opportunity by my friend and mentor, John D. Greeley, has made me very grateful to this day. I was able to land a job in lower Manhattan simply because the daily trading volume on the New York Stock Exchange had expanded all the way up to the breakneck level of 5 million shares a day. The Street was having a hard time keeping up with the increase in activity, so hiring new blood was the order of the day. It was an era of new trends in business and in our social lives. Innovation in technology was touching every single area.

This atmosphere was a result of a very healthy economy, low interest rates, low inflation, and a recent military success, a la the Cuban missle crisis. It was hard to argue with success, for the United States was running on all cylinders. The rate of unemployment would drop in the 1960s from 7 percent in 1959 to as low 3 percent by 1970. Leading economic indicators were strong, especially in the first half of the decade. Money supply was plentiful, which helped finance a rising stock market as well as a hot IPO (Initial Public Offering) arena.

I listen today about stories of the Internet and how it will change my life forever and that the world will never see another period like this again. Perhaps this will turn out to be a true statement, but I can assure you that I've seen it before. I have to shrug my shoulders and laugh a little sometimes. I can't help but remember one night when my mother came home from work where she was employed as a secretary. She told us about the excitement in the office that day because a new machine had arrived, and it seemed that it could make copies of documents and memos simply by touching a button. Up until that time, if management wanted a few extra copies of a report for distribution, those copies would have to be made by a secretary simply by repeating the task over and over again. Sometimes they could use carbon paper if they were lucky to have a boss who didn't mind a little ink stain on the reports. It seemed, however, now with this new-age gadget, no more carbon paper for that woman. It was the 1960s and they were getting their new machine. She could not remember the name of the company that made this awesome machine, but she thought its name started with a letter X.

In those days it seemed like there were an abundance of new opportunities opening up every week. They were going to change our lives and in fact they did alter almost every facet you can imagine. New "everything" was the order of the day. There were concepts from fast food stores to color TVs, calculators, supermarkets, and even computers were being introduced to the public. Up to then, these superbrains were only known to us via badly made sci fi movies. I don't believe that many people realized how much this tool called a computer was about to alter the landscape. It seemed like the sky was the limit and all you needed was a concept and Wall Street was there to finance your dreams and help you go public with a new offering.

In 1961 and 1962 they reached a level of approximately 70 IPOs a month, and in 1968 and 1969 that level was increased to more than 100 IPOs a month. This level was the record until the start of the next great bull market in 1983. Even with that, the 1968 level was only exceeded three times over the next 30-plus years. Given the fact that the capitalization of the total market in the 1960s was a lot smaller than today, I'd have to say those were very impressive numbers indeed. Of course, with all these new deals hitting the market on a daily basis, the average trading volume exploded. The explosion of volume was Wall Street's way of expressing its acceptance for any new idea. Between 1960 and 1970, daily trading volume on the New York Stock Exchange increased from approximately 2 million shares a day to over 15 million shares a day.

From my vantage point there were a number of events that occurred on the Street within a fairly short period of time that helped to shape modern technical analysis. For one thing, with the sharp increase in daily volume, Wall Street brokerage firms were pressured to answer more requests for stock ideas from the customers, who were getting more aggressive as the market rallied. The public wanted to enter into the stock market, and technical analysis was there to fill in the gaps. This also was the time when analytical computers first appeared on the scene that would prove to be the launching pad for many new technical indicators. Finally, the advent of a major long-term bear market in the second half of the 1960s moved technical analysis into the spotlight and propelled the art to center stage of the financial world. You see, a technician's function is to interrupt charts based on the "price" facts. To a good technical analysis, a sell opinion is the natural progression in a stock's life. A stock will rise in price, then flatten out, and then start its decline. At the time not only were sell ideas a no-no on Wall Street, but many fundamental analysts feared for their jobs if they did tell accounts to sell. It just wasn't done, for the simple reason that technicians were better suited to sell stocks on breakdowns of chart patterns that made us more popular during bear markets.

Despite the bear markets from 1966 to 1974, most of the technical analysts I knew did fine in those days as long as we kept to our knitting. I recall once that I tried to stray off the path and did not recommend a sale of a stock that had broken a support level because it was a "good company." Also, I believed that it was a "solid value" and perhaps a small violation of a support could be overlooked. My friends reminded me that I was a paper trader, meaning I was dealing with stock certificates and I was not asked to give my dissertation on some company's long-term prospects. That fine company stock eventually sold off 75 percent.

The stock market was in a full retreat, and fundamental analysis was getting a black eye almost on an hourly basis. Unlike the scandals in our recent history, the analysts back then were folks, I believe, that were trying their best. The only scandal was that most had never seen a long-term bear market and as a result could not fathom how deep a sell off could go. Wall Street is noted for its "gallows humor" and I will say that by the time the bottom in 1974 appeared, the quality of the jokes about the business was the best vintage that I have ever seen. I remember going out to lunch one day during the 1973–74 bear market and running into a friend that had just been promoted to research director at one of the firms (life expectancy was about 1 year). He said he felt like he was promoted to first mate on the Titanic.

A MISSED OPPORTUNITY

I must say that as technicians, we knew from firsthand experience that certain price patterns had implications that were totally rational. A stock breaking down from a top pattern on expanding volume was not only a clear sign showing the sellers overpowering the buyers, but also an early warning that some negative corporate news was about to be announced. We didn't know "when" and we didn't know "what," but we knew if the stock was falling away and breaking supports levels that any upcoming news wasn't going to be good. This response to upcoming developments was reflected in the increase in daily volume and the price movement on the chart.

Indicators carry the same predicative qualities. It is not strange to me that an increase in volume accompanied by a positive increase in price in the housing market index might have a secondary implication generated about lumber prices or perhaps the health of the market in general. I remember an analyst came out with a recommendation on the auto industry one year after the stocks had already rallied for more than 6 months. My response was to recommend the tire and oil sectors, mainly because the charts looked better, but also the Street hadn't gotten around to those groups yet. The last time I looked you can't run a car without four tires and a tank of gas, therefore the tire and oil stocks had to benefit from a boom in auto sales.

This kind of thinking was second nature to most of us. It was the fault of the technical community, and I include myself, that we never took the time to back test many of our theories or indicators and tools, but rather relied on street knowledge to get us through the day. Had we devoted more time to back testing and proving our work, we would have had a much easier time in many board meetings during the next 20 years. One major problem at the time was that we had limited access to price history. The vast majority of technical analysts had all their data and their notes in old dusty books. It was impossible to go to any university with that type of data and expect to be given an audience.

Besides, the campuses at that time were more concerned about demonstrators against Vietnam rather than any indicators that my colleagues and I could dream up. Wall Street was in trouble, as a great bear market had taken up residence in lower Manhattan.

In the 1973–74 period the Dow Jones Industrials Averages would drop from a high of 1047 in Dec. 1972 to as low as 577 in Oct. 1974, a 55 percent decline. There have been enough books written about that time, but as perverse as it might sound, technical analysts thrived during that period. After all, this was our type of market, a market of multidimensional movers. Technical analysts, on the whole, helped many a firm avoid some very nasty pitfalls during those times. Most of the people that worked in the finance community had only seen stocks move up for most of their careers. Brokerage houses that never had an official TA department up until then found it to be a good idea to have someone in the research department that actually watched the stock market. Many of the senior people in the firms felt that having their own technical department was an irrational move. They felt that the stock market would bail you out of any bad positions over time. Keep in mind that from Pearl Harbor to 3

FIGURE 1-1

Chart of the Dow from 1942 to 1966. Drawn by The Chartstore.com.

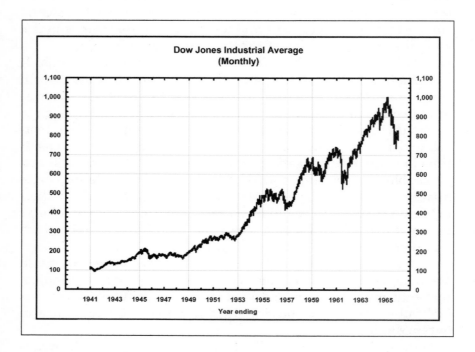

years after the Cuban Missile Crisis, the stock market was nothing but up, up, and away. The idea of a declining stock market, for any meaningful period, was not really a viable opinion for many of the old timers. Like the man said, "In a bull market, who needs *any* analysts' help." The typical thinking of the times was, "If prices always went up, why worry about the market?" Over time that expression was changed to, "In a bull market, who needs *any* analysts, and in a bear market, who can afford one?" (See Figure 1-1.)

The bear market of the late 1960s to the mid 1970s showed the world that attention must be given to the overall markets and thus focused attention on technical analysis. New indicators were beginning to appear in the marketplace. Negative volume, MACD, Stochastic, and the Arms Index were all offshoots during this period.

The growth in technical analysis that I spoke of came with the growth of financial markets in general. By the late 1970s, daily volume had expanded to more than 30 million shares a day, and public interest in the stock market was once again on the increase. The start of the 401k programs was a great driving force in this increased interest.

It gave the public a vested interest in stocks, and along with that interest came the demand for more information. It had been a long time since stock tips were a source of conversation at cocktail parties, but here we were again. This time, however, the information was much more meaningful in nature. Investors weren't looking for the next "hot idea" as much as they were looking to understand what the investment process was all about. The demand for information exploded on the financial front. The investor of the 1980s wanted to know the reasoning for purchases and sales. They wanted to know about all the terminology that sounded like so much double talk from the brokerage houses, the fundamentalists, the technicians, and the economists. They were willing to invest, but they wanted to know the whys and wherefores of their investments. (See Figure 1-2.)

After the shellacking we took in the 1966–1974 bear markets, the market came back slowly. The damage that was done to the big indexes such as the Dow Jones and the S&P 500 was obvious. The declines for these major averages were on the nightly news shows and on the front pages of morning papers. The worst damage, however, was felt in the smaller companies, where losses of 70 percent to 90 percent were registered during that same period. These issues that were not well known suffered from being overlooked by investors because of the general fear of the market and the lack of liquidity that smaller stocks generally carried. They had gone down much deeper than their nationally known counterparts. If Chase Manhattan Bank could fall from the mid $62 down to $21, a percentage drop of 65 percent, what chance did much smaller, regional banks have in attracting buyers?

However, in time these overlooked and washed-out stocks did attract buyers as investors began to recognize two facts: First that the general market had bottomed, which meant that

FIGURE 1-2

Chart of 1966–1974. Drawn by The Chartstore.com.

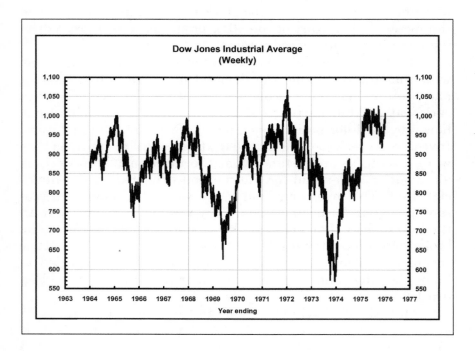

it might be safe to go back into the market. Second, that in making the bottom, many of these underowned issues were drastically oversold and offered a better bargain. This shift in thinking first showed up on the charts in 1975–1976.

Conclusions that had never been attainable before were now showing up every day. The breadth index is the net difference between stocks that are advancing minus the stocks that are declining over a given time. It is one of the best indications of the overall health of a market. It gave us a view of a sum of all the issues in the marketplace. For 8 long years the advance/decline line had fallen, which reflected the bear market and the faltering economy. But once that A/D line began to reverse and move up, technicians had a more constructive outlook on the market. It was showing that for the first time since the top of the Dow Jones in 1966, more stocks were advancing rather then declining. There is only one way to make that indicator turn up, and that is to have the buyers overpower the sellers. We all started thinking maybe that light at the end of the tunnel wasn't a 900-pound gorilla with a flashlight coming at us to give us another beating. Again, here was a typical example of bare bones indicators that was lost on many people on Wall Street. The one unshakable truth about the financial markets is that the forces of supply and demand are the ultimate keys to understanding the market. Without a doubt there are other forces to contend with, but they all come in second place compared to supply and demand. (See Figure 1-3.)

Overall, money was flowing into stocks, and demand for these overlooked issues had absorbed the supply of stock for sale. This time money was going to value issues rather than the very narrow group of favorite brokerage stocks that were called the "Nifty Fifty." These were issues whose earning and growth rates were never questioned. These growth stocks were

FIGURE 1-3

ADV/DEC. Courtesy of MetaStock.

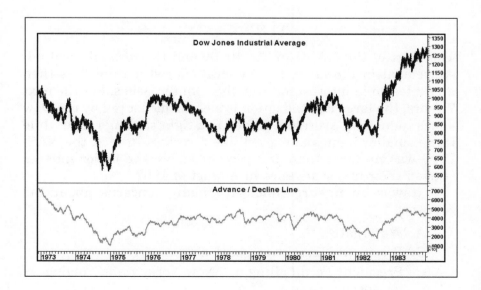

publicized as simply one-decision stocks; you always buy them. Wrong again. The day of the one-decision stock was over. The markets once again were growing, and so was technical analysis about ready to have another growth spurt.

One of the causes of this growth was the availability of data and the computer. Some of the new tools that we were using helped us in spotting shifts in investor's psychology. These were created by men like Gerald Appel on the development of MACD, George Lane on Stochastics, and Wells Wilder on RSI. These were all part of the new landscape. By no means is this a complete list of innovators.

Investors were getting smarter and realized that many of the smaller capitalized companies that had been hurt in the bear market would be one of the first beneficiaries when the economy began its resurgence. So a reaccumulation of secondary issues became the new mantra for the market. For most of this century, the New York and American Stock Exchanges were the two key marketplaces. In the mid 1970s plans were underway to move trading for non-NYSE issues upstairs off the floors and into the trading rooms, which nearly spelled the death knell for the American Stock Exchange. To this day the Amex, which once was a powerful force in the business, is hardly even remembered.

THE NASD

The start of the NASD in the 1970s and the technological advancement in the market in general caused nothing less then an explosion in interest for over-the-counter issues. For the next 7 years, the large capitalization issues, as measured by the Dow Jones Industrial Averages, traded in a tight trading range while these smaller names advanced like a rocket. In fact, the NASDAQ was up more than 450 percent before the major indexes started their major advance in August of 1982.

It was an unsure time with many concerns about the country:

A. Watergate

B. President Nixon's resignation

C. President Ford bailing out New York, via arranging for special loans

D. Iran and the Ayatollah Khomeini

E. The Three Mile Island nuclear accident

But through it all, the technical indicators were improving despite the disconcerting news.

NEW INDICATORS

The new work that was appearing on the scene showed new ways of looking at the same old data, and the personal computer was the reason we were able to go to the next level of analysis.

At the time, economists were interested in a totally difference set of numbers like the Gross National Product, earnings growth projections, and signs of economic improvement. Many of those types of numbers didn't even begin to turn strong until the 1980s. There was not a lot of interest in something called the A/D line. The fundamentalists were looking at falling earnings and the traders were just hoping their telephones wouldn't ring. If they picked up a phone it might be an account wanting to sell stock to them, and the traders wanted no part in building up their inventories. So studying technical indicators was not popular at the time.

Between the bottom of 1974 and the explosive breakout in 1982, the Dow Jones Industrial Average was stuck in a trading range of approximately 500 points. It did nothing but rally and fall and rally and fall. But under the surface, stock prices generally were increasing. The NASD from the end of 1974 to the summer of 1982 rallied nearly 400 percent by the time the Dow finally began its upward move. In August of 1982, the Dow Jones exploded on the upside with more than 100 million shares of volume, and the race was on. Not only was the stock market back, but also it was back with a vengeance. And the appetite for equities and knowledge about the markets was insatiable. The daily volume in the first half of 1982 swelled to more than 60 million shares on a daily basis, and once again new indicators and techniques were created.

This hunger for information was not going to be held back. The street needed a new way of communicating with the public because the demand was too great to be handled in the same old-fashioned way of one company research report at a time.

Similar to the time I first got my job on Wall Street, the volume
and interest was overwhelming. The financial markets and new
methods of communicating had to be forged if we were going to
prosper. Some of the new tools of the stock market were televi-
sion shows dedicated to the stock market. Shows like *Wall Street
Week*, *Financial News Network,* and the *Nightly Business Report* were very popular in the mid 1970s.

But the real quantum leap was with the improvements in
the personal computer and the coming of age of the Internet.
The computer gave the public a chance to gather information
and make decisions on their own. Although the PC was around,
it had not yet reached a level of being user friendly. Once that
leap was made, the public no longer had to rely solely on the
opinions of the others. The Internet was the natural extension
to the PC. Although it had been around for 30–40 years, the access to this tool was very limited and not available to the vast
majority of the world. As computers became more people
friendly, the public became more engrossed with the opportunities. Once the public got interested in the www's of the world,
we had another explosion on our hands. It led to online trading,
information research, order placement, more activity, and a reduction in commissions and the discount brokerage house.

ACADEMIA

With the introduction of the World Wide Web, we were also introduced to vast amounts of information and databases on almost any subject. We could now build anything from a sailboat
to an atomic bomb on information pulled from this system. We
were also able to obtain data from Wall Street with some very
long term history behind it. In the 1980s and 1990s, we began
to see a marked increase in white papers on the subject of technical analysis because finally enough data could be gleaned to
have some real value. I remember that a long time ago I was
asked to draw a 2-year chart of IBM with a high–low close and
volume as well as a few indicators. That one chart took me 5
working days to build. Now we're able to pull thousands of charts
and hundreds of thousands of data points at the touch of a button. For the first time, academics had an opportunity to roll up
their sleeves and go to work. With almost no effort, data was

available in mass quantities to allow studies to be performed. For the academic community, there was another side to this new interest in technical analysis. In this subject they had new, fertile ground that had not been overanalyzed and written about ad nauseam. There had been little in the way of "white papers" or studies published on this part of the financial markets, and now that they could get their hands on long series of data going back 50 years or so, they were much more willing to pursue the task. In the university system the adage "publish or perish" has some very real meaning, and now there was a whole new field to be written about. With technical analysis, they now have indicators, techniques, and stock chart patterns to test and study.

As a result, technical analysis is being put into the spotlight, and the interest has never been so great. The new books that are being published on the subject mean that we have new eyes looking at the same data. This is great because we have begun to see new indicators and new approaches to the stock markets. Also, many of our old indicators have begun to be rediscovered and put to some real test. A good friend of mine, who happens to be a professor at a major university, came to me one day and made an announcement that he had *found* one of the true pearls of wisdom about the stock market. Of course I was eager to find out this new revelation and ask him to share his findings. He told me that after going back over 30 years of data on his new powerful computer, he had discovered that by tracking a simple set of numbers that are reported in the newspapers daily, an investor could get a real handle on the age-old question as to the direction of the markets. The gem that he found was the New High/ New Low index. He discovered on his own that when the number of daily new highs was larger than the number of new lows, a positive market outlook was justified. Conversely, when the new lows exceeded the new highs, a danger flag was given. I was reluncent to tell him that indicator was one of the oldest in the field because he had done his own original research and was proud of the results, just like I had been 30 years earlier when I was first told of this barometer. The difference was that when I was told about the indicator, I accepted it for the truth on its face value because it made prefect sense to me. My professor friend had to prove it to himself before he would believe it. Big difference. Doing the legwork on an indicator and back testing the results so that we could have quantitative proof on even one indicator was a great step forward. That was the kind of proof that my generation had failed to produce, and/or they just never took the time to do the necessary work to show TA in a true academic light.

THE BEGINNING OF IFTA

Another major step forward for modern technical analysis was the launching of the International Federation of Technical Analysts, which I am proud to say I had a major hand in launching in 1985 in Monterey, California. Never did I dream that we would end up with a worldwide organization for technical analysts with a membership of 7000 plus and growing. This society has been a great boost to technical analysis around the world and demonstrates its global appeal. It offered, for the first time, a platform for technical analysts to present their new ideas and approaches and to proselytize the subject at the same time on a global basis. All of a sudden we were thrown into the international arena and exposed to a new set of challenges on the international front. At the outset we had only a few member countries: Japan, England, Canada, and the United States, and again the word spread quickly. We also saw that most of the technical work that was being done in other parts of the world used the same tried-and-true methods that we use in the States, but every now and then a new idea would bubble up and catch everyone's eye—like the Kagi charts or Filter Trading rules of Minoru Eda from the Nippon Technical Analysts Association in Japan. These are just a few concepts with new perspectives that we have come across in our contact with IFTA.

Now that I have laid out the background of technical analysis during the past 50 years, let's get started on some of the old and some of the new aspects of this profession. Technical analysis is a combination of both science and art. The numbers generated from price and volume carry the aspect of science, while the interpretation of how these numbers interact with each other shows the art function of TA. I will try in the coming chapters to turn many of the chart patterns and indicators into common sense and common language for you.

Chapter 2

The Forces of Supply
and Demand

There are two general approaches to analyzing the various markets that an investor might choose: fundamental and technical analysis. There is a third avenue called "quantitative analysis," but because it is nothing more than technical/fundamental analysis by the numbers, I'm going to let someone else spend the time explaining the difference. I think it was Shakespeare who said, "A rose by any other name would smell as sweet." I promise I will not quote poetry again unless it's a limerick.

There is no question as to the camp in which I belong, but at the same time I believe that fundamental analysis has its place and I recognize that it is an acceptable approach in the business of financial analysis. The business of money is very difficult indeed, and in my opinion anyone who ignores pertinent information concerning his or her investments is a plain fool. I am not a fundamental analyst, but I know the general outlook and earning of my companies and I have a working knowledge of the economic overview of the current market. Anyone who tells you they don't use one side or the other is simply playing Five Card Stud with four cards. You must be able to understand how the two styles differ in their handling of the stock market.

Technical analysis is the study of the forces of supply and demand and how they relate to financial markets and instruments. The media we use to accomplish this study are charts created from the data generated in those markets. We believe that following the price and volume of any financial instrument and then analyzing its chart enables us to forecast future price movement with a high degree of accuracy.

The fundamental approach is the study of economic statistics and the data concerning the corporations within the general economy. The fundamentalist studies the corporate books and pertinent information about an industry and/or a company, thereby trying to determine the company's valuation price. If it is determined that a stock is above the valuation level the analyst placed on a stock, then it should be sold. If, however, the perceived value is at or below the current price, then a buy would be warranted.

In my mind there are a few problems with the fundamental approach. One major glitch that is hard to overlook is the time delay between the "market and the fact."

It is generally accepted that the stock market is a discounting function. In the government figures, the Dow Jones Industrial Average is listed as a leading economic indicator because it points the way that the investors' expectations are leaning. The reason is the market is the sum total of everyone's opinions and outlook. This makes the "market" something that will respond to the question of "What is a discount or an overvaluation?" much faster than it takes for a research report to be released or the actual news to be read in the newspapers or seen on TV. Therefore, the fundamentalist is always behind the times. Being somewhat late to react in a market is not a fatal flaw, as the fundamentalist tends to be geared toward very long term investments and there is certainly nothing wrong with dotting the "i" and crossing the "t" before you invest.

Another difficulty that I have with fundamentals is that many times I have the feeling that what is being analyzed is incorrect. There is a huge difference between the company ABCD Inc. and the stock ABCD. The fundamentalist works hard studying the company while the technician works hard studying the stock of the company.

The technical approach studies the markets themselves for knowledge. Instead of corporate books and news items and a mountain of government statistics, they tend to the let "price" do the talking. By following the forces of supply and demand, we believe that we can project the likely trends of markets or stocks. We technicians study market indicators and chart patterns to forecast the markets.

Many of the tenets of technical analysis were first put forward by Charles Dow at the turn of the twentieth century, and from his general observation, modern-day technical analysis was born.

DOW THEORY

Charles Dow (1850–1902) was the founder of *The Dow Jones News Service* as well as the first editor of the *Wall Street Journal*. As the editor, Mr. Dow wrote articles for the *Journal* based on his observations of the stock market. He never wrote his ideas in a book, but his articles were in many ways the bedrock for today's technical analysis. It wasn't until after his death in 1902 that Mr. S.A. Nelson, a writer himself, published Dow's articles. He was the first to use the term "Dow Theory" and it apparently stuck. In 1922, William Peter Hamilton, the editor of the *Wall Street Journal* put Dow's work together in a general framework in his book *The Stock Market Barometer*. But it was Robert Rhea that formalized Dow's work into rules that are still in use today. Arthur A. Merrill, a fine technical analyst, wrote in his book *Behavior of Prices on Wall Street* a brief biography for Mr. Rhea.

> Because of an airplane accident in the first World War, Mr. Rhea was bedridden from 1918 to the time of his death.
>
> In Colorado Springs, he began a study of the Dow ideas—first as a hobby and later as a profitable vocation. His own wealth accelerated from the practice of his (Dow) ideas. He was long stock through most of the 1920s: he had no stock at the time of the 1929 crash; he thereafter sold short for two years.

The vast amount of the credit for his success was given to Charles Dow's theories.

The First Steps

Charles Dow built an index that was made up of the major industrial companies of the day. His thinking was that by following the "right" stocks you could create a barometer of the business trends.

At first many of his efforts towards designing an average met with less than the level of success he desired, and he was sent back to the drawing board to do a rethink. He reasoned that a second group would be needed to act as a confirming element to the action of the industrials, and he developed the Dow Jones Railroad Averages comprised of 20 issues. The thinking was straightforward and made all the sense in the world. The industrial companies that he first worked with "made" the goods that ran the economy, but it was the rails that delivered those goods to the public that enabled the sales to take place. At that time, railroads were the major mode of transportation in the United States. The rail acted as a double check on the industrials. Therefore, a fully engaged bull market would have both the industrials and the rails traveling in the same directions and making new highs together. On October 7, 1896, for the first time *The Wall Street Journal* began publishing a piece called the "Daily Movement of Averages" and ran an average price for both the 12 industrials and the 20 railroads. Just for your information, those first closing numbers were

12 Industrial $35.50
20 Railroads $48.55

There are dozens of great texts on the life of Charles Dow, but for our purpose allow me to hit some of the high spots. Dow had a number of principles, but I believe the most important was that closing prices reflect the sum total of all investors' current feelings towards stocks. Outside of the acts of God, like wars or earthquakes, etc., the collective thinking of investors is shown in today's closing price. In other words, it is price that gives us knowledge. By the close of the trading day, everyone who wished to make their feelings and analysis known has had their opportunity to do so by purchasing or selling shares in the open market. Therefore, the closing price of a stock is, in theory, the sum of everyone's outlook for that instrument.

Stages of the Market

Charles Dow also believed that stocks had three phases of trends

a. Primary bull and bear stage, lasting over a year and setting the general directional tone of the market

b. An intermediate phase lasting 4–6 months, which acts as contra moves to the longer term move

c. A short-term phase, which was considered noise lasting a few days to a few weeks

In his works he compared these stages to the ocean, and even though his explanation is a cliché, after all these years it is still very good imagery. The primary move is the tide coming in or going out, while the intermediate moves are the waves that made up the tide, and finally the short-term moves are like the froth on the top of the waves.

Confirmation

Some of the other observations that Mr. Dow made were equally amazing when you remember he made these findings in 1900–1902. He further stated that volume confirms price moves. If we look at this statement from the standpoint of supply and demand, it is a very same belief found in every economic textbook ever written. If a stock is in demand by the public because it is felt that the price will rise, then the amount of stock being bought must increase to reflect that demand. Mr. Dow felt, therefore, that an expanding volume pattern during a rising price trend was the confirmation you wanted to see for a strong stock. Just as important, he also noticed that during periods of normal retrenchments, the volume slowed. Although he looked at volume as secondary to price, it was still an important part of his theory. He felt that if the volume was expanded while the stock was in a decline, then that might be an indication of a major top. In a minor pullback, demand should gain the upper hand because supply will slow, not because supply has increased. He also felt that a rally without volume behind it was suspect. A price rally would seem to suggest that there is positive thinking about a stock, which should in turn attract buyers. If, however, we witness a stock lifting on low volume, we must assume that the rally might not have a long life. Again, I believe he was watching the basic rule of economics, which states that the principle of supply and demand will dominate price action.

Of course he felt that the industrial and the railroad averages must confirm each other. The industrials moving to new highs without the rails was reason for concern. This is only one of his findings, but it is the one fact that I believe most investors are most aware of when talking about Dow Theory.

Today, many people think that Dow's Theory might be antiquated and very slow to respond to changing market conditions. That might or might not be true, but it still is a solid method of avoiding major declines or missing major advances.

THINK ABOUT AN UPDATE

It might also prove to be a great place for some energetic person to mix and match some new names in order to do a little updating of the indexes to keep pace with the times. To the best of my knowledge, the last time the Dow Indexes were seriously adjusted was on January 2, 1970 when the Dow Rails Index was replaced by the Dow Jones Transportations. In this new index, nine railroad stocks were deleted and the new, modern means of transport were added, which included truckers and airlines issues. Up until that time the DJRs were strictly 20 homogeneous railroad issues. For me, the 1970 version still works quite well, but perhaps if we were to look to the index once again with an eye to update its function, we might improve on a great tool. By adding a few service areas like the Internet or Bio-tech Index to the industrials, and perhaps something from the information highway to the transportations, we might come up with a new look to a very important piece of research. Over the years there have been dozens of small adjustments, which for the most part have been a correct step. What I am suggesting is taking a giant leap on the scale as they did in 1970, when they lessened the dominance of the railroads and modernized the purpose of the index. It's just an idea.

Keep in mind that Mr. Dow's work is considered to be the base from which modern-day technical analysis was built. Without his early observations and the subsequent work done by people like Nelson, Hamilton, and Rheas, technical analysis might have taken a completely different path.

THE MAIN DRIVING POWER

There are many fine books on the subject of technical analysis that are in-depth and cover the subject from top to bottom. A curious thing, though, about most of these market books is that the concept of the forces of supply and demand are always treated as secondary to price movement. It's not that these forces are overlooked, but rather they are de-emphasized in favor of techniques or some new tool that appeared on the financial scene.

Let me state early on in this book that it is my belief that the constant struggle between these two dynamos of supply and demand are the primary engine to the whole market. I really don't care if it's economic, fundamentals, technical, or some other form of analysis that we are talking about, it is the tug of war that goes on between buyers and sellers that causes price change, patterns to be formed, and economies to expand and contract, even earnings to rise and fall. So I'd like to spend a little time exploring these forces to demonstrate why we need to place them in a paramount position in your analysis of the market.

It is surprising to me how often people will forget their common sense when entering into the financial markets. Because of the availability of powerful computers and access to large pools of data, novices to the business come up with the most outlandish systems and approaches in their efforts to understand the markets and stocks.

In today's society, we teach people how to land a rocket on the moon, but we neglect to teach them how to fly an airplane. The people who enter the financial markets are the same. The level of their sophistication is much higher than ever before, but I do get the feeling that the level of understanding is not what it should be.

With that in mind, I would like to say that I believe that the major thread that we should carry through our analysis must be that supply and demand are the most powerful, overriding factors in our decisions.

This thing we call technical analysis is part science and part art, and I believe that if you understand the interaction of these forces, then the patterns that are formed and the price action of indexes just might come alive to you. Charts almost take on a quality of being alive after awhile because they tend to get into a rhythm, and for long periods of time you can follow their footprints easily.

THE MARKET

Let's look at the stock market from ground zero and see if we can make some sense out of it all. One of the items that you will be dealing with from now on is the concept of "the market." When you are asked for your opinion, usually the first question out of a person's mouth will be, "What do you think about the market?" You might as well get used to it because it's going to happen. But the question is not as important as it once was.

In the 1950s, 1960s, and to a great degree the 1970s, there really were only two markets that both institutional and retail accounts employed. You either went to the stock market or the bonds. Today, however, with the power of computers and our chances to enter options, commodity markets, the international arena, ETFs, currency pits, etc., I have all but reached the conclusion that there is no such thing as "the market." Which means, of course, that when you respond to the question, "What is your market opinion?" your answer should be, "What segment of the market do you mean?"

Any historic textbook that you read about the Dow Jones Industrial Averages mentions that one of the reasons that that index had only 30 stocks in it was because it was a much easier job managing a 30-issues list rather than a 100-issues list. Everything was done by hand and in pencil at the turn of the last century. So the "KISS" method was vital. Today, however, there are averages and indexes on anything and everything you can imagine. They even have an index on Zimbabwe to the price index of Adzuki beans.

The net result is that you can find large pools of stocks trading in opposite directions at all times regardless of "the market" opinion. It is true that there have always been places to hide money during hard times, and a few groups that would offer some yield havens. But what I am referring to is a segmentation of the entire market so that we can follow a multitude of markets all within the same time frame. When the 2000 bubble popped for the technology issues and all of those day-traders' plans for early retirement faded, the midcap and secondary markets for both the NASDAQ and the NYSE enjoyed a significant rally. (See Figure 2-1.)

Two years earlier in 1998 we saw the advance/decline line on the New York Stock Exchange go into a nosedive that lasted more than a year, while tech stocks exploded in their parabolic patterns. A few years earlier we had to deal with a stealth bear market while the Dow Jones average only declined 9 percent for the year, while the rank-and-file issue was suffering a much worse pullback.

Understand that we will always be seeking sectors, groups, or styles of investing for ideas to sell or to buy. But the days of telling your customers or some TV show that the market has

FIGURE   2 - 1

S&P 500 versus S&P 600. Courtesy of MetaStock.

topped or bottomed might be over for good. This belief comes
from the fact that there are just as many places and investment
choices that can be made today that allow investors and traders
the alternatives that have always been lacking. I haven't even
mentioned that the difficult entry into international markets
has been all but removed, so not only do you have many new
choices of investments domestically, but internationally as well.
Taking your money and putting it in the bank vault is just not
a smart move even in a bear market. Sure, I know if we go into
another depression then all bets are off, but because I don't believe that one is around the corner, I'll take my chances in making that statement.

Let's look at some numbers. In the area of institutional accounts, by some records they make up roughly 85 percent of all
daily trading volume on the NYSE. With the advent of 401k retirement plans and the growth of the mutual fund business,
John Q. Public has turned a great deal of their funds over to
professional portfolio managers. While it is true that there is a
much larger percentage of the public in the stock market today
than in the past, the vast majority of that money is handled by
the professionals. These managers are paid to invest the funds
and not to hold cash for long periods. The majority of these mega
accounts are unable to build up much more than a 10 percent
cash position even in the worst of times. So the institutions that
make up the lion's share of the daily trading are required to invest the money regardless of any directional move by the market. On one hand, during declining periods, this tends to slow
any decline, as their buying will absorb a large part of the selling as they invest cash on hand. It is also the case that as the
stock market declines, these long-term investors get to buy shares
at greatly discounted levels, and if they can hold long enough,
they tend to reap the benefits of buying at those discounts.

I am not trying to reinvent the laws of the stock market by
thinking that bear markets can be avoided. Be advised that once
a market is in a declining mode, there is no amount of cash that
will stop it from declining until a final low is reached. I am not
proposing that we will not have declines. But money can flow
into sections of the market both foreign and domestic that can

mitigate a drop. In the bad old days, there weren't many choices one could make; not so today.

THE NEW PLAYERS

A hedge fund is a fund that can take positions in the market on both the long side (buy side) and the short side (sell side), depending on their outlook.

Most of the time they maintain positions on both sides at the same time and simply overweight one side for leverage. These accounts can act as a great stabilizer during overbought/oversold market conditions. The popularity of these funds has been remarkable, but when you consider that investors want the flexibility to defend their portfolios in case of a major downturn, maybe their popularity is not so hard to figure out. The latest numbers available show that there are approximately 7000 hedge funds in the market. That can make for some very interesting market action when you get these new players working in the same direction.

The point is that simply saying we are in a bear or bull market is no longer good enough. Segmentation is most likely the newest trend that we are going to witness in the early part of the twenty-first century. The word segment means "a section or a division of a thing." Segmentation is therefore the act of forming into sections or divisions. That seems to be what is happening to the internal workings of the markets. Between the dozens of market indexes and the ETFs and group and sector funds, we have broken the marketplace down to many smaller markets, and most of those markets are electronic, which makes their accessibility simple. A large portion of the trading today is done away from the established exchanges, and that trend is growing.

You must know at least what indexes are available to you and what they are designed to accomplish. To list them here would be a pointless effort because every day new products are coming into the marketplace. The purpose is to allow for diversification of funds and to offer the investor dozens of ways of avoiding financial calamities.

When you look at an index, know what that index represents. Products are too specialized in today's market. One size does not fit all. If you were to buy the QQQQs, you're buying an index that reflexes the NASDAQ top 100 issues, which are mostly technology stocks. Therefore a purchase of the QQQQs is a bullish comment on technology. If you buy the Diamonds (DIA), another popular derivatives product, you are buying a proxy for the Dow Jones Industrial Averages. So you must know what you want to buy and then you must know what product will give you the desired mix to attain your goals.

Pattern Recognition

Pattern recognition is a term you will hear from here on if you decide to choose technical analysis as a career. When we look at charts, we are actually looking at a visual record of the transactions that have occurred in the marketplace for that day, week, month, etc., depending on the time scale of the chart. It makes no difference what type of financial instrument we are referring to: stocks, bonds, commodities, currencies, etc., but for the sake of consistency I will be mostly talking about stocks or indexes. The combination of a stock's support /resistance, trend lines, volume patterns, human emotions, and many other factors all add up to form price patterns. These patterns have repeated themselves over the years enough times so that they have become highly predictable, which in turn can be quite valuable to your pocketbook.

We will cover the major categories of chart patterns to make the point. If you can understand the *"why"* of these patterns, then you will be able to understand what forces are influencing a stock and you will find that you are more than halfway to your goal of winning in the stock market. Never, however, think you can replace your brains and common sense with a chart pattern. These patterns are tools, not sacred scripture from the mount. Rather, think of the patterns as road signs that are there to guide you on your way.

Patterns are created as a result of the interaction between the forces of supply and demand. When I say forces, I use the word to reflect a real battle situation where buyers and sellers in the marketplace pull and tug at each other all the time, trying to gain the best price. Perhaps it's not as intense as a Blue Light special sale at Kmart, but you get the picture.

We used some examples in Chapter 2 and hopefully they should stay with you as we look at patterns. Markets and stocks, and pretty much anything that has a bid and an ask connected to it, can do only three things: go up, go down or trade sideways.

If there were a general shape of a stock's typical price pattern, it would be contained in four segments:

a. A base-building period
b. The breakout and uptrend stage
c. A period of distribution and loss of momentum
d. The declining stage

The technical analyst must look for and spot the transition from one phase to another. We find that past is prologue, and by studying the various patterns that have continually been repeated over the last 100 years, we can maneuver with a greater amount of conviction through all trends of any market. This is not to say that mistakes can't happen; there will be mistakes, but in our business you can fix a mistake easily by admitting your error and cutting your losses before they get severe. Here comes a Brooks' truism: "The market is never wrong; it's you." Many a great trader or analyst has been carried out on a stretcher thinking she is right on a position and the market just doesn't understand. I promise I will not tell too many war stories, but this one might help you understand that you must listen to the stock market and not to the noise that is always buzzing around that market. The best example of the indicators and fundamentals telling you one thing and the market telling you something else is found in my distant past. In the mid-1970s I was running a fair-size portfolio that was 100 percent on the short side of the market. It was 1974 in October and we had already turned in a very solid performance, more than doubling the money. (See Figure 3-1.)

FIGURE 3-1

The DJIA Market 1968–1976. Drawn by The Chartstore.com.

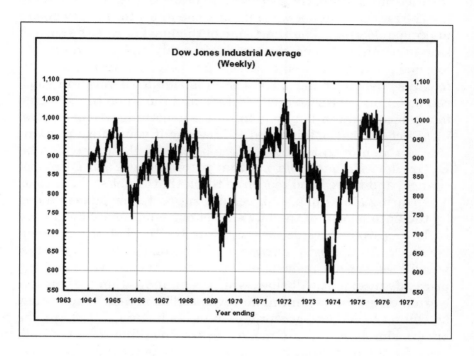

All the right stocks had been shorted and the market had the glide path of a brick. The news could not have been worse, and the ticker tape looked like 10 miles of bad road. Fundamentally, the earnings numbers were falling and the economy had the distinct appearance of the Titanic breaking apart and sinking. For a "short seller" it would be difficult to ask for a better atmosphere.

At the end of each day my last job was to calculate the profit or loss of the portfolio and report that day's results to the head of the firm. On October 4, 1974, after the market had fallen 100 points in one week (which back then was a big deal), the net gain of that portfolio of $42 million dollars was $112 net. The boss and I looked at each other, and we both said, "Tomorrow we cover and go long." You see, the market was telling us that it was drained out, and after almost 24 months of down-side pressure, there was little left for sale. The stocks were making their lows before the averages. In other words, we were reading the market and not waiting for some indicator to turn before making a decision. The short side of the market was the correct side to be on, but then the forces of supply and demand began to come into balance and reverse, and therefore our market outlook also had to change. The lesson is simple: If you find yourself swimming with an anvil—*let go*, and the same thing is true for an incorrect market opinion. There is nothing wrong with an incorrect market opinion, but it is wrong if you refuse to fix it.

My mentor in the business is a man by the name of John D. Greeley. He once told me that a technician's job is to spot change, and there is no reason to think that is not still the case.

During a bull phase, prices are supported or pushed along by the enthusiasm of the buy side of our equation. New money is flowing from the sidelines and into the market or a particular stock. As the price advances and becomes more expensive, we will see the enthusiasm of the buyers start to wane and the price advancement will slow, which is an indication of their forward momentum beginning to reverse. The investor might now be willing to sell and accept a gain in his holdings. Perhaps the buyers simply ran out of money or are unwilling to pay a high price for the issue that had run up so far. As technicians we really care little why investors have changed their collective minds. It is more important to know that they have in fact changed their minds and for us to take the appropriate action. What we find is that as the forces of supply and demand come into balance, the stock price will flatten and eventually turn down.

PATTERNS

When you examine the market overall, there are two major divisions of patterns. Either a stock is ending a trend or it is working within a trend. By ending a trend I mean that a major top or a major bottom could be developing. These are known as "reversal patterns" and have long-term implications connected to them. Usually, when a reversal pattern is completed, we expect a significant magnitude move, as well as a longer time period in the opposite direction of the previous trend. Calling a pattern that is two weeks old "a reversal pattern" is silly to me, but then again I'm not a short-term trader. "One man's meat is another man's poison," as they say.

We will look at one category at a time and try to make the point that in all the patterns we are looking at opinions, emotions, and supply and demand.

a. The stock market would not be the stock market without opinions. Everyone, and I mean everyone, has an opinion. You will get bombarded with them from early morning until the 11:00 o'clock news. Being able to stay on top of events and keeping abreast of things that affect the markets is a key facet to this or any business. The problem with our area is "information overload." I wonder sometimes if I really need to know the prices of pork bellies while I'm eating my breakfast. But then all opinions and world events that are influencing investors should be known to you in order to accomplish your task. So it becomes a necessary evil and something we live with.

b. Those overloaded opinions we just talked about can create quite a stir with investors' emotions in short periods of time. There is a whole new method of investment analysis that has sprung up over the last 10 years or so called behavioral finance. This is a study of why people do what they do. They hope that by studying the investor habits, we can become better at the investing game. We'll see.

c. The culmination of opinions and emotions leads us to the most important element in the world of technical analysis—supply and demand. Emotions are not real; they are simply emotions and if not acted upon, dissipate over time. Opinions are just that, opinions, and everyone has one. In fact, most people have two. I remember back a long time ago Alan Ableson, editor of *Barron's,* wrote in his column that there were only two people in the world that positively knew what the price of gold was going to do. He added . . . "One said up and the other said down." That's about par for the course. But supply and demand can't be ignored. These powers determine price, and price is what determines chart patterns. So in your daily work, get caught up in the moment, listen to other people, and learn. *But* before you open your wallet, look at the charts and find out what is really going on in the marketplace. If demand is more aggressive than supply, then prices will rise; however, if supply is able to overwhelm the demand, prices will fall. Often it can be as simple as that.

Reversal Patterns

When you look for reversal patterns, there are a few general characteristics that should be present for a reversal pattern even to exist. For us to have a reversal pattern there is an assumption that there was a preexisting long-term trend in the first place, and of course the longer a trend has been in existence, the more significant the reversal. Reversal patterns are considered major in scope. When we refer to them we are usually speaking of something that can be signaling a change of direction for a number of months or perhaps a few years. Remember, a technician wouldn't automatically call a top of a two-week rally a major reversal pattern.

There is another traditional element that goes hand in glove with a reversal pattern. There must be a break of an important support or resistance level as a prerequisite for this pattern to be completed. We could see a trend channel or long-term trend line violated, but there must be signs that the existing supply/demand picture has not only slowed for our stock, but that the predominate forces have in fact been overtaken.

I think I'll stick in another Brooks's truism here. It seems in our business "God takeith away much faster then he giveth." It seems that for major patterns, and in all patterns in general, tops are made much quicker than bottoms. Once that uptrend is violated, action is required relatively quickly. In the case of major lows, however, you'll find that after a long period of decline, investors might not be so eager to reenter the market. If that sounds like the words of experience, it is. Been there, done that.

That statement makes solid sense when you think about the dynamics involved. We are dealing with OPM, "Other People's Money," so I can cavalierly say to get out of a position or to buy into a bottom. The reality is that when it comes to real money, people tend to protect their cash much faster then they will risk it. At major bottoms it is usual for a period of consolidation to occur in order for investors to be convinced that it is safe to reenter the market. Many times we will see a number of tests of a low point before a reversal takes hold. Finally, after some time in a base pattern, buyers become aggressive enough to push prices above an important resistance level.

These patterns are created and can be explained just by thinking of it as a constant battle of supply and demand for dominance. Many times when we work with pattern recognition, you will find that "volume" will be the determining factor in your decision. Patterns can look alike and leave a lot to be desired as to predictive powers, and you will learn how to include volume as a confirming indicator in your studies. I will cover the question of volume in a later chapter. (See Figure 3-2.)

F I G U R E   3 - 2

A Bottom with Volume Indicators. Courtesy of MetaStock.

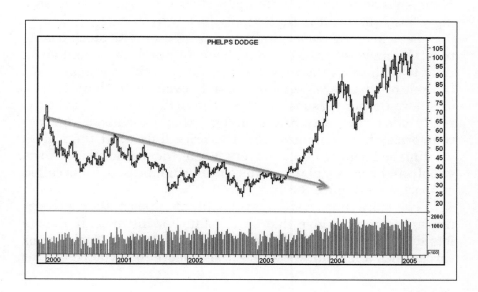

Support and Resistance

I have introduced new terms into this talk that I need to spend some time explaining. The terms resistance and support will have to become second nature to you if you ever intend to earn a dime in this business. The names of these tools are straightforward, which is saying lots in a profession that has gone out of its way to use obscure terminology. Here is where the rubber begins to meet the road in a study of the forces of supply and demand. The word "resistance" means exactly what it is intended to imply. A stock price will rally as buyers chase after the shares due to their belief that the price will continue to lift, based upon whatever information they are using. The stock is in an uptrend because we witness a series of higher highs and higher lows. At some point the buyers begin to be satisfied, and they start to feel that either they have all they want or that the price has risen high enough as to exceed any reasonable valuation. There's a word that will get you into a lot of trouble, valuation. I save that discussion for my next book, entitled "What, Am I Nuts?" Anyway, we see the sellers begin to gain the upper hand and they turn the stock back down. That equilibrium point has just become "resistance." It is a point in the stock's price history that will have to be penetrated in the future if the price is going to continue its upward rise. Another way of saying what I just said is that supply has overcome demand.

Let's keep the concept alive for a minute. The stock begins to fall because sellers wish to take advantage of the recent stock rally to cash in on their good fortune, or possibly the reason for the selling is a news item, or possibly even some short sellers, or a dozen other reasons. Always keep in mind that technicians really don't care why prices change; they care about the fact that prices have changed. But the price falls until the sellers are finished selling or the buyers, a.k.a. "demand," absorbs the supply and prices stabilize. This equilibrium price point is called support. (See Figure 3-3.)

The more times a stock level holds at support, the more significance we must give that data point. For instance, if a stock found support at 25 and successfully tested that level two or three times and held, we would assign more importance to that

FIGURE 3-3

Support/Resistance.

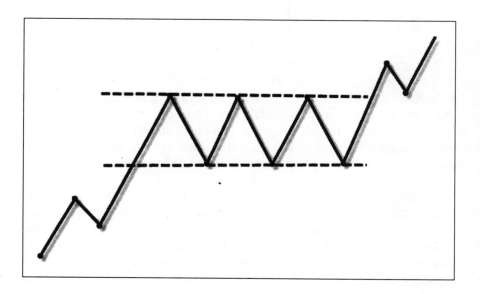

level than if it were a single test. Having touched an equilibrium point a few times and then to violate that point would carry more negative implications than if we were looking at a simple downtrend developing. The same is true for resistance points. If a point has been tested a few times on the upside and then is penetrated, a technician will assume that a new up leg is unfolding. To state it clearly, the supply of stock that had been present at that certain area has been removed and the stock is now free to lift to its next supply area. Where that next area is will depend on the forces of supply and demand again. We now watch for the sellers to impose themselves on the tape with enough force to halt the buyers, at which time a new resistance point would be spotted.

If a price stabilizes at a point higher than its last low, then we have the start of what could be an uptrend, but at this stage all we really have is a support area. Like resistance, we now have a point in this stock's price history called support, where sellers were halted by the demand side of this equation. This constant struggle between supply and demand is what creates support, resistance, trends, channel lines, and just about everything else in technical analysis.

Broadening Patterns

Broadening tops or bottoms can best be described as a failure in price to continue the established prevailing trend. They usually have the appearance of a triangle, but the apex of that formation is to the "left," which gives the pattern the appearance of a megaphone. In other words, you continue to make new highs or lows, but each pullback or rally cuts across the whole trading range back to a support or a resistance point.

In the case of an uptrend, we should have a series of higher lows and higher highs. But in a broadening pattern, we have the higher highs, but the lows are now showing support violations. This loss of forward momentum is very important for the long-term outlook for the stock. Let's look on the other side. Let's say that we are in a bear market (declining market) for say 6 months and prices have been falling day after day, establishing a clearly defined downtrend. We finally reach a support zone that halts the decline, but we have no idea if that support is strong enough to stop the decline or just another respite before continuing lower. We need a period of testing before we can make that determination. In a broadening bottom, which is harder to spot, you would see a penetration of a resistance level and then a retest of the support. You might see a few new highs and retests before the pattern is recognized, but once it is spotted it is an indication of a major reversal.

Think of the logic of a reversal pattern from the standpoint of buyers and sellers. In the case of a downtrend being reversed, we have the supply side of our equation in complete control. More sellers appear each day to overpower any demand that shows up in the marketplace. There will be occasional rallies that are short lived and happen on light volume, but those usually are relief lifts and have little in way of real power behind them. One day, however, the price halts and fails to drop to a new low. In itself there is a large change in the existing pattern, but a rally and then a penetration of a previous high is your signal that the reversal might be underway. To accomplish a penetration of a previous high during a bear phase, buyers need to have confidence enough in the market to be willing to "pay up" for something that a few days ago they could buy at reduced prices, just by waiting.

Double Tops and Bottoms

Double tops and bottoms are another type of reversal pattern that is commonly found after a major move in the market. The name of the pattern seems to tell you what to expect. After a long-term move in a direction, a stock or market will reach a high and experience a run-of-the-mill countermove to relieve some of the short-term overbought or oversold condition. This action is normal and raises no major concern. It is when a second attempt to move past the latest resistance or support point fails that we become concerned. With a momentum failure in the price, the pattern is no longer in an uptrend or downtrend but rather has changed into a sideways pattern where the tops or bottoms are the same price. Usually the volume patterns reach their highest point on the first test. Like the broadening pattern, we need to have a break above a previous high or below a support for the pattern to take on the characteristics of a double top/bottom reversal. An important element is that on the break, volume should expand, giving a higher degree of confidence in the opinion. (See Figure 3-4.)

There are triple tops and bottoms also, although they are seen less frequently. Lots of times, however, instead of making a new category out of them, I'd rather place them in the same grouping as the double top. The rules remain the same, namely a failure to extend an existing pattern, a test or retest of a top or bottom in the direction of the prevailing trend, and a penetration of a support or resistance point going in the opposite direction of that long trend. Volume should also increase on that penetration move. I've said this before, but let me emphasize it again. In a declining market, volume patterns in general will decline. Again, it makes perfect sense to expect lower levels of activity if prices are going down. The increase in volume in a bottom appears on the reversal breakout (upside).

FIGURE 3-4

Double Top.

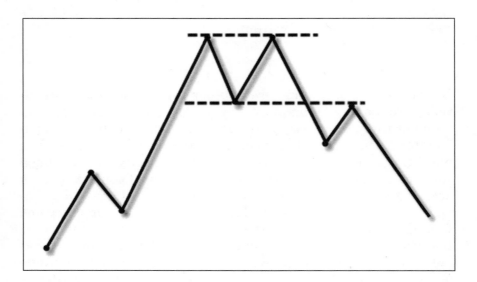

Head and Shoulders

A head and shoulders formation is by far the most misunder-
stood and overused pattern in the business. It is true that this
pattern can be included in both reversal patterns or within a
move sometimes called continuation pattern. Let's look at the
major reversal pattern first. It can be characterized as an exhaustion rally with two smaller rally attempts on either side,
which tends to explain the terminology, head and shoulders.

In this pattern, volume plays a key role and is often the
reason people misinterpret the pattern. Without the volume signature, the H&S pattern does not exist. The volume is usually
the heaviest at the left shoulder of this pattern.

I will attempt to walk you through a normal head and shoulders formation as it would unfold. To begin with we have a stock
in an uptrend running on its normal pattern. It will develop a
short-term correction still within the framework of a normal
move. The next rally that develops penetrates into new high
ground, but this rally is accomplished on lighter volume.

Usually a new high should be accomplished on rising volume and not lower volume. This would be the first warning sign of a possible long-term problem developing. After a normal correction, a third rally attempt is made, but this time there is a failure to reach new high ground, and the volume levels are the lowest yet. What you have is the loss of forward momentum in price as well as loss of demand for this issue.

The failure to attract buying interest during another rally attempt is telling us that the stock or market has run out of the power needed to continue this move. The way we use this pattern to predict price is by drawing a line between the two troughs in the pattern. This is called the neckline. The drop below the neckline is the completion of the pattern. We would measure from the neckline to the highest point in the head for a measurement and then project that down from the neckline. This pattern is usually the one that nonprofessional people abuse and misdiagnose the most. The main reason is they fail to study the volume pattern in conjunction with price, and without the volume pattern of lower highs, you don't have a head and shoulders pattern. (See Figure 3-5.)

FIGURE 3-5

A Head and Shoulder.

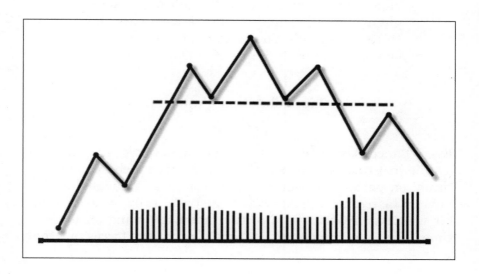

Fan Principle

There is another reversal pattern we should cover. This particular pattern I have always used as a major reversal signal. It usually takes some time for it to fully develop and give us a reliable reading. The fan pattern or principle gets its name because it resembles a "fan." Sometimes when a stock violates it trend line, in either direction, the stock or index will rally back to the bottom of the violated line. A second trend line can be drawn using the original starting point as the first point. Eventually, that second line will be violated and a third trend line can be drawn and again is violated. The main point here is that it is the third violation that gives us the confirmation of a directional move.

Reason out three points to this formation:

1. With the all the rallies back to previous trend lines and the violations in this pattern, there is usually not a drastic loss of price action before you can make a decision. It is true that time has been lost, but usually price has been somewhat stable.

2. Taking that long to form a pattern (up or down) tends to imply a more serious implication as far as magnitude is concerned.

3. This is a perfect example of a shift in power between supply and demand. We can see the two forces struggle in the rallies and the breakdowns. By the time the third violation happens, the fan pattern has been decided. In Figure 3-6, it is decided to the upside.

Consolidation Patterns

Triangles

Even Lance Armstrong has to take a break every once and awhile just to catch his breath. That pretty much explains continuation patterns in general and triangles in particular. A financial instrument finds itself in a strong rally or decline, and for whatever reason the direction has been going on for some time. What will happen many times is that the forces of supply

FIGURE 3 - 6

A Fan Pattern.

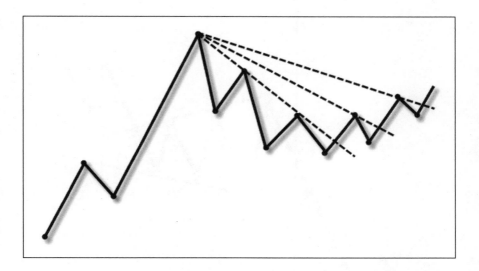

and demand will reach an equilibrium point, and it will form a triangle pattern to allow the buyers and the sellers time to re-group and reevaluate the price action.

There are three types of triangles: symmetrical, ascending, and Descending, and all three are considered continuation pat-terns. There shapes tell a lot about the potential price action.

Symmetrical triangles are resting points for a longer-term pattern. The pattern forms two lines converging. The bottom trend line connects at least two higher lows and the top line must have at least two lower highs.

As the price works its way through the formation, the vol-ume within the pattern declines, which makes perfect sense be-cause this a supposed to be a price level of "balance." The point where the two lines meet is called the "apex of the triangle," and the breakout above or below the trend lines will determine the direction. In symmetrical, they tend to go in the direction of the prevailing longer-term trend, and the breakout of the pat-tern is usually accompanied by an increase of volume. In all

F I G U R E   3 - 7

Symmetrical Triangle.

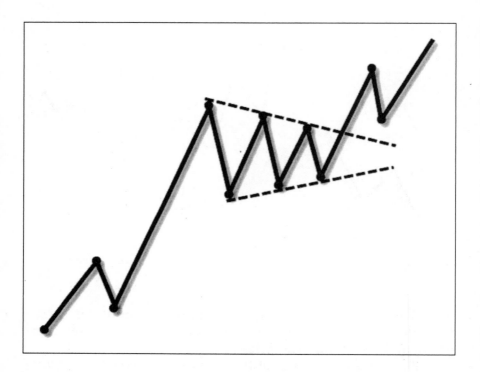

three types of triangles, you will see that a breakout of the pattern tends to occur before the "apex" is reached. Extending into or past the "apex" is a weak sign that there is enough confusion on the part of the investors and traders to stall any decisions. (See Figure 3-7.)

Ascending Triangles   These triangles have many of the same traits as far as needing at least two points on its top line and two points on the lower line. We have the line meeting at an apex, and within the framework of the pattern the volume tends to decrease.

The schematic of the lines are where the real story is told. In the case of the symmetrical triangle, we have lower highs and higher lows. In the ascending triangle patterns, however, we see that the top line is horizontal or flat while the lower line of the triangle has a series of higher lows. Think about the action in the pattern for a minute. A stock will reach a resistance level where the supply and demand for the stock is balanced. The next move should be to downside as buyers ease off for another assault on the top. The next rally is turned back again at the same resistance point, but the following selloff doesn't quite get back down to the support, and it establishes a higher low. The pattern is telling you that the forces are tending to the upside. This rising lower line is key to the outcome of the pattern. (See Figure 3-8.)

Descending Triangles The descending triangle pattern is just about the opposite case of the ascending triangle. The shape of the pattern is the signal you want to watch. Like the other triangles, we need at least two tests of the upper limits and the lower limits to give us the pattern. Here, however, we see that

FIGURE 3 - 8

Ascending Triangle.

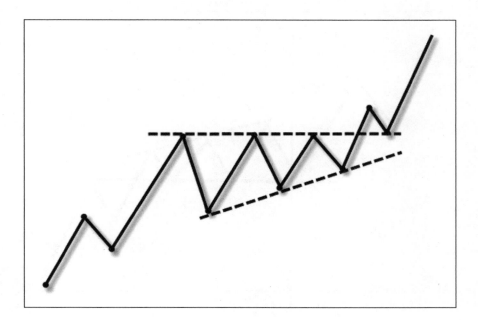

a stock will reach a support line and rally. After being turned down from a rally high, the sellers push the stock back to support, and another rally attempt occurs. This time the buyers run into more aggressive sellers, and a low high is established. The shape, therefore, is a declining series of highs for the upper line to the triangle and a flat lower line. The break is usually to the downside on an increase of volume. (See Figure 3-9.)

Wedges

These patterns are akin to the triangle patterns we have already referred to earlier. The difference with wedges is that they have two trend lines that converge at an apex, but both trend lines are going in the same direction. Wedges can be either rising or falling. A rising wedge is usually found in a longer-term declining pattern. It can seem like the beginning of an uptrend but in fact is it a temporary stabilizing attempt. We have a

FIGURE 3-9

Descending Triangles.

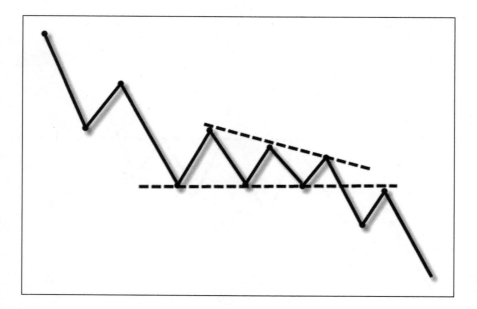

series of slightly higher highs and higher lows. The trend line will meet, and the result is usually a sharp break to the downside. The volume pattern during this respite is declining, and the break is accompanied by heavy volume. The opposite is true for the "falling wedge." After a period of rising levels, a stock can form this falling "wedge pattern" where we see lower highs and lower lows. The trend lines meet at the apex of the triangle, and volume is declining until they reach the apex. The moves for both patterns are accelerated on a volume spike out of the apex. The key point is that the wedge pattern goes against the long trend of the series you're watching. A falling Wedge is bullish, while a rising Wedge is bearish.

Rectangles

A rectangle pattern is as simple as they come. It really is nothing more that a trading range between a resistance point on the upside and a support price below. The tops and the bottoms in the price action chart should allow you to draw parallel lines. The end result is that the pattern resembles a rectangle. This formation is considered a continuation pattern and should break in the direction of the longer trend. That point is not a hard-and-fast rule. The signal for the next move is given with the penetration of either resistance or support. Again, the only way the resistance will be broken on the upside is for the demand side to overpower the supply. Conversely, to violate support we need to see the sellers increase their aggressiveness. But once the price moves outside of that pattern, it will indicate, the direction it is going to take. The length of time a stock is in this pattern will give us an approximate idea of the projection that you might expect from such a move. It is very important that volume increases on the breakout or breakdown, as it is supposed to be making a meaningful signal. If volume remains stationary, you should be concerned about a false signal.

Flags and Pennants

These two patterns are most often locked together in a discussion of patterns. It is an unfortunate fact that much of the terminology that is used in technical analysis is inane and unprofessional, but in the case of flags and pennants it's hard not to use the terminology because that's what they look like.

The shape starts with price having a few days in almost a parabolic move. Because of the sharp swing in price, the stock needs to cool off, as it has gotten ahead of itself or is oversold, depending on the direction. Either way, you will notice that the volume shows a reduction of activity through the pattern.

The differences are a flag will have prices in a rectangular pattern, meaning two parallel trend lines for the week or two before breaking out. The "flag" will be in the countercyclical direction of the major trend. A "pennant" will have the same basic shape, except that the consolidation portion will take on the shape of a symmetrical triangle.

The measuring technique is the same in both cases. The parabolic move in both patterns is called the "flagpole," and on the breakout or breakdown, we extend the length of the pole in that direction for a price target. Both of these patterns are considered short-term pattern.

Gaps

Gaps are best described as vacuums in a price chart. It is an area where no trading occurred on the chart during the course of normal trading, usually because of a sudden shift in thinking about a stock or index. Just as a note, gaps have no place in P&F charts or line charts. A gap is ignored in these two types of charts simply by extending the price points on the P&F and line, so there is no sign of an interruption. So when we speak of gaps we are generally talking about bar charts. Candlestick charts have their versions of gaps called "windows," but by and large it is the same approach.

A downside gap appears when the highest price of a certain period is below the lowest price of the previous day or on the upside when the lowest price on one bar is above the highest point for a previous day. The space created by this action is the "gap." The rule of thumb is that most gaps will be filled eventually. It can take a few days or in some cases a few years, so trying to wait for a gap to fill can be a waste of time. At the very least your reaction to a gap should be to establish a partial position in the direction of the gap. Too many times a move can be missed waiting for a fill. The important implication is that because the demand side or the supply side has exploded with enough force to cause a gap with their aggressiveness, we must respond. A gap takes on more importance if it is accompanied by a large increase in average trading volume.

There are four types of gaps:

a. Breakaway
b. Continuation
c. Exhaustion
d. Island reversals

They all add a different twist to the chart puzzle, and all of them deserve your attention. Their importance is that on a temporary basis the buyers or the sellers have been shoved aside on an emotional investing public, and when that kind of furor is unfolding we need to pay attention.

Breakaway Gaps

Breakaway gaps appear at the conclusion to a price pattern and the start of a new directional leg. Whether the move is up or down, the implications are the same. A typical example would be a consolidation pattern where a stock had been trading in a sideways formation. Your opinion must be neutral until a move over a resistance point or below a support level is successfully accomplished. That directional move can happen by the stock simply trading to new levels and giving us a simple buy signal, or if it happens on a "gap," the implication is that the expectations are explosive enough to create a gap in the price. Increasing volume is key to an upside move, as it acts as a confirming gesture. Downside gaps need not have that characteristic of heavy volume, as sometime traders will walk away from an idea a let the stock fall under its own weight. There are periods when the public simply can't make up their collective minds, and the volume is less important on the downside. In these cases, how-

FIGURE 3-10

Gaps. Courtesy of MetaStock.

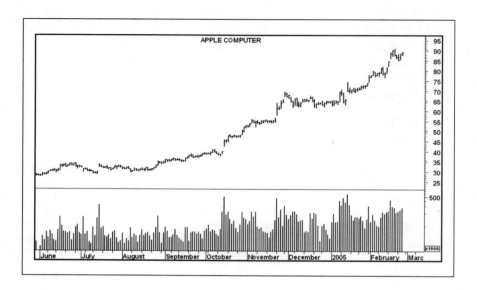

ever, a down gap out of a pattern will still carry a major sell signal regardless of volume. (See Figure 3-10.)

Continuation Gaps

Continuation gaps develop during hot running patterns in either direction. As the name suggests, a gap like this is a signal of a continuation of an existing trend. These gaps seem to appear at the halfway point of a stock's total move. If a stock is in a full retreat and simply cannot find support except for the 4:00 o'clock closing bell, we will sometimes see fear build into a crescendo. It's human nature for people to try to hold onto a position in an attempt to avoid a loss. As the market pressure builds, so does the fear for the ones still holding, and people will panic, causing a gap in the price. This action can be used as a method of measuring for an ultimate price target. We can measure the distance of the original breakout point to the gap as halfway and extrapolate the rest of the move.

Exhaustion Gaps

An exhaustion gap does what its name implies, namely it exhausts the buyers or the sellers, depending on the direction the stock is taking. Say a stock has been having a strong upward advance. The market is great and the news in the company is good and the buyers can't stay away from it. One day we see an upward gap as the stock takes its last hurrah. The volume in this type of gap is usually extremely heavy, and often ends the day with a small price increase. After a few days of consolidation, we might see the price fall below the low of the gap. This is the time that we have a high probability that we have a turning point and that we have, in fact, witnessed an exhaustion gap. The end of the move is now.

I mentioned a fourth type of gap—the island reversal. This example of a gap will be found at the end of a major move. It is distinguished by having a combination of gaps surrounding a neutral price pattern. After a major move, we can witness an exhaustion gap followed by a few days of the forces of supply and demand in balance, and then a breakaway gap. The logic of this pattern is obvious. A stock has run a long way, and after a gap move, the investors see no further progress. In an attempt to lock in profits, there is a rush to sell, which recreates a downward gap. This pattern is considered a major reversal pattern and cannot be ignored.

These patterns are not the only ones you will run into in your studies, but they are the basics that you can build your experience from. I believe that every new major market move will carry with it a signature that can and must alter your expectations of these patterns. There are very few unbreakable rules in technical analysis. An example of this would be at the various stages of a market move. Two stocks that are comparable in pattern and price levels will have more potential of running ahead of a price target early in the bull market rather than a stock that is being traded in the late stages of that same bull market. The point is that we must always be ready to adjust our thinking as to chart patterns, depending on the overall market stage.

The Tools of the Trade

This chapter covers the types of charts that are available to the technical analyst and will introduce you to the varying styles you may choose. The style of chart that you select is strictly a personal choice, and your pick will depend on two items:

a. What is visually appealing to you

b. How complicated or in-depth your requirements are to complete your task

I have worked extensively with all forms of charts and will say that they all have valuable attributes. After all, a chart is nothing less than a pictorial historic record of actual price transactions that have occurred in a financial instrument such as a stock, bond, option, commodity, etc. Charts are constructed to show investors the price progress, or lack thereof, for the particular stock or index they are considering buying or selling. If you stop and think about it for a minute, what you are looking at are the forces of supply and demand in their basic forms, struggling for domination. Therefore all of the following styles have some basic similarities and show slightly different slants of behavior.

I have laid out three charts to illustrate this point. The sellers and the buyers, or the supply and demand if you prefer, are motivated into action by news or fundamental and/or economic changes for so many reasons it can make your head spin, but it's the reaction of these forces against each other that eventually creates the chart patterns. I think it was Michelangelo who said, "Every block of stone has a statue inside it, and it is the task of the sculptor to discover it."

VERY BASIC RULES

When a stock has a heavy supply of shares for sale with little demand to buy, it will find itself in a full retreat until a point of equilibrium is reached. That price point where demand finally enters the picture with enough power to halt the selling is called "support" and will act as a pivot area on the chart. In a position like this, technicians don't look for "why" the stock has declined but simply note that it has occurred. The only thing of interest to them is where it might stop and find support. Once we have that recorded on a chart, it will act as a road marker for us in the future. We will be able to see at what price buyers were willing to commit funds in the past. As long as that level is not violated on the downside, we can use that price level as an indication of where we might wish to enter a new position. This reference point is also useful in a study of reward/risk because we can at least determine where our downside risk is found. If support is violated, the stock would be considered a sell. (See Figure 4-1.)

Inversely, heavy demand for a stock when there is a limited supply to be offered will force the price of the stock to rally until a greater force on the sell side appears to halt the advance. After an upward run, the price will reach a point where sellers are enticed to let go of their shares, and that in turn stops the advance. This equilibrium point on the upside is called "resistance." Like its counterpart, resistance points show us a price at which buyers were no longer able to influence the stock price and allowed sellers to take control. (See Figure 4-2.)

We can also have a stock that has reached a neutral area, and a trading range is formed. Until one side or the other takes the upper hand, the existing support and resistances areas will act as boundaries. Many times this pattern is found after a strong move and an overbought or oversold condition needs to

FIGURE 4-1

A Stock at Support. Courtesy of MetaStock.

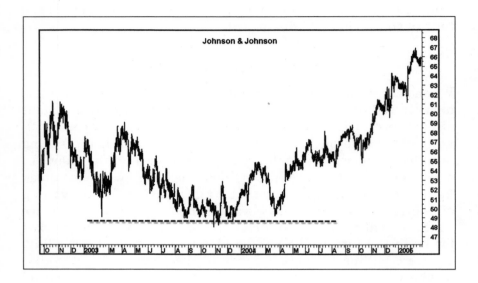

be digested. The longer a neutral pattern is in force, the more significant the move once the stock has broken out of the pattern. The point to all of this is that support and resistance levels show us the prices that are essential to a stock's outlook. A penetration of a resistance level or a violation of a support carry with that action the implication of either falling to the next lower support point or starting a new upward leg. How long those levels were intact many times will determine how far a move is likely to be.The study of supply and demand is the most basic element in economics and the main reason that technicians believe that charts reflect everything in the marketplace. Let's take a minute and explain a bit more about that thought. Technicians look at a chart as the end result of the sum total of all investors' feelings toward a particular financial instrument. Everyone has a chance to buy or sell a stock on any given day in the open market. News stories, TV interviews, government announcements, overall market fears and optimism, plus a hundred other facts influence investors' reactions towards a stock

FIGURE 4-2

A Rising Stock. Courtesy of MetaStock.

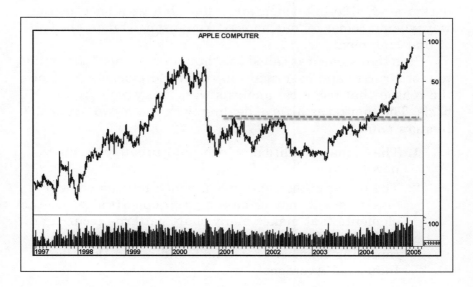

or the market. When the buyers and the sellers meet and come to an agreed-upon price is when technicians look for real knowledge. We look for answers in price.

Another major concept that must be accepted by any student of the market is that "stocks trend." Once again we will have to go back to some basic concepts. Just like Sir Isaac Newton, many new investors need to be hit in the head with an apple from time to time to have them come around to the idea that a "body in motion will tend to stay in motion until a force greater than the prevailing trend causes a halt to occur." He was speaking about gravity, and I am talking about supply and demand. A price will move in a trend or general direction until there is a shift in the supply/demand equation and the domineering force is alerted and overpowered by the other.

I believe that it would be impossible to go any further if we didn't touch upon the belief that price patterns repeat themselves. Again, like most things in technical analysis, we like our basic truths. In the financial arena, no matter which one you choose (stocks, bonds, currencies, etc.), we cannot get away from human nature and the awesome power of fear and greed. An investor might dress differently, have different surroundings, background, different beliefs and habits, but we all act the same way when it comes to "our" money. You just can't deny the truth of that statement.

It is that sameness called the "human condition" that tends to reoccur over and over again in the world markets. It is also the reason that technical analysis works very well on a global basis. The market is always dealing with these two major motivators namely:

1. The human condition, which unfortunately seems to never change.
2. The power of fear and greed, which tells us we will lose all our money or miss a great opportunity, are the elements that makes many chart patterns recur again and again. One of the clearest examples of patterns repeating themselves can be found in the Dow Jones Industrial Averages.

Figure 4-3 shows the Dow Jones from the beginning of the Korean War to the present. During that 50+-year span we have seen good times and bad, Democrats and Republican administrations, high interest rates and low interest rates, high unemployment and low unemployment, earnings rising and earnings dropping like a stone in a lake; you get the idea. In all that time, with all those forces seemingly pulling on stock prices, we still witnessed an important bottom registered roughly every four to four-and-a-half years. Keep in mind that the stock market is the original 900-pound gorilla. No one can tell the markets what or when to do anything. Yet we are faced with the fact the Dow Jones Industrial Averages does seem to have a repeating pattern to it.

If we look at the Dow Jones bottom of 1938 as a starting point, we can see the next meaningful low was established in April of 1942. After World War II, the market made a low in 1946 and, because of the shifting from guns to butter economy, the price activities during that cycle were neutral until we came into late 1949 to mid-1950. In June of 1950 North Korea invaded South Korea and the market took a hard hit for about

FIGURE 4 - 3

The 1949–2004 Dow. Drawn by The Chartstore.com.

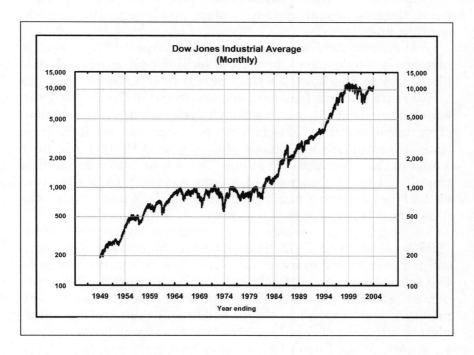

one month when it lost roughly 12 percent but finally bottomed at 1954. In January of 1958, 53 months later we witnessed another major low for the Dow at 416.

In 1962 the world was really coming unglued. Early in the year President Kennedy placed price controls on the steel industry in an attempt to head off inflation. This action sent the stock market into a decline. Later that year that decline turned into a nosedive due to the Cuban Missile Crisis and the real possibility of starting World War III. All in all a fairly nervous time. The Dow Jones, however, made another major bottom almost at the moment that the Russian merchant ship turned around. In 1966 in the middle of the Vietnam War, the Dow bottomed in October of that year at 736 and again in 1970. Despite the expansion of the War into Cambodia, the Dow managed a major significant low at 627 almost exactly four years from top to bottom. By the time the DJIAs made their lows in 1974 at a price of 563, we had been in a solid two-year selloff that truly did look like the end of capitalism. After a rally from that low point, the next 4-year cycle took place and by late 1978 we had another low.

August of 1982 was the start of the largest bull market in history. It would usher in a new secular bull market that is likely to stand as the best rally period in the record books for many years to come. Our next low was found in October of 1987, which made that a 5-year cycle. All cycles do have the element of variation to them. The market made us pay for that extra time on the upside in October of that year. I think I still have a nervous tick because of that one. The low in 1987 was the first time in 40 years that we had a 5-year cycle, possibly because we had just started a major longer secular bull market, and the first thrust upward was the largest.

Going forward we saw another market low in 1990, 1994, 1998, and again in 2002. The fact that the market repeats itself is not amazing to me at all. After 40 years in the business, I've seen countless chart patterns that keep repeating. I've witnessed seasonal patterns work year after year. I've seen commodity prices respond to the calendar and the planting schedules. So the concept that "patterns trend" and repeat themselves does work. What I can't figure out is how more people don't see the same events. I guess it must be that left-brain/right-brain thing. I gave up a long time ago trying to convince anyone about things that are right in front of their noses.

If we take these few basic ideas that history repeats itself and therefore patterns should also, then it is a short jump to the idea that the market is a discounting mechanism and that the market/stocks do move in trends. It seems to flow that studying those trends and patterns would be the next logical step. So let's take a look at our first instrument in our toolbox: charts and their construction.

BUILDING CHARTS

Relax, I am not going to tell you to get a number-two pencil and start drawing charts. All the charts you are ever going to need are found on computer systems today and can be altered as to their scaling to fit your needs. But I do believe that everyone should have at least a working knowledge of what goes into a chart and why it means what it does. There are several types of charts that technicians can use in their daily activities. As I have already stated, the selection of the type of chart style a person uses is as personal as the type of clothes you wear. As far as I can tell, they all have their good points as well as short-falls. Let me put down a few rules for your consideration in choosing a format.

a. The technician should feel comfortable with the choice of chart or else the results will be poor. If I were you, I would try them all before you make any lasting choice. Some firsthand experience is always a smart move. Get familiar with how the different charts move before deciding. If you were buying a new car you would take it for a test ride, and trust me, in this business you will be risking more than just the price of a car.

b. The chart should be easy to read. Some people feel very comfortable with many indicators on a chart while others might opt for the simple approach. There is no right or wrong answer here. When I say it should be easy to read, I mean easy for *you* to read while still answering your questions.

c. You need to feel that you are in control of the information you are studying. Whatever indicators you place on a chart, you must understand every aspect of the tools you have chosen to appear on the chart. I say that because I have seen many times where technical students will use very sophisticated software that is capable of producing complicated charts with many in-dicators. The problem is that they have no more idea of what information they are looking at than I know how to breathe underwater.

d. The charts should match the time frame you intend to work within. You must be given the information you need to accomplish your goals, for example, if you are investing on an intermediate-term basis (6 months to 9 months), hourly or even daily charts might not yield

the answers you need. Charts can be of any length:
daily, weekly, monthly, or yearly.

So before diving into a chart book or a piece of software,
take a look at you choices and decide what design fits your
needs.

The types of charts available to you are:

a. Line Charts
b. Bar Charts
c. Point and Figure Charts
d. Candlestick Charts

Line Charts

A line chart is simplicity itself and in every way the technician's
classic tool. It would be difficult to have a chart much more basic. We are dealing with a chart that records the closing prices
only of your stock. Because the technician believes that the closing price is the most important piece of data in a day's trans-
action theoretically, the line chart will yield the most pertinent
answers. On the vertical, we have a price grid and on the horizontal the time line. Of all the charts that technicians employ,
this is the one that usually ends up in front of the public most
often. You will see these types of charts in your day-to-day life
and in advertising campaigns or listening to some politician
telling us that her plan is better than the next guy's. But it does
seem to be the one chart that requires the least amount of explanation to the public.

One of the values of this chart style is its ease of interpretation. The message that the chart is designed to deliver is the
"general direction" of the time series you are studying. You will
find that any chart can be made as complicated as you want.
Many technicians in fact do like filling a chart with data, trend
lines, indicators, etc. to help in their decisions. But the line chart
really is made for just the opposite. It can quickly answer the
question: Is this series that I'm looking at going up or is it going down? You will notice that the more time that the chart covers, the less important minor swings mean. Therefore, line

FIGURE 4-4

A Line Chart. Drawn by The Chartstore.com.

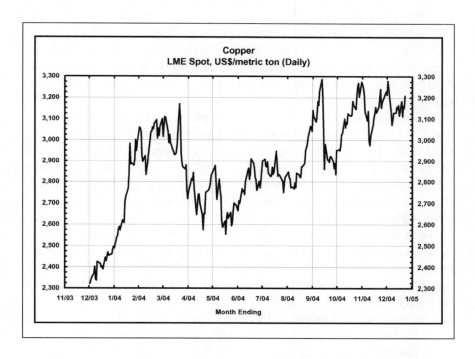

charts are perfect in studying trends in groups, sectors, and indexes to gain a better perspective.

The one major drawback in a line chart is its simplicity. With all the tools at your command, choosing this type seems to limit a chart's depth possibilities and informational capability just to price. They are great in presentations, but for analysis you will want a little more firepower. (See Figure 4-4.)

Bar Charts

The bar chart is the true workhorse of a technical analyst. Here we have a chance of getting more information in a chart while still keeping its construction relatively simple. The data points contained in a bar chart are the high price, a low price, and a closing price for the time series plus the volume on the bottom of the chart along the horizontal. The high and the low point will be connected with a line indicating the price spread for the day, and the close will be represented by a dash line off to the right. Some services include an opening price. That piece of data will appear on the left side of the bar, while the close will appear on the right side. With this extra piece of data, we can analyze the difference between the open and the close. We'll cover that later.

On the bottom of the chart we plot the volume. If we have a daily chart, it would be the total amount of shares traded for that day. If we are looking at a weekly, then the weekly volume would be assigned one vertical line that matches the price bar. So in one plot we have five key points of information. These are the pictorial representations of the actual transactions for whatever series you're watching. Keep in mind also that each bar on the graph represents the time period you have set for a chart. A daily chart means that all the bars are showing daily high, low, close, and volume information for that chart. Obviously, weekly charts represent weekly data, monthly charts represent monthly data, and so forth. For the sake of this chapter, let's try to stay with a basic daily bar chart.

As more bars are added to the graph, you will quickly see that patterns begin to take shape. These patterns are not confined to price only. The volume patterns also emerge, but we will handle volume in a later chapter. Technicians believe that these patterns repeat themselves into recognizable patterns. And why shouldn't they? In most cases we have the same elements being mixed together. We will always deal with some combination of human emotions, fear, greed, the current news, and current known facts about the economy and political environment. Why would we expect to get anything but similar results? A cook will add ingredients together to make an omelet and will expect to get a reasonably similar result most of the time. A good cook will try variations on the theme from time to time, but basically an omelet should emerge. It's the same with chart patterns. They are created by supply and demand, which is always stimulated by the above factors.

As far as their negative side is concerned with bar charts, I find little to complain about this tool. Possibly we can overfill a chart with too much information, but that's not the bar chart's fault. Overall, this is a very useful tool and tends to be a major part of a technician's equipment.

Point and Figure Charts

The P&F chart is the granddaddy of all charting techniques in the United States. When it comes to charting, the point and figure chart is another excellent example of the KISS system as it reduces the chart down to price alone. Towards the end of the nineteenth century, Charles Dow first used this technique. Mr. Dow would follow the progress of a corporation's common stocks traded on the exchanges by plotting the company's price movements on pieces of graph paper. The actual price (rounded off to the nearest full point) would be placed on the chart in the chronological order that the transactions took place. If a company's share were to trade at a given price, the actual mark would be placed in the first column of the chart paper. The clerk would post subsequent trades in the same column, either up or down, and each of the subsequent trades would remain in that column until there was a full-point reversal in price. To mark that one-point directional reverse, you would move to the next column to your right and continue in *that* direction until that trend was reversed again by a full point. Each reversal would move you to the next column on the chart paper. One major caveat is that every column on the graph paper has to have at least two postings before you can move on to the next column to the right. Obviously, after a short while, patterns would develop and certain assumptions were made based on patterns analysis. At the turn of the century, the actual price marks were replaced with Xs if the stock price advanced and Os, if the stock declined. (See Figure 4-5.)

When I started in the business in 1964, my job was to post these Xs and Os on chart paper, and at the time it meant absolutely nothing to me. Soon I came to realize exactly what I was looking at—the buying and selling pressures that investors

FIGURE 4-5

Point and Figure Chart.

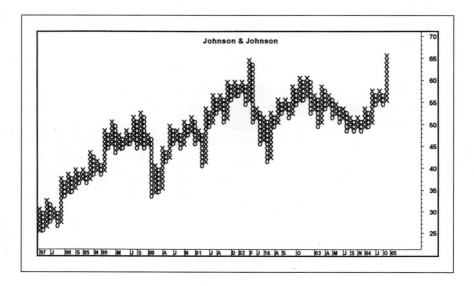

were placing on stocks based on their opinions of the fundamentals or news of a corporation. I noticed that I would get a
feel for the trading patterns of a stock, and then the chart formations took on new meaning. All the technicians of the day
would maintain their charts by hand, and everyone would lit-
erally be able to recall almost perfectly the pattern and opinion
of 600–700 chart patterns in their heads as a matter of course.
But that was a function of the "relatively" light volume of the
day. Compared to today's world of finance, in the limited markets that we dealt with, you could commit many of the price actions to memory. To keep a good perspective of the times, remember that for all intents and purposes, there were only two
market vehicles available to the public—bonds or stocks. To
make things even narrower, most Wall Street firms of the day
only allowed one opinion—buy! As far as foreign markets were
concerned, the Philadelphia Stock Market was about as foreign
as most American portfolio managers would venture away from
Wall Street. When I look back on those times, I sometimes feel

like Bob Cratchet in *A Christmas Carol* bending over my 4000 charts with my pencil in the early morning light.

Candlestick

Candlestick charting is one of the oldest styles of charting from Japan. It has increased in popularity in this country over the last 15 years as western technicians have discovered this eastern type of analysis. Many computer services have added candlestick charts to their systems. The exposure to these charts in part can be credited to the efforts of another fine technical analyst, Steve Nissin, who has written the basic text for this style of charting, entitled *Japanese Candlestick Charting Technique*. That's about as straightforward a title as you can find.

When you read about candlestick charts, it doesn't take you long to realize that many (not all) of the patterns were developed perhaps two centuries ago, and yet there are many similarities between these patterns of the 1700s in Japan and modern technical analysis in the United States. The names are different, but the concepts are the same. People using candlesticks are still trying to gauge supply and demand using the price patterns to interpret the struggle. What difference does it make if we call something a "gap" in the West and a "window" in the East? In both cases we are dealing with an opening in the price picture that represents an emotional move either up or down. The candlestick chart deals with high-low price points, and like the bar charts we have already studied, we connect the data points in order to have a representation of the day's trading record. This line represents the range of movement for the day. It is called the "shadow" because it is a simple line. (See Figure 4-6.)

The candlestick chart does offer a bit more information in its construction than the bar chart, as the candlestick will depend on the relationship between the closing price to the opening price to determine its coloring. This spread between the open and the close is called the real body. If the stock closes higher than the opening, then the "body" of the candle will be clear or white. If, however, we get a lower close compared to the opening, then the technician will indicate that action by blackening in the body of the chart. The intraday high and low that will

FIGURE 4-6

Chart of a Shadow.

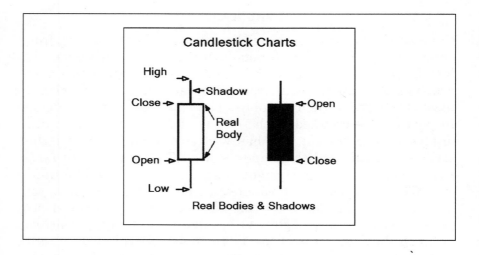

extend past the open and close on either side are called the upper and lower shadows.

Stop and think of the difference. In a bar chart you can have a stock that has a 25 High, 22 low, 23 close. Last night's close, say, is 24. On a bar chart it would correctly indicate that the stock closed up 1 point from its previous day's close and would be a positive. But suppose the stock opened at 25 and closed the day at 24. On a candlestick stock, it would show black as a negative.

Another major positive with these charts is the powerful visual message they convey. Areas of accumulation and distribution patterns tend to jump out at you. Distribution is colored black and accumulation is clear.

I believe one of the strongest attributes of the candlestick charting technique is its flexibility, as it can be used with almost any other indicator or tool for confirmation purposes. Some other charts, like the P&F charts, are not as mobile.

The Japanese names for the patterns are quite descriptive: hammers, rising stars, three crows, and the ever-popular three river bottom. These names are no more bazaar then rising wedge, cup and saucer, or the ever-popular head and shoulders formations that we Westerners employ.

This is a great time to put your mind at ease. All of these charts are available these days on many computer programs. Please get rid of the idea of slumping over a draftsman's table in order to use charts. I would say, however, that there is nothing like drawing your own and getting a feel for the chart. I am well aware that doing hundreds or thousands of charts is impractical, but keeping a few key charts or indexes by hand can be very rewarding and profitable. An old-time block trader, Tommy Murphy at Edwards and Hanly, told me once you should keep hand-drawn charts on your favorite stock and your biggest positions. Maybe it's only 10 or 15 names, but you will know those charts better than anyone else after a short time. That's also what many, if not most, of the upstairs traders are doing, and many of the floor specialists.

All of these styles of charts can work in any time frame: daily, weekly, monthly, and yearly. With the rapid rise of all the new trading vehicles, it is not uncommon to see hourly or even shorter-term charts. It is all a matter of knowing your needs and the limitations of your computers.

Here are a few final points I'd like to make about charts. There are a number of other types of charts that you will be able to study as you delve deeper into technical analysis, such as Gann charts and equivolume charts, for example. These chart techniques I would save for later after you have mastered the basics. My advice is to take this one step at a time. Learn the basics and proceed with caution. As long as I have suggested to use caution, let me also state that as you go along you will run into or hear about many new approaches to the market. Be very careful. There are many get-rich-quick systems in the marketplace that are just no good. They are developed by crooks and can cost you lots of money. I strongly advise you to stay with the basics until you have mastered the tools.

Scaling

There are two scaling methods that are available to the technical analyst. A chart either can employ an arithmetic or logarithmic scale. The most common method is the arithmetic scaling. It also is the one that investors relate to easily. The scale on the left-hand side of most charts shows a given range for the instrument. Let's say 0 to 50. Each point on the chart shows the same interval so that the distance between 15 and 20 is the same as 45–50. This is fine and on most occasions will be the type of chart you will be using. However, when you are studying long-term charts of indexes, sectors, or groups, and you're looking at 20 years' worth of data on one chart, you will find that many times a log chart is more useful. Log charts can also be helpful in following individual issues that trade well above $100 and can have wide swings during the day. It will show large moves on a chart in percentages and cut down on the size of a fluctuation. A price move from 10 to 20 represents a 100 percent gain. On a log chart, that move and a move from 500 to 1000 would be the same vertical length. All the same rules and regulations apply to both types of charts because you are looking at the same data in either case.

Chapter 5

Channels and Trends

John Greeley was the person responsible for giving me my first job as a technical analyst. He handed an armful of books to me one day and said to read them and we would talk. At the time I was working for F.I. DuPont & Co. and the books were all the leading texts of the time: *Technical Analysis of Stock Trends* by Edwards and McGree, a few of Joe Granville books, William Jiler's book *How Charts Can Help You in the Stock Market*, and Alexander Wheelan's work *Study Helps in Point and Figure Technique*. These were the books that started my education and introduced the various techniques of technical analysis to me. To this day they would still be some of the first authors I would recommend to anyone eager to join the technical ranks. All of those volumes, and many more, are on my bookshelves and are referred to on a regular basis even today. One of the texts, en-titled *Wiped Out*, however, had a profound impact upon me. I was young and could relate to the author's mistakes.

I remember the book had a yellow cover and large black print. It was a story of a young man who had inherited a good sum of money at the market low in 1962 and by the top in 1966, he was *Wiped Out*. He said on the book's jacket that all he was trying to do with his book was to recover some of his losses. But there was a quote that I have always kept with me, and I want to pass it on to you. At the time it answered many questions about investing or trading

Folly transcends all market conditions.

That one phrase has stayed with me longer then most words of wisdom that I have picked up over the years.

One major way of avoiding being wiped out in the stock market is to recognize the trend of the market. Knowing which direction the market is moving is vital if you are planning to be investing or trading for any length of time. That might sound a little simplistic and trite, but believe me, more money has been lost by people thinking that a market should be doing what they think rather than what it is actually doing. Here comes another Brooksism: "The market is never wrong: it's you." If you learn nothing else in this book, learn that fact.

In their pursuit of excellence in the marketplace, I have seen the great and the near great get taken out behind the woodshed and never heard from again. The idea that you have a better mousetrap or a superior market indicator other than what the market itself is telling you is almost laughable. It would be a great source of humor if it weren't sad to see someone lose it all because they felt they were smarter than the market. If you spend any time in the financial marketplace, you will run across people who will make all sorts of outlandish claims about "their method" of trading/investing. To be fair you should at least look at many of these approaches. That just goes with the territory. It makes no difference where outrageous promises of great wealth come from, a brokerage house or a market letter writer. As soon as someone starts telling you things that make no sense to you, run, don't walk, to the nearest exit.

All of the markets are based on supply and demand. The aggressiveness of the buyers and the sellers and the perception that those forces have on the investing public is what we need to follow. This touches on the subject of "top down" analysis, which I'll cover in a later chapter. For now let us simply use the stock market for our examples.

TRENDS

The elements that make up a stock's trend are obviously price and time. If you were to look at any chart of a financial instrument, it wouldn't take you long to realize that stocks do not travel in a straight line from point A to point B. Even if the

investors believe that a market or a particular stock is undervalued, we never see an immediate leap up to a point that is
considered fairly valued. Their movements are stair-step in nature. As the stock moves higher, some people are willing to accept a small profit and sell to the buyers, while others choose
to hold in the hopes of higher profits. Although the reasons are
varied, the results are always the same, and what we end up
with is a series of highs and lows over a given period of time.
In studying trends, the direction makes little difference, as the
results are the same for both sides. The longer a stock remains
in a trend, the more important that trend becomes. Of course,
any instrument—bonds, stocks, commodities, currencies, etc.—
can travel either up, down, or sideways, and that's about the
extent of their dexterity. So let's look at some definitions to aid
us in a study of trends.

REFRESHER

I want to make sure that we understand the terminology. The
terms support and resistance are given to price levels where
the forces of supply and demand have come into equilibrium.
Remember, a price will remain in the direction it's moving until a greater opposite force halts it progress. At that point we
will see the price trend stop and often reverse. The upside is
called resistance and represents a point where supply is sufficient to halt a price movement and cause at least a temporary
decline. Once a decline has started, it will remain in that trend
until the price is low enough to attract enough buyers to absorb the supply and halt the decline. That price level is called
support. It is the position of these supports and resistances
that make the patterns and the trends. The more times a resistance point or a support level, is tested the more important
and reliable it becomes.

An uptrend is a series of higher-price highs and higher-
price lows. What defines the uptrend is the pullback after the
first upward move. The low point of that pullback must be above
the previous low, and there must be a subsequent new high
point reached in order to start an uptrend. This is very basic
but is part of the bedrock of technical analysis.

A downtrend would be just the opposite. Here we would have a stock registering a series of lower-price highs and lower lows. The same type of experience will be found in downtrends. This trend direction will remain in play until an opposing force can be mustered to halt the series of new lows.

A neutral trend would be a trendless market. Prices establish an upper limit that is called resistance that match each rally attempt. Lower limits called support match each preceding low. This represents a market either reversing its long-term trend by making a top or a bottom, or a consolidating pattern to catch its breath after a strong move before continuing in its primary trend. (See Figure 5-1.)

All three patterns have their importance in our work, as they tend to give us entry points in a market. It's fine to say I think the market is headed lower because of my economic outlook. But unless you're planning to pull all of your money out of the market and into a piggy bank, you're going to have to learn where and when to buy and sell. Like stocks, markets don't

FIGURE 5-1

Three Charts.

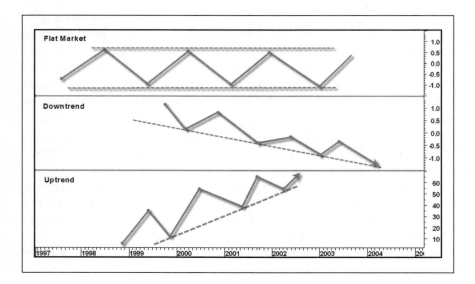

usually simply collapse. They tend to rotate lower, and by following the trends of the sectors and groups, you can very often navigate around hard times and capitalize on the good ones. I believe the only market that I remember having very few places to hide was the last few months of the 1974 nosedive. Trend lines can give us the information we need as to where stocks have reversed before and where they are headed. Remember, even a neutral pattern can be quite profitable if the spread between the high and the low is wide enough. A stock that swings back and forth in a 20 range can be valuable even if the stock itself has no progress of its own. Knowing where a support or a resistance area can be expected is a major tool in our business. It can be the difference between having a target to guide you or not. Picture yourself at sea in your boat and having the choice of knowing where the next harbor is or sailing blind. Trends give us boundaries that can be turned into profits.

TIME PERIODS

When we look at charts we find that time becomes a major factor in our work. We must know in what context we are working and know the correct tool to choose to guide us to our answer. Charts are usually divided into three time categories:

   a. Long term is usually considered about 1 year
   b. Intermediate term approximately 4–6 months
   c. Short term could be 2 weeks to 1 month

These grouping are very flexible and can be lengthened and shortened depending on what you're trading. When we start looking at monthly charts and patterns, we find they are of the most use for general overview items such as in a market index chart. Perhaps a long perspective of sectors or groups works.

Intermediate-term weekly charts are very popular and can cover as much time as you need but are mostly useful in the 4 to 6 months' framework. This is the time frame where most institutional money managers are interested in spending their efforts. Their situation is somewhat different than an individual investor due to the amount of money they deal with and in most cases their charter restrictions. Many of the large institutional accounts cannot move their capital more rapidly than on an intermediate term because of turnover and liquidity reasons.

Finally, short term can be monthly or less time. Trading in today's markets requires firsthand experience and plenty of discipline. Another one of those old sayings comes to mind. "There are old traders and bold traders, but there are no old bold traders." So before your get started in the world of day trading, be prepared to take some hits as you learn. We all have gone down that road and if I could talk you out of it I would, but knowing human nature I will let experience be the teacher. The number-one rule was taught to me by an ex-floor trader who is now an MIT visiting professor. This principle is key to surviving the trading world: No matter how much of a sure thing you think you have going, never expose all of your money to any one trade. Another main rule in daily trading is to be disciplined in your obedience to your rules. Most traders will tell you that the secret to the trading game is that during the course of the day you can have many losing trades as long as you keep the losses small. You must develop the ability to cut your losses, and when you get that once-in-awhile solid running stock, you have to be disciplined enough to let it run its course instead of locking in a small gain just before it becomes a big gain. Letting discipline go out the window is the fastest way I know of turning a short-term trader into a long-term investor. Please keep in mind that many who read this book might be trading options or futures, in which case a long-term position could be a day and short term 10 minutes. All of this is just a question of knowing what *you* want to do and then adjusting the time frame. An interesting point about the market is that, generally speaking, markets have three important intermediate-term action points (inflection points) a year when purchases and sales may offer the most advantageous entry points. One sell point and two buys or two buy points and one sell.

Know what tools to use when. You must learn which tool to use for separate jobs. This again goes to the point of knowing what you want to do and then staying the course to attain your goals. If you wanted to get a long-term overview of the Dow Jones Industrial Averages, you would likely want to look at a monthly bar chart going back 5 to 10 years. This would give you a general idea of direction for that index. Weekly bar charts and three-point reversal P&F charts would be used for intermediate-term work, and daily charts such as a one-point reversal P&F chart and daily bar charts could be used for this work. You would never use a daily bar chart to look at long-term information. You'd find yourself with a 7-foot-long chart. That's a joke. However, during my 40 years in the business, I have had charts that were even longer then 7 feet.

TREND LINES

As we have already covered, stocks prices move in trends, and when the forces of supply and demand come into balance, we can spot support and resistance points. Now let's talk about trend lines and how they fit in our tool chest. In order to draw a straight line, you must have two points. To draw a bullish trend line (rising), the same idea is employed. We first find a low to the left of the chart and extend the line upward to the next reaction low.

Now that we have two lows connected, we have what is called a tentative trend line. To have a trend line that we can rely on and consider valid, we must have a third point that connects all three points. The theory is that the rising trend line has proven in the past to be the point where the stock has stopped its decline, and we will continue to use that assumption going forward. This rising trend line is very important, as it now becomes an indication of where support can be expected. It goes without saying that the more points on the trend line that respect that line, the more relevant that line becomes.

A downtrend employs the same principles except now we are looking at a falling stock price. For a valid downtrend we must have two highs and a correction low in between to give us our starting line. Then we can connect these two lower tops and draw the preliminary trend line. While we wait for the third test of that line for confirmation of its validity, we can prepare our trading strategies. These are what I like to call my "what if plans." (See Figure 5-2.) For either directional trend line, a violation of the line, usually by a full point, often proves to be a great price level to reverse your positions. Flipping a long position over to short position because of a trend line break can be

FIGURE 5-2

Trend of GE. Courtesy of MetaStock.

very profitable. It's like one of General MacArthur's quotes from the Korean war, "We are not retreating; we are advancing in another direction." You always want your portfolio advancing.

Violating Trend Lines

This is a simple concept. If we are tracking the Dow Jones Industrial Averages, let's say, and that index has been able to maintain a trend long enough for a valid trend line to be established, then it deserves our attention. In this example, we might have seen quite a number of tests of the uptrend. A violation of a trend line is very important, as it is telling you that there has been a *change* in the makeup of the buyers and the sellers. That, of course, will change the direction of the index. If we consider that the trend line has been showing us where to expect to see the demand for the index, then a violation of that pattern is telling us that we must be prepared to readjust our opinion. I say readjust our opinion and not reverse our opinion because we could be looking at an index that is moving into a consolidation pattern before it continues in its long-term, established direction. Time will tell whether it is a reversal or a consolidation pattern, and usually that answer is reached by looking at the internals of the series you are following or the general market conditions. Evaluating the first rally attempt after a break can supply many answers as to the power or weakness of the longer-term pattern. A weak attempt as measured by volume and prices' ability to regain previous highs or lows can be quite enlightening. In Figure 5-3 we are looking at a rising trend. This one has been in existence for some time. Notice that the first rally we see failed to extend back to the old high and quickly faded. No action can be taken until we see a violation of a support for our confirmation. Once that has occurred, however, the path is set and a new strategy can be planned. As long as we are here, let me add to my last comment that "a new strategy can be planned." Never fall in love with your own opinions. They will and must constantly be changing to roll with the market. Yesterday's market opinions are good for wrapping fish. (See Figure 5-3.)

F I G U R E   5 - 3

Violation of a Long Trend. Courtesy of MetaStock.

CHANNELS

The concept of channels has not been mentioned yet, but it is nonetheless a very important tool that should be mastered by the professional. Earlier I spoke of trend lines and their importance in giving us the overall direction of a stock or any time series we are studying. I have said that these trends also can provide us with areas where support or resistance might be found. But now let's take that one step further and draw a parallel line to that existing up or down trend. We have built a channel.

For example, in a downtrend we first must draw the basic trend line from the two lower consecutive tops, and then using the intervening low we create a second trend line that runs parallel to our original line. We should never lose sight of the main point—that the basic trend line that was drawn first is the more relevant of the two lines. The parallel line that we put in after the direction has been established is simply there to set targets and limits. The same rules apply for channels as they do for trend lines, as far as having three points of the channels to confirm the validity of the channel. The part of the chart in between the trend lines is called the channel.

Many times when a long-term channel for a major index is nearing a support or resistance zone, it will be in the news and will be talked about on the trading desk. The pros know that a reversal or a penetration of a time-tested trend channel can be an important event. This type of excitement is usually geared towards major market indexes such as the Dow Jones Industrial Averages, Standard and Poor's 500, or the NASDAQ rather than a stock or a single option, but if its *your* stock or option that's reversing a channel, it becomes the most important thing for you.

Keeping Your Eye on the Trend

Channels cover the full gamut of direction and trends. They can be up, down, or neutral. All three movements can make you money if you recognize your opportunities. The object of our profession is to make money, and using channels can prove to be a discipline that takes much of the guesswork out of your decisions.

An interesting point about trend channels is that it makes no difference what direction they are going in for you to make money. There are stocks that trade in neutral channels for years, and as long as that channel is respected, a trader can buy at the lows and sell or even go short at the tops. Believe me, it is not as simple as that, but employing one or two other indicators in addition to a channel chart, and waiting for a confirmed turn *before* you act, can be quite profitable. (See Figure 5-4.)

Recently I have seen commercials on TV for just such a program. Some guy is retiring early because of his channeling talents. Well, life isn't exactly that easy, but it doesn't have to be that hard either. If we bother to examine the markets, we all can spot stocks that trade between some levels and capitalize on the pattern.

These could be stocks that trade strictly on valuations or seasonal factors. But they do exist. As to investors' reactions to these issues, they can vary greatly. Some people will note the fact that these stocks are around and think no more about them.

FIGURE 5-4

A Neutral Stock. Courtesy of MetaStock.

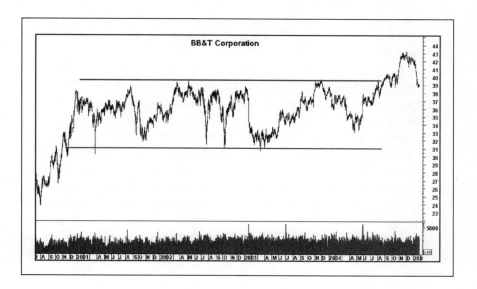

Others will choose to ignore them, as they are dull and unin-teresting. Yet others will think it's a sign of weakness that the stocks can't get ahead. Beauty is in the eye of the beholder. It all depends on what goals you set. Once those goals are set, we need to use the correct tools to reach our ends. One person might feel that hitting singles and doubles by using a trading channel is a much wiser strategy than trying to go for the homerun. It's all a question of how you work. Sometimes I refer to an approach called "your pillow pressure," meaning how much pressure you want when you lie down on your pillow at night. Many people on the Street have made careers out of hitting singles all day long.

Tip-offs

These channels have another very important aspect to them. They can provide us with an early warning system all their own. Many times these warnings are not going to jump up and wave a big red flag in your face and say "look at me." They are a bit more subtle than that. When a stock or index is trending and we can draw a channel that meets all the criteria we have talked about, then we should be justified in expecting that either the upper or lower bands should be reached. A momentum gauge in a sense has been created that must be viewed as having mini-mums and maximums. Take a stock that is in an up channel and has been in that channel for a few months.

A failure to extend all the way up to the top of a channel line can be a warning that the force of demand for this stock is beginning to run into more supply than the stock has seen in the life of that channel. When we see this loss of magnitude, we must now shift from relying on that trend line to watching our support areas for signs of violation of those zones. Obviously the violation of the trend channel would be the confirmation that the long-term trend has been shifting, but the failure to extend to the upper limits would be the first warning flag. This is the reason that we say it is vital that you have other technical tools at your fingertips. If there is going to be a loss of demand for the stock, then we should see a few basic items popping up. For instance, support levels being violated, volume expanding on the downside, moving averages turning lower, shorter rally power. All of these will be covered in later chapters. For now let us say that a channel lays out upper and lower boundaries, and a breakout or a breakdown should give the heads up to be prepared to shift your outlook.

Other Channeling Techniques

We have looked at the concept of building a channel trend line to aid in our overview. There are many other methods and variations of that theme that attempt to accomplish the same goal. Two, however, are widely accepted and have earned a place in the chapter. Let's first look at the "percentage envelope." (See Figure 5-5.)

This approach is based on the idea that stock prices "trend," and within that trend there is a reasonable movement both up and down in the overall pattern. By calling a moving average line the center price of a stock, we could then place two other

FIGURE 5-5

Percentage Envelopes. Courtesy of MetaStock.

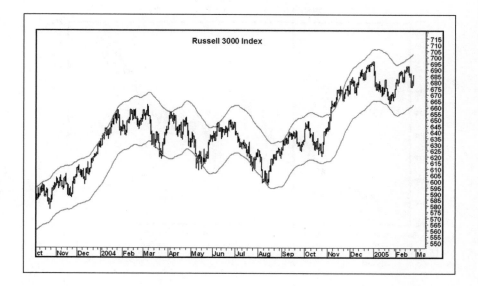

lines at equal distances above and below the centerpoint and place that envelope around the price chart. What we assume is that a price will tend to stay within that envelope for the vast majority of the time, swinging back and forth within a normal range. Even on directional changes an envelope will tend to bend with the price.

There are occasions where stocks or indexes will push past their boundaries of the envelope, but most of those moves happen because of major news and tend to be short-term happenings. When that occurs, usually an overbought or oversold condition develops and a reversal quit often follows. But barring those outliers, you will find that an envelope will contain most of the action in a stock. There are no hard-and-fast rules as to the percentages used in drawing the lines. Today many people use a 3 percent envelope when looking at the larger indexes like

FIGURE 5-6

Bollinger Bands. Drawn by The Chartstore.com.

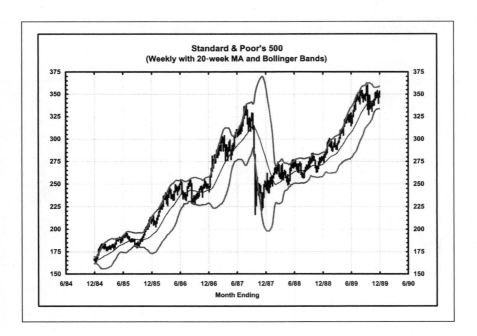

the S&P or the New York Stock Exchange and a somewhat larger band for individual issues. The more volatility a stock has, like a technology issue, the more room you should allow yourself. An envelope for the NASDAQ, for example, would most likely need a 6 percent upper and lower limit, as the NASDAQ has higher volatility than the Dow.

Another powerful method of "banding" a stock was developed by a very fine technician, John Bollinger. In the envelope we have two lines at an equal distance from the moving average line. John Bollinger took a new approach by employing the concept of "standard deviation" in his calculation. This concept of standard deviation is another way of capturing almost all of the price swings around an average. The usual length of that average is 20 days, but it can be used on weekly or monthly charts as well. Bollinger uses a two standard deviation in his work in order to capture all but a small percentage of the stock's move. The main difference between his approach and envelopes is that the Bollinger bands expand and contract depending on the volatility of the average. In a period of slow-moving markets, the bands tend to narrow, and when the action increases, we see the bands widen once again. Like the channels and envelopes when the upper and lower bands are touched, a reversal back towards the other side of the bands could be anticipated. Another point is that when the bands find themselves closing in on each other, it is an indication that a directional change could be at hand. (See Figure 5-6.)

Chapter 6

Volume

The study of volume as it relates to price activity should be a significant part of your technical education. For reasons that will become clear, it is the second most studied piece of information, outside of price, an analyst will use. The most important data in technical analysis is price, but if we want to measure an investor's intensity in that price movement, then volume is the best overall piece of data to follow. This data point is the technician's confirmation device and is employed in almost all facets of our work. Some of the techniques in technical analysis do not use volume such as point and figure charting. If you recall from Chapter 3, that approach is strictly price oriented. In P&F charting, volume and time have no place. Other styles of technical analysis use volume in varying ways to spot trend moves, confirm price movement, or to zero in on where the money is flowing. Remember the great line in the old movie *All the Presidents Men* when Deep Throat told the two reporters to "follow the money." In our business the money is represented by the volume. If you keep your eyes on it and combine that knowledge with the price action, you can improve your odds greatly.

When I speak of volume, I am referring to the total amount of shares traded in a stock or a market for a given time period. Of course, volume can be measured for almost any time frame—daily, weekly, monthly, etc. The basic rule is in order. For an upward price trend to continue, you should see a volume pattern that is increasing in the same direction. If we have a rising stock price, volume should expand in that prevailing direction. The confirming nature of volume carries into periods of short-term contra moves as well. Any rally will have short-term reactions because of a temporary overbought state. The volume patterns during these interruptions should decline and rise again once the longer-term pattern resumes its original upward direction.

Downside volume tends to take a different path. In the beginning of a decline, we may well see volume expand above the average trading volume level. The problem with declines is that as a stock or a market becomes entrenched in its fall, volume also tends to fall away.

There are a number of explanations for this behavior. The most obvious one is that as the reason for the drop becomes known to the public, they tend to avoid the problem. Unlike many professionals that must trade a certain stock, John Q. doesn't have to invest every day. So a stock can simply waste away because of lack of interest. An example of a common trap that you must be on guard against is the concept that if a stock is going through a light volume decline, it is suggesting that a positive move to the upside is at hand. It might be true that having a light volume decline could be a constructive development, but you cannot tell until you examine the move closely and use other technical indicators before reaching a decision. In a normal short-term contra decline to relieve an overbought condition, a light volume decline is bullish. That fact has been distorted over the years so now people, trying to be positive, have said that all light volume declines are good. They are most certainly not good. Most of the 1960s saw nothing but light volume declines that nearly shut Wall Street down permanently.

In a long-term decline, however, many times a pickup in volume will occur after a bottom has been reached. Even then it usually takes a few tests of support zones and improvement in price before a real increase in volume is noted.

VOLUME ON THE DOWNSIDE

As a rule of thumb, during long-term declining periods, total volume tends to decline quite a bit. Bear markets by their nature will have lower volume because investors are concerned,

and they tend to hold off new purchases and reduce their portfolios overall. The ending days of a prolonged decline usually
see volume expand, but it is marked as a capitulation by investors when they toss in the towel finally. A market that is
clearly in a decline will witness many investors pulling out of
the stock market and into safer instruments, like the bond markets or money market funds.

I have firsthand knowledge of this from the 1973–1974 bear
market. That period was very negative for the stock market, as
the Dow Jones fell from a high of 1060 down to a low of 563
over a course of about 24 months. The selling was relentless and
the daily news during that time would pound the tape. The only
support was found at 4:00 o'clock when they made us go home
for the night.

I was fortunate to have called the top correctly and missed
much of the damage and in fact spent most of the time on the
short side of the market. The firm I was employed with at the
time, Edwards and Hanley, allowed me to express my views on
the markets to our accounts, and I believe their courage to state
a negative opinion, in concert with others in my firm, saved our
customers vast amounts of money. The problem was that we
would get many letters from our accounts telling us that they
appreciated the solid market opinion and they agreed with our
declining market call. And therefore please close out my account
and send them the proceeds. It's like the man in the street calling for the end of the world. If you're right, there will be nobody
around to thank you for the heads-up. (See Figure 6-1.)

We use volume much of the time to spot divergences and
to give us an early warning for possible reversals. When prices
rally, it is believed that the forces of demand are rushing in to
buy up shares at a more aggressive rate then the supply side
can offer shares for sale. Therefore, prices tend to lift. If volume
does not expand with this enthusiasm in price, then we have to
begin to wonder if perhaps an equilibrium point might be ap-
proaching. At the very least, given these facts, we should be
forewarned. There are times when a stock will jump ahead on
light volume, such as short covering or a bogus piece of news.
In the summer of 1967, during the first Middle East war, the
market was in a full retreat and the best ideas of the day were
to be found on the "short side." One day a news flash came out

FIGURE 6-1

DOW in 1965–1976. Drawn by The Chartstore.com.

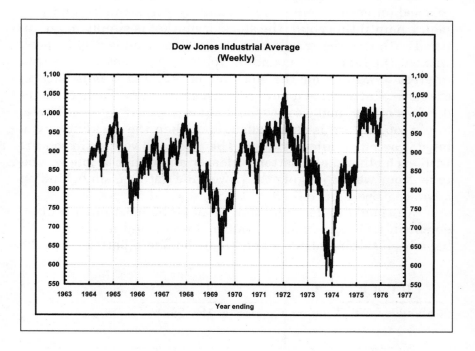

over the Dow Ticker that the two sides might be willing to sit down at peace table together, and the market exploded (possibly a bad choice of words) on the upside, sending all the shorts for cover. This rally lasted for about 20 minutes when the rest of the statement came out saying they could sit at a peace table after they had driven one army into the sea. I forget who said what to whom, but no matter, the point is that the rally was accomplished, based on a false piece of news, and propelled by short covering and *not* bona fide buyers. Of course the market took a drop-dead pill and we finished the day in a nosedive.

PATTERNS AND VOLUME

Volume analysis is, of course, used in many of the chart patterns that we have already mentioned. In the head and shoulder pattern, for instance, we know that a volume pattern in conjunction with price is vital. The rallies on the head and the right shoulder are lighter than in the left shoulder. The reasoning is simple enough. The first high (the left shoulder) is reached on good volume and is running hot, straight, and normal. Up until this point, the stock or market is simply in an uptrend with the proper volume pattern. The head is a spike peak without the luxury of expanding volume. We must assume that interest is waning for the stock or market and it falls back in the hope of attracting a new group of supporters. The left shoulder fails both to make a new high and to increase volume. Therefore a top pattern is established, and when the neckline is violated it becomes officially a top. The price and volume in concert with each other make patterns clearer and easier to follow. Volume is our way of judging the power and enthusiasm behind an advance. (See Figure 6-2.)

We should understand that price is the most important element in technical analysis, but a close second is volume. We have been talking about a head and shoulders pattern, but the

FIGURE 6 - 2

Shoulder with Volume. Courtesy of MetaStock.

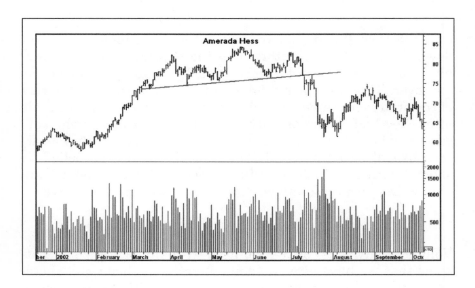

essence in this one pattern carries to all patterns. If you have a rally without volume, it can be very dangerous because it is basically saying investors are not impressed or are not willing to pay the higher prices for the stock.

Another perfect example of price and volume working in harmony within a chart pattern is found in the triangle patterns. These triangles are usually continuation patterns, which represent a resting or accumulation period. The theory is as the price trades within the triangular pattern (a series of lower tops and higher bottoms) it digests and consolidates its recent move. As it approaches the "apex" of the triangle, it must make a move out of that pattern, hopefully in its original direction. On that breakout, volume should expand and that directional move would be confirmed. If it does not have supporting volume, then the pattern is questionable. The triangle is a consolidation period for a stock and is looked upon as a temporary resting time. It is not a good sign to see a stock trade its way all the way to the "apex," as it would represent too much uncertainty. Usually when the pattern is extended that long, we see a price failure and low volume, as either the investors do not care about the stock any longer or they believe that whatever problem the stock had is not resolved.

VOLUME PRECEDES PRICE

We have stated that by watching price and volume in tandem we can get advance warning of a shift in the price of a stock. Watching price alone is one dimensional. It can answer a certain number of questions, but to understand the power or validity of a price move, we must incorporate volume into our work. There have been many academic studies on this subject, to say nothing of lots of on-the-job training that I have done, to bring me to the belief that "volume leads price." (See Figure 6-3.)

If you examine volume activity closely, you can see that volume can signal shifts in investors' thinking. Simply watching the demand and the supply forces fight for domination can give us all the advanced warning we need to be successful. There are a few general observations you need to be aware of when watching price and volume working together. I am not implying that

FIGURE 6-3

Chart Volume Precedes Price. Courtesy of MetaStock.

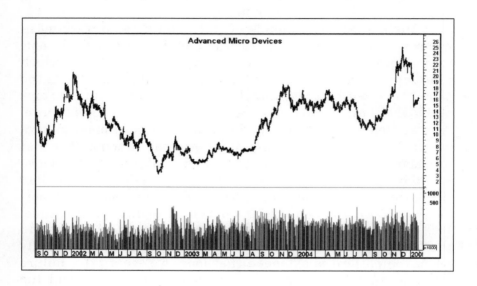

these are the only rules, but these ideas will give you more than enough information to ponder.

a. For one thing, if price and volume both are showing an expanding pattern, this gives us a normal and healthy picture and requires no action except to sit back and enjoy. This is a perfect example of the old saw "the trend is your friend." As long as these two factors are working together, we should let the position run its course and only on a deviation from that pattern should we even consider removing the position.

b. A price rally that has contracting volume is waving a big, red flag. The forces of supply and demand are sending a clear message that there is a problem. It's like a car moving fast down a highway and running out of gas. Despite the fact that the engine has shut off, the car will continue forward for a while before coming to a halt. What we can spot, however, is the loss of momentum. That's the same idea here when it comes to volume. If a stock runs out of buyers, its top is not too far away.

A corollary to this is that a stock in a long-term downtrend will show volume drying up as the sell side is exhausted. Investors will react to negative events rapidly. So as the outlook for a market or stocks turns down, volume tends to be heavier early in the decline. Remember where you heard this next concept: "If you're going to panic, panic first." As the negative news or world events unfold and knowledge of these events becomes commonly known to all, fewer and fewer people will want to own the stock and you will see daily and weekly volume decline. Many times most of a stock's long-term decline is characterized as drifting lower from lack of interest rather then being beaten into the ground. The expression is that traders make the tops and investors build the bottoms. Investors and traders will simply walk away from an area and not come back until things improve. This shows the differences between fundamental and technical analysis. Often technicians will act much faster than fundamental analysts because technicians are following the market's reaction to news events instead of waiting for complete verification of news. The market tends to discount corporate news much faster than the news can get digested and disseminated by fundamentals.

c. If you have a stock with a large expanding volume pattern but little price advancement or even lower price action after a prolonged rally, then you are looking at an accident searching for a place to happen. This churning action is distribution and can signal a top. It is saying that despite high demand for this stock, the supply side is rushing in to overpower the buyers. The net result is a reversal.

d. A price breakout above a resistances level or moving average line on an increase of volume is always a welcome sight. This is the confirmation that says that the demand for this instrument is building, and the implication is that the advance is likely to be sustained.

e. On the other hand, a breakdown below a support zone on expanding volume is your signal to look for lower prices until the sellers (supply) are exhausted and the buyers (demand) can find value in the price. Then the stock will stabilize. (See Figure 6-4.)

f. Blow-off tops or selling climaxes are found at the extremes of market moves. These characteristics can change somewhat, but the basic elements are high emotions along with violent price swings. At these points volume can expand to two or three times the normal volume as investors panic. On the upside people are scrambling into the market because they are afraid they will miss an opportunity to become wealthy, and people will pay any price to get into the market. You need not look back in history very far to see what greed can do to common sense. Simply look

FIGURE 6-4

Volume Breakdown. Courtesy of MetaStock.

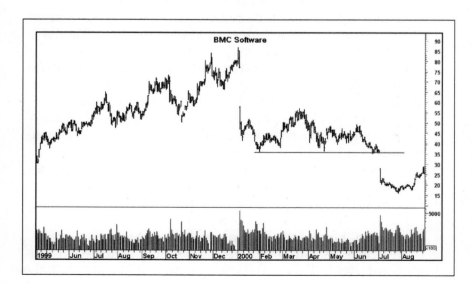

FIGURE 6-5

A NASD. Drawn by The Chartstore.com.

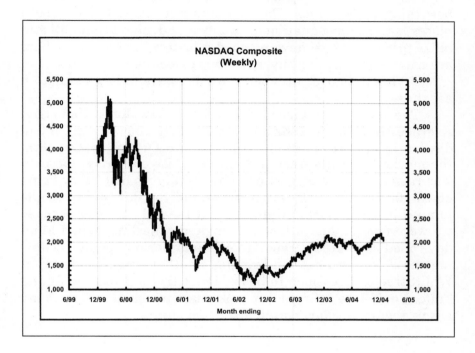

up the numbers at the 2000 top on the NASD. Do you remember that TV ad with the guy in the tow truck and his picture of his private tropical island? (See Figure 6-5.)

There is no thought of using fundamentals or technical, or even trying common sense. This is herd mentality at its best. The most recent example was the week of March 10th 2000 when the OTC exchange registered a closing high of 5132 on volume of 1 billion shares, and the Street couldn't get enough of the Internet stocks. Well that didn't work out very well for many people.

The selling climax is just the reverse, of course. Investors are selling at any price in fear that they will lose their life's savings. These selling panic lows are trickier than I can make them sound in print. I could illustrate many charts to explain the event, but the truth is that until you've gone through one, nothing I say will count for much. It's like being in a bar fight. The best thing to do is duck. The only constant that is found at both places is the same equation of supply and demand that will stabilize price. Once we have reached a price where all the sellers are satisfied, then the buyers reappear looking for values.

Trying to figure out when the sellers are finished is not an easy task

The selloff of October 1987 saw the Dow Jones Industrial Averages fall from a 2662.38 intraday high to a 1616.21 intraday low in 11 days, a loss of 1046.17 points. On Friday, Oct 16th, the market was in a freefall. Near the close of Friday, the Dow was registering the biggest one-day drop in its history by being down 108.37 points. Towards the end of the day, many people jumped into the market thinking that the fall was over because we were trading on an historic single-day decline. When Monday rolled around, the Dow dropped another 567 points, eclipsing the Friday record and bringing another one of those great Wall Street expressions to bear: "Don't try to catch the falling knife. You'll lose a finger." It took years of repair before many issues regained their footing after that drop.

Confirmation

We have already talked about support zones and resistance areas in an earlier chapter. These levels are prices where supply and demand have come into balance and they give us an exact idea of where we can expect selling or buying. A breakout on either side has a certain amount of important information for us as far as price is concerned. If, however, a move beyond one of these levels is accomplished on large increases of volume, then the implications are that the move will extend further and last longer. The fact that the move was accomplished in an aggressive style, as measured by an increase in volume, is grounds enough to have confidence that the action is real. This reasoning can be extended throughout most of the indicators that are used in technical analysis. It is the elevated level of activity that confirms the desires of the buyers or the sellers and can give us a higher level of trust about a move.

On-Balance Volume

I mentioned in Chapter 1 that I began my career in technical analysis in 1964. A year earlier, a well-established and respected technician by the name of Joe Granville wrote a book that I was required to read, entitled *Granville's New Key to Stock Market Profits*. In that book he stated that a closer study of volume and its relationship with price could prove to be of major help to stock market success. He called the indicator On-Balance Volume. It was profound and sad all at the same time. Profound from the standpoint that this concept of On-Balance Volume is still used in most chart services and computer programs today, 40 years after the book was published. It's sad from the standpoint that I've been around long enough to remember when that book was a new edition.

The indicator was designed to grade the quality of a rally or selloff. It is to be used in concert with a price chart and to act as a warning of divergences. The word divergence itself means to go in a different direction, and that's what OBV was developed to spot. It is a method to gauge whether or not the volume in a stock is keeping up with the price action. The formula for OBV is quite simple. The total volume of a day's trading is counted as a positive number if the closing price of an index or a stock ends on the plus side at the end of the day. If, however, the price is lower from the previous close, then the volume is given a minus and the volume is subtracted from the total. The technician runs a cumulative total, and by adding up-volume and subtracting down-volume, a line will be built.

The OBV line's function is to give validity to the price movement, and what is desired is that the cumulative volume line should have the same general direction as the price chart. Like the moving average line, the actual number on an OBV has no meaning by itself; rather it is the direction that interests the trader. If the price movement is to have legitimacy, then the volume pattern should show that buyers and the sellers are in agreement with the overall price chart. If in fact volume leads price, then On-Balance Volume is considered a leading indicator and should give us early indications of a divergence. (See Figure 6-6.)

One problem with OBV is that it gives a somewhat erroneous reading and can be misleading. As for myself, I do not find this abnormality a major problem and still use the original format every day. The problem that arises for some is that total volume is figured with a plus sign or a minus sign, depending on the closing price. The questions come up when the daily action has a twist to it. For example, what happens if the stock opens on a gap high and trades lower for the rest of the day but still ends positive for the day? We would calculate the total volume as a plus because the stock ended the day on the plus side, but in truth most of the volume was traded on downticks. In an attempt to override this flaw, people have tried many different methods of calculating volume. Some of these approaches multiply the amount of gain in the day by total volume, while others go to the actual tick-by-tick

FIGURE 6-6

OBV. Courtesy of MetaStock.

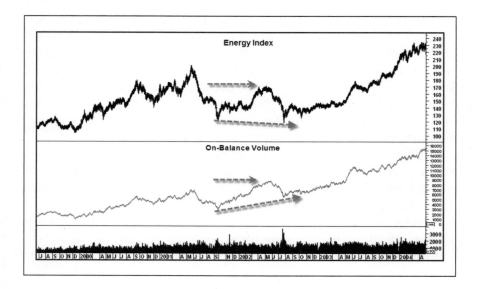

approach, adding up the rises and subtracting the downticks. These approaches can be helpful, but to a large degree I find that the regular OBV indicator performs very well on its own.

UPSIDE/DOWNSIDE VOLUME

The practice of using upside volume and downside volume to help in our judgment of the quality of the market is another attempt on the part of technicians to spot market tops and bottoms. Again we base this type of analysis on the belief that volume is a leading indicator and can give us insight into the aggressiveness of both the demand side and the supply side all at once. A trader that has an informational edge like that at a turning point can be very profitable.

One way to accomplish this is to split volume into its basic parts and run separate cumulative totals for both sides of the supply/demand equation. Upside/downside volume is used in market analysis rather then individual issues. On any given day you can take the total volume traded in all the stocks that end the day on the plus side. That total volume number will represent the upside volume for that day, and we can add it to our accumulative total. On the other side, a total of all the volume in stocks that traded lower on that day is totaled up the same way for the negative issues. Like the moving averages, the actual number has very little meaning. What we want to be aware of is the direction of the lines and what is important is to watch for nonconfirmations. A market that is making new highs in price but is failing to maintain the upside flow of volume into the market is giving off some very negative signals. Also, a market that might be treading water and acting as if it is stalling out but whose upside volume is forging ahead may very well be telling you that all's well, and continuing higher highs should be expected. One of the biggest proponents of this type of analysis is Lowry's Reports, Inc. in North Palm Beach, Florida. They have been working with volume on a daily basis as well as on a 30-day basis for more than 70 years, and it is an important part of their trademark for that service. The 30-day moving average of upside/downside volume indicators are dealing with intermediate-term data. Therefore the signals generated here are not meant

FIGURE 6-7

Lowry's Up Volume/Down Volume.

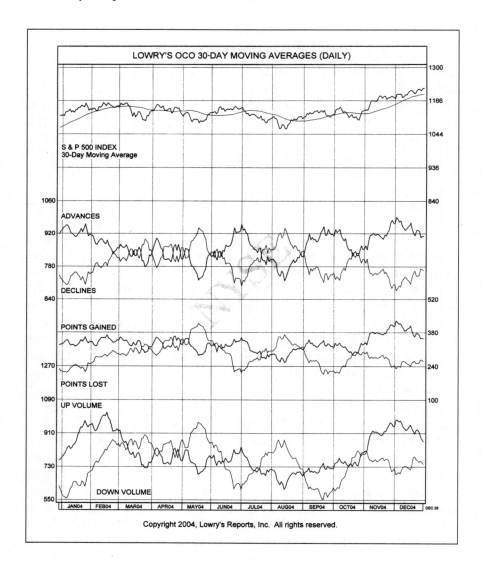

for short-term signals but rather to spot reversals or confirmations for important market turns. With this tool you can watch for trend line violations and crossovers to serve as confirmations of the existing moves. (See Figure 6-7.)

TICK VOLUME

It's hard to speak of tick volume without a mention of Don Worden, who in the 1960s had a service by the name of "The Worden Report." It is my memory that Mr. Worden had this idea of dissecting stocks and markets with tick volume before there were ways of getting the information that is needed. But the concept of looking at every tick and coming up with a plus or minus volume result was quite revolutionary at the time. Tick volume is measuring every trade whether up or down and the volume that accompanies those trades. This calculation is found on many computerized technical services today, and the rules for tick volume are the same as on balance volume. We are looking for divergences and confirmations. We can use trend lines and support and resistance points for signals, but what is sought after is a trader's edge concerning divergences.

One reason for tick volume is to remove some of the misnomers that pop up in volume analysis. Let's take a stock that closes at $24, and the next morning we see a gap open to $25. For the rest of the day we trade lower then $25 and close at 24¼ that night on 1 million shares. Under normal upside/downside volume, it would record 1 million shares of positive volume when in fact most of the volume was really on downticks.

The truth of the matter is that both methods are valid, but if you are a day trader or someone whose plans call for very short term trading (a week or less), then tick volume analysis is well worth your time. Investors might find that the extra effort in this type of study can cause more whipsaws than would be welcomed. It's a trader tool and often depends on your objectives.

MOST ACTIVE ISSUES

A very old and still relevant indicator is the most active list. Every day there is a published list of the stocks that were the most active issues in the previous day's market. Most of the financial newspapers will report on the 20 most active stocks traded on the NYSE, AMEX, and the NASDAQ. The importance of this listing is to show us the issues that have attracted the most interest for that day. Regardless of why, the stocks that have made it to the most active list are indicating that they have the eye of the investing public. This is a snapshot peek into the current market's profile, and we can use this data in a few different ways:

a. We can use the numbers as an indicator of price/volume momentum, which we will talk about in a later chapter.

b. We can examine the areas that are attracting trading volume. It is not unusual for a group or asset class, like preferred stocks, to cluster on the active list. Many times a news event will affect the stocks found on the list. For example, a news story concerning Middle East oil could have the effect of having all 10 most active issues energy related. Simply looking at whether the stocks closed on the plus side or not will tell you about the news story.

c. We can study if the prices are finishing higher or lower for the active issue. It might be obvious, but just in case it is not: seeing 10 out of 10 issues with price gains and very large volume is much stronger then only 5 issues gaining ground or none being to the upside. In a glance you can see the direction of the aggressive part of the market.

d. From a pure level of activity, we can examine if total volume is rising or falling for the issues on the list.

e. Finally, many times by looking at the price level of the issues we can see whether high-priced issues are in favor or whether low-priced stocks are what are attracting traders. We know that there will always be a few low-priced stocks on the list simply from people taking a gamble, but a powerful message is sent when the average price of that list rises. For one thing, it is suggesting that the so-called smart or big money accounts are active.

You need not toil long hours over these numbers, as the active list is another simple tool that can keep you up on the correct direction of the market. You will find that after a short while you will be able to spot sectors, groups of stocks, and styles of stocks that are clustering. Volume moving in or out of certain areas can be spotted, and all in less time than it takes to have your morning coffee.

COMPARING EXCHANGES' VOLUMES

Years ago technicians would compare total volume on the New York Stock Exchange to that on the American Exchange. The thinking was that the traders and the issues on the AMEX were more speculative in nature than those stocks on the New York Stock Exchange. Therefore by comparing the two exchanges' volumes and expressing it in terms of percentages, we could gauge the level of risk the market was able to handle. If the index would get too high, the indicator would be flashing a warning sign that there is too much speculation. If the numbers were low, it would suggest that there was plenty of room to move higher due to the low levels of investors willing to take a large risk. By measuring the volume levels one against the other, it was possible to estimate whether money was flowing into high-grade or low-grade issues.

Well, using those two exchanges today would be silly because the two markets are not what they once were. Besides, if you want to do only what I spoke of you could use the NASDAQ and the NYSE. But thanks to new areas like the Exchange Traded Funds (ETFs) and all the derivative products, we can contrast and compare all night long. The same exact concept is the goal, but now we can look at the market with a much better and stronger microscope. Today, following volume and therefore finding out where the traders are most interested has become a much more reliable and insightful tool than we have ever had before. International markets, sectors, asset classes, and groups are all fair game and arrive at conclusions that are many times sharper than back in the bad old days.

CONCLUSION

Volume can be a very helpful tool in trying to judge the validity of a price move in a time series. The level of activity, in connection to price action, can add another layer of confidence to your outlook by enabling you to conclude that the action caused an increase in volume levels. Volume can also serve as a warning if it fails to keep pace with price or we see too much volume with no price action. The bottom line is that this tool that we label volume can provide us with more pieces to the puzzle and needs to be a part of your tool chest if you ever expect to master technical analysis.

Chapter 7

Momentum

On June 22, 2004, we witnessed the first commercial flight into space by pilot Mike Melvill, and perhaps someday we might look back on that date as historic. But that's beside the point. When the ship was launched it was attached to a larger plane that took a slow, gradual, upward path. Once the ships were in position, Melville's craft, SpaceShipOne, was released and fired its own rockets to propel itself into outer space. For a non-NASA flight you had to be impressed. The plane stayed at those lofty levels for about 3 minutes and started its descent back towards earth. It reached its zenith and declined to its nadir. We saw the slow advance, a rapid increase in altitude on a spiking power thrust, a stage of gradual leveling out, and finally its rapid descent.

I felt that this is a perfect way to think of momentum and explain what we are trying to measure. The fact that during part of its leveling-out phase the ship was still rising is not important; what is relevant is that the rate of ascent was slowing compared to the acceleration stage. That slowing of the rate of acceleration is the information that we seek. If we witnessed a slowing of forward momentum in a stock, as we did with the spaceship, we would have advance warning that the stock might be reaching an end to its rally and it might be time to take profits or at least be ready to act upon additional signs.

What momentum indicators measure is the speed at which price is changing rather then price change itself. The same type of thinking is used in determining the momentum of a stock or a market. What we want is to know whether the rate of ascent or decline is maintaining it's power or losing thrust as the price picture unfolds.

OSCILLATORS

The moving average concept, which is covered in depth in the next chapter, was briefly mentioned earlier as one of the tools to be employed during a trending market. In nontrending markets, however, the oscillator is the weapon of choice because it is designed to signal when the limits of a trading range have been reached. Oscillators, which are extremely useful in trading/ neutral markets, can be harmful at the beginning of a major advance or decline. The signals that are generated at the outset of an important move show the market as being either overbought or oversold. I will speak later of the differences created at these turns.

These tools are a way of examining momentum and not just a simple average of price. Oscillators are trying to give us advance warning of a turn by examining the rate of change in the price action. They look at the internal power of the price by comparing the current price with the price at a fixed period in the past, therefore warning us of market extremes.

When that rocket ship reached its highest point, it stopped climbing up, but it did not immediately drop out of the sky. It hung there in space, although it had lost its forward push and was in the process of changing direction. That's what oscillators are trying to measure and trying to warn us about the prices.

While oscillators are very versatile, there are really only two formats for this tool. They usually appear at the bottom of a price chart and are fairly easy to interpret. Depending on the math you employ, an oscillator can be set up to have a scale of 0 to 100 or we can use a 0 line as a midpoint and plot the oscillator above or below that 0 mark. In the case of the 0 markers, we would run the numbers like this. Working with a 20-day rate of change, we simply would compare today's price with the price 20 days ago. If the current price is 35 and 20 days ago it was selling at a price of 30, then a plus 5 would be plotted on the grid. On the reverse side, if the price today was 5 points lower then 20 days ago, we would plot a minus 5 on the grid. By looking at the price chart and the oscillator chart, we can compare the action of both to determine if the momentum is giving us the proper indications.

The other method is to show the same type of number, but in this case the scale would run in a band from 0 to 100. To judge its overbought or oversold condition we would set upper and lower parameters to gauge the extremes. (See Figure 7-1.)

I mentioned earlier that moving average lines are very helpful in trending markets. A generally declining market with a stock that is in a well-tested down channel can be money in the bank simply by "shorting" into each test of a downward-slanting moving average line. The same can be said for a strong issue in a bull market phase. However, trend-following tools during neutral or nontrending markets are as useful as a library card for

FIGURE 7 - 1

Overbought/Oversold Oscillator. Courtesy of MetaStock.

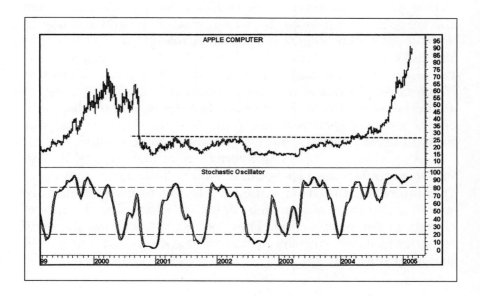

your dog. At the beginning of a major move, an oscillator will become overbought or oversold very quickly and generate a false signal. The reason for these erroneous readings is that many times as we come out of a major bottom, the action on the tape will be in the form of a power thrust for both price and volume. The net result is these large increases in the market numbers will give warnings initially to the traders. At market tops, we will find the same conditions. In the early stages of a rollover, the number will signal that the market is oversold and in a possible positive state, while in fact we are just starting a move lower. The way around this is to follow the other indicators, such as pattern recognition, moving averages, trend lines, etc. in combination with oscillators.

Oscillators, however are made for markets that are confined to a range and swing between the resistance and supports. These tools help us identify overbought and oversold zones and any loss of forward or declining momentum.

The velocity of price is what we are after in our measuring of a stock's price movement. The technician is always running a price comparison for the time span he has assigned to the oscillator. So we are looking at today's price in comparison to an earlier time. If you construct a 20-day momentum line, for instance, you simply subtract the closing price of 20 days ago from the current closing price. It is then plotted around a 0 line to show a positive or negative reading. A reading that shows that the current price is lower than it was 20 days ago would register below the 0 line and have a negative implication. However, if the current price were above where it was 20 days ago, it would be above the 0 thresholds. Like many of the other indicators we have spoken about, remember, the shorter the time period that is used, the more signals will be generated.

A moving average is an average price history, and its signals occur after the fact because we are looking at past data. Oscillators, on the other hand, are trying to give us advance warning of a turn, either up or down, by examining the rate of change in the price action. They look at the internal power of the price by comparing the current price with the price at a fixed period in the past.

Let's try to put some realism into the oscillator. Say we have a stock that is in a strong rally mode, and day after day our 20-day oscillator is showing that the current price is ahead of the older price point. We would have the oscillator in a powerful uptrend until it starts getting into an overbought territory. Overbought and oversold zones are judgment calls, and we would look to the left of the chart at the history to spot past levels that were the upper and lower limits for the particular item we are following. One index might have very different volatility characteristic than another index. These oscillators can lead price because you are comparing current to past prices and seeing visually whether or not the price is maintaining its internal momentum. It's our old friend supply and demand again that is being measured. Buyers make stocks rise and sellers cause them to drop. As long as the index can stay ahead of its most recent past, then upward momentum is maintained. When we see the oscillator's line begin to roll over and start its descent, that's when the red flags should pop up. The demand side is exhausted as the buyers are satisfied, or as a result of the rally the index has gotten so overbought that sellers became aggressive enough to stop demand.

Overbought/Oversold

The words overbought/oversold can be very tricky to say the least. These oscillators are designed to measure extreme levels for whatever financial instrument you are following. There are two main methods of showing OB/OS levels. You can set up a trading scale that runs between 0–100 where O is on the negative extreme and 100 is the positive limit. Usually a technician would set a band on the grid to indicate the overbought and oversold level, such as 30 on the low end and 70 on top. The other style is to construct an oscillator that swings above or below a 0 line. We can spot these limits in many cases by looking backwards on a chart and spotting levels in the past that had acted as turning points. These oscillators are your best working tool in a market that is flat and trendless, as they can show when to move in or out of positions. They spot extremes and give advanced warning that a change in direction might be at hand.

A word of caution: During markets that have defined directional movements, these oscillators can do more harm then good. One failing that we all go through is that, as a market switches from a neutral state to a bull or bear mode, we must switch as well to trend-following tools. I have seen markets in an oversold state for months. Just look at any old chart of the 1970s to get the idea. On the other end, the latter part of the 1990s saw nothing but overbought readings for much of that advance. You will find that because of modern computers, you are able to run many oscillators on many sectors of the general market. There are many different formulas to accomplish this task.

Stochastic

This type of oscillator is another perfect example of a supply/ demand study that can add depth to your technical analysis. Stochastic is an approach that was introduced to the Street by George Lane in the late 1950s. His idea was quite interesting and, like most really sound ideas, once you hear about it you say, "Oh, yeah, why didn't I think of that?" Math is complicated for stochastics, but the concept is straightforward. During periods of a rising bull market, closes tend to be very near the high levels of the day. The reason is that if demand for stock is strong, then that demand should last right into the close of the day. On the other hand, during negative times or a prolonged bear market, the closing prices should be nearer the lows of the day. The question is how to measure this action and place it on the chart. Again let me put your hearts to rest; most technical software carries stochastic as a standard feature. Two lines are employed to attain our goal. One is the %K line and the other is the %D. George Lane suggested that you use a 3-period smoothing of %K to create %D. The %D is the line that generates the signals and therefore the more important line. This technique is a very common tool, and most services use a 14 period as the default. The formula is $\%K = CCP\text{-}LLPn \times 100$

$\qquad\qquad HHPn\text{-}LLPn$

Where CCP = current closing price

LLP = lowest low price during whatever period you set, usually 14 days

HHP = highest high price during whatever period you set, usually 14 days

n = number of days

$\%D$ = %K smoothed over three days

The main problem with this calculation is that it is very sensitive and will give you too many signals. That's as bad as none at all. To reduce the level of whipsaws, some analysts will change the %D line, which has already been slowed by the smoothing, to the %K and then run another 3-period smoothing of %D to develop a "slow stochastic." Many services use a solid line for the %D and a dotted line for the %K. By multiplying the results in the formula, you reach a percentage number that can run from 100 down to 0. (See Figure 7-2.) The 100 level is in the overbought area and the 0 is, of course, oversold. You also

FIGURE 7-2

Slow Stochastic. Courtesy of MetaStock.

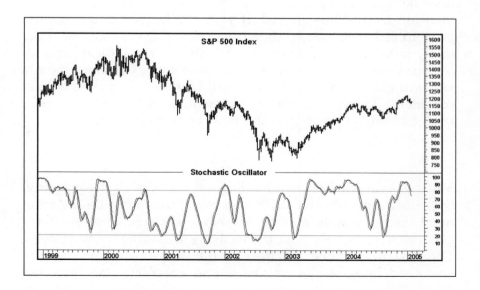

want to employ the crossover rules for this oscillator. If the %K crosses above the %D (slow), it generates a buy signal. If the fast line, %K crosses below the slower smoothed line, then we have a sell signal. A stochastic oscillator can be useful in longer-term charts. This tool is best suited to flat, trendless markets, or markets that are slowly trending.

Rates of Change

ROC is simple enough to understand and interpret. We take the current price and the closing price of the same item for a given date in the past. To create a 40-day ROC indicator, we take the current closing price and divide it by the closing from 40 days ago. The formula would be ROC $= 100 \ (P/Px)$. P is current price and Px is the length you choose. 100 acts as the threshold in the oscillator. If the current price is higher than 40 days ago, then you would be above 100 and have a positive reading. Conversely, if the price is lower now than 40 days ago, then it would show below 100 and we would have a negative reading. The indicator should mirror the price movement as a sign of healthy momentum. It is when we see a divergence that we can start to make some assumptions. The major assumption is that the balance between demand and supply is about to shift as the momentum picture has shifted. If your ROC starts going against price in either direction, then a warning flag is triggered. Like many indicators, the choice of the length of the indicators is up to you. Remember, the shorter the time span, the more signals you will get and the sensitivity will increase. Investors should consider a longer horizon (a few months up to a year), and a trader could get down into the days or perhaps hours.

MACD

Moving Average Convergence/Divergence was first configured by Gerald Appel in the 1970s and was intended as an improvement on the simple moving average approach. This oscillator generates its signals from the crossing of moving average lines. The first line, called the MACD, takes the two exponentially smoothed lines of closing prices and subtracts one from the other. The computer services today use the default of 12 and 26

FIGURE 7-3

S&P 500. Courtesy of MetaStock.

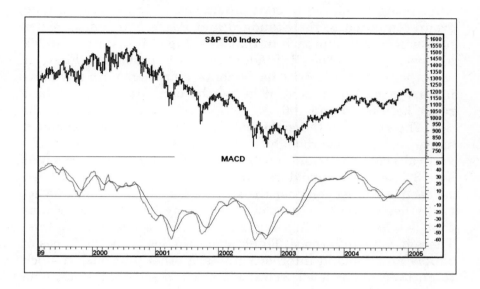

weeks or days for the calculations. The slower line, called the signal line, is nothing more than an exponentially smoothed line of the MACD, so in reality we are dealing with three exponentially smoothed lines of price but only looking at two. The signal line is usually 9 exponential periods of the MACD line. (See Figure 7-3.)

The signals are given when the MACD and the "signal line" cross. When the fast MACD crosses above the "signal line," which is slower, you have a buy signal enforced. On the other hand, when the MACD falls below the signal line, a sell signal is given. The signals are generated by the crossing of the slower line above or below the signal line. The moving above or below a 0 line often is a confirmation of the direction, and usually by the time we reach a 0 line cross, the trend is well established.

Relative Strength Index

The Relative Strength Index, better known as the RSI, was developed by Wells Wilder about 30 years ago and has become a mainstay in many computer services today. The name, however, leaves a lot to be desired. The reason is that when we hear the words "relative strength," we start thinking of two separate entities being compared to each other. For example, the banking group compared to the Standard and Poor's 500 Index. Wider took a different approach in that he compared a stock or index against "itself." The RSI addresses two problems: First, it smoothes out erratic price movements, a problem with any moving average. And second, it keeps the oscillator in a constant range between 0 and 100.

The rules are the same as the other oscillators inasmuch as we set up an overbought and oversold band on the 0 to 100 vertical grid. The usual levels are drawn at 70 for overbought and 30 for an oversold reading. Once either level has been reached, we must consider the state of the stock or index as actually being overbought or oversold. I say it that way because that is when a warning flag goes up. *Not sell or buy signals.* There is a big difference. Think about the logic. As the forces of supply and demand interact with each other and push a stock to an overbought level, you don't want to sell that stock. The reason you are overbought is because there is a good deal of power in the instrument, and that power can last longer than you think. So don't jump too fast. Let your other indicators lead you to a sell. On the other hand, buying a market or stock just because it is oversold is not the smartest thing in the world. Most times I did it, I wound up losing money. The reason something is oversold is because nobody wants it. Here's another Brooks truism: "You don't have to be the first one out of the foxhole." We have to be able to adjust our thinking when it comes to all of these oscillators, and maybe this is a right time to bring this point up. When you use indicators, you must use them in combination with all your tools to reach a decision.

Average Directional Index

The ADX is a method developed by Welles Wilder to determine if a market is in a trending phase or in a neutral phase. The index is designed to grade the strength or the lack thereof in a trend. This is not a market-signaling device but rather a way of judging if a market is trending or not. The ADX ranks the directional move of a market from 0 to 100. Again, keep in mind that we are talking about the trend of the market and *not* the market's direction. The importance here is that there are a number of tools that we can use in a trending market that are very poor tools in a neutral or sideways trading market. So knowing if a market is likely to continue trending can be key to your success. (See Figure 7-4.)

A lifting ADX line signals that the trending process is likely to carry on in the existing direction. A dropping ADX line gives

F I G U R E 7 - 4

ADX and Stock Market.

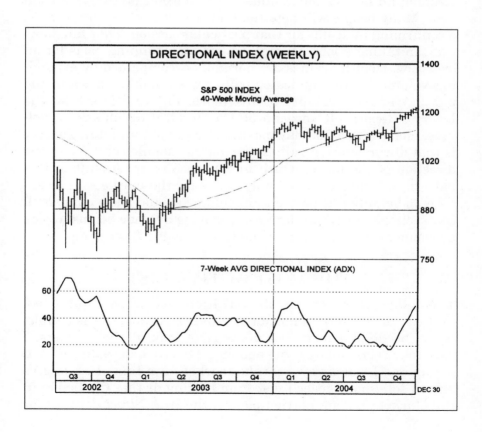

us the opposite indications and suggests that we could be entering a market period suited for possibly our oscillator tools rather than trend-following ones.

This index is an average, as the name suggests, and the usual time frame that Wilder uses is 10 to 14 periods. The index has 20 and 40 as its usual upper and lower trigger points. When the index drops from above the 40 mark, it is a red flag that the trend is beginning to turn soft and might be in for a reversal. On the other hand, a rise above 20 signals the start of a new move. I will say this again: we are not talking about up or down but rather a trend shift.

VOLUME

Keeping an eye on the volume of the market is always a solid idea. Many people will note the total volume on certain days as a confirming indicator for that particular session. They fail, however, in taking a look at total volume on a running basis for an overview. Healthy rallies are normally accompanied by expanding volume, so this indicator will give us another piece to the puzzle as to the validity of any move. Figure 7-5 is from the Lowry's Reports. It shows a 30-Day total of up plus down volume, along with a 200-day moving average of that total. The key is that during market rallies, the volume should continue in the direction of the move, which in this case is up. A shift in this pattern can have serious implications for the markets. If a sell-off is to be minor, then the total volume should show only small contractions. It's when the 30-day moving average begins to pick up momentum on the downside that warning flags go up.

THE MOST ACTIVE LIST

This indicator is very simple, but it does serve as a quick tool that can be mastered in about 3 minutes. Although it is simple, it can be helpful in taking a snapshot look at the markets. I once told a class many years ago that if Scotty had really beamed me up and I was away from the market for a time, I could give a good solid-hour speech just from looking at the "C" section in the Markets Lineup portion page of the *Wall Street Journal* for

FIGURE 7-5

Up Plus Down Volume.

5 minutes. A major part of that boast would have been a scan of the most active names. What we get to look at are the 20 stocks with the heaviest volume of that day for the New York, Amex, and NASDAQ markets. Many times you can spot patterns in the names as far as sectors or groups are concerned. Another element that you can cull from the numbers is the price level of the majority of issues. It is usual that low-priced names will find their way to the list on a regular basis, and most of these you can eliminate as permanent residents of the list because of their low price. The rest of the list, however, can give you a feel for what the buyers and the sellers are up to in their

daily business. Remember, talk is cheap, and the most active list is showing you where and what the people are doing.

PERCENTAGE OF S&P 500 STOCKS ABOVE THE 200 DMA

Another simple indicator is to follow the Standard and Poors 500 Index and its moving average line. There are a number of services that follow this indicator for you, so again you're not going to have to do the math yourself. But if you want that pleasure, all you need to do is to run a 200-day moving average for 500 names in the index and calculate how many issues are above or below their own 200 DMA. To remove the wide fluctuations, a 10-day or 4-week moving average of the percentages would be recommended.

An easy rule of thumb for this momentum indicator is to follow the trend. If the indicator is moving higher, stay long. When the 4-week average turns lower, go short or simply sell your position and stay on the sidelines. I think I feel another Brooksism: You can go to the sidelines and wait. There is no law that says you always have to be active in the markets. "When in doubt, stay out."

Chapter 8

Moving Averages

A major problem that investors and traders face when looking at stocks and market indexes is trying to handle volatility. Trying to distinguish between a short-term reaction or an important bottom or top can be illusive even at the best of times. We are living in an age of instant communication and information overload when it comes to being confronted with events that can affect our lives. These two facts of life can be a blessing and a curse at the same time. The phenomenon has been a part of the background in the U.S. markets since almost the first day someone traded a stock under the Buttonwood tree in lower Manhattan. The dissemination of information has been a major reason for the success of our markets and has been part and parcel of the expansion over its 120+ years of history.

Here's an interesting fact that can be found when you read books about the Depression years: People blame the invention of the telephone, to some degree, for the great crash in 1929. It seems that with the introduction of the telephone, sellers were able to place their liquidation orders at a much more rapid pace than in the past. At the time this new invention must have made the order flow seemed like it was at the speed of lighting. So I guess it's all relative compared to today. The point is that we have always learned how to adapt to speed in the markets, and we will always be faced with faster modes of communication. Always be prepared for change.

The markets today can trade in wild swings influenced by current events from global news, an election, war, or invaders from outer space, etc. Stock prices can trade in many different directions and sometimes in a very short period of time. As a result, a person can fall prey to moves in price that prove to be a false start or an early sign of weakness. When you are in the trading day and things begin to happen around you, that is not the time to start wondering if you should buy or sell. A general game plan should have already been thought out. There are ways to protect yourself from some of the emotions that go hand in glove with these swings.

If I haven't said it already, let me stop here and tell you that none of these tools are infallible. A very excellent technician and a good friend of mine, Alan Shaw, once told me years ago that "Everything in technical analysis works, sometimes." So when you use this tool or any other, use them in concert with other indicators and know that nothing will work well if you fail to use your common sense.

A powerful instrument that technicians have in their tool chest is the moving average. This technique, which can be applied to any area of the financial market, allows us to smooth out price data and obverse the general direction of the series we are studying. If we are following a stock and want to construct a basic 150-day moving average line, we would simply add up the closing prices for the last 150 days and divide by 150. This will give us one data point or average of that stock's closing price for the last 150 days.

By adding the next day's closing prices to the total and subtracting the first day, we move the data point forward, thus the name moving average. By smoothing out the price, especially of a very active moving stock, we can get a very clear picture of the general trend of that stock. Then when we do see a sharp move, we watch the moving average to help us determine what action should be taken. (See Figure 8-1.)

These moving averages can be any length of time. We have talked about the 150-day moving average, but it could be just as easily a 50-day, 10-day average, etc. The time period for these

FIGURE 8-1

Moving Averages. Courtesy of MetaStock.

averages is selected according to the goals you set. If you are trading options, a 150-day moving average might not be of much help to you except as a general overview. Many short-term traders use them on a 2-week or even on an intraday basis. So once you have a handle on your time horizon, then a proper moving average length can be selected.

I'm going to say this again, although by this time you should know this on your own: Do not use MAs as buy or sell signals. They are called indicators because they indicate something is in the works and needs looking after. My own preference is to get a signal from a MA and then react only when there is a penetration of overhead resistance or a violation of downside support for a confirmation. Finding the correct combination of tools is the trick that you must seek. One size does not fit all. Discovering the correct combination that works for you is the secret and the goal you are trying to reach. Some folks will run separate P&F charts and use them for confirmations. Yet others will use trend lines as their confirmation tool. Just like my kids say to me all the time, "Whatever floats the boat, Pop."

SELECT THE PROPER TOOL FOR THE JOB

Know what you want and use the tools that will get the job done. Short-term traders should stick with MAs of about 20 days or less, while longer-term investors would be best suited with 150-day moving averages. Making these changes is simple with today's computers. Back in the dark ages, I was told by my boss to construct a chart of IBM for him. The task he gave me was a 2-year daily bar chart with volume. He wanted an OBV (on-balance volume) and a 50- and 150-day moving average. After getting 2 years of *Wall Street Journal*s out of the library, I gathered the high, low, close, and volume for IBM and drew the chart in pencil, by hand. The OBV and the two MAs had to be done on an old, crank-handled adding machine. The job took 7 business days and my eyesight (just kidding). I am happy to report that all the moving averages that I have been talking about come ready to order on today's computers. What was at one time a backbreaking task is now a push of a button. If you want to study the subtle differences between the various time frames, feel free to explore. I believe what you will find is that the shorter the time frame, the more sensitive the movement. Make the computers work for you, and like me and most good technicians, don't take anyone's word for what's best for you.

My advice is to experiment with different lengths of time for your moving averages. You'll find that different instruments need different time intervals. Also, in a market rally or decline, one area or sector of the market might require a shift in parameters because of their velocity. Technology issues might require a shorter moving average then say a utility issue. Moving averages are very helpful, and with today's equipment, you can get wonderful use from this technical mainstay. (See Figure 8-2.)

I want to make a few more observations about MAs. The reason this tool is employed so much is that it's hard to argue with its success. The theory behind this indicator simply makes sense. If after you have constructed a line of the average closing prices for this stock and that MA line is going up or down,

FIGURE 8-2

Tech Stocks, Intel. Courtesy of MetaStock.

then it's impossible to reach some other conclusion about its direction other then the trend in which the MA is headed.

If a stock is in an uptrend and has been running strong for a time, then the moving average will be rising along with the price pattern. The movement of the price and the moving average line in lock step simply means that the uptrend is intact and all positions should be maintained. Obviously, those small contra drops that appear should be used to add to a portfolio.

If eventually, for whatever reason, the current closing price falls below the average closing price, then we have a warning flag as to the health of that uptrend. The moving averages are not to be used as buy/sell signals but rather as a warning of a possible reversal. Other tools must be applied together with the MA information to reach a decision. Imagine the chart and what is happening just for a minute. A cross below a rising MA tells us that the stock's price momentum is losing ground and supply is beginning to beat out demand. (See Figure 8-3.)

FIGURE 8-3

A Moving Average Bottom. Courtesy of MetaStock.

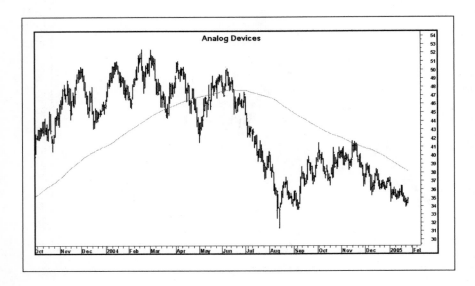

I realize this can be a simple tool, but it is usually the easy things that elude us. This business does not have to be complicated, although that's what we all tend to do from time to time. Our problem (I include myself) is in thinking that maybe the indicator isn't working this time. Perhaps we think we know something that the market doesn't or that the market just has the wrong idea about this stock. Believe me, all these thoughts and more will crop up. And they are all wrong. Ignoring basic indicators might be one of the largest failings you will face in the business. Thinking that this time, it's different.

A FEW HIGHLIGHTS

Because you will be using moving averages in this line of work, let me highlight a few more points about moving averages. The MA will act as a potential support or resistance area in a trending move. What does that mean? Let's look at a stock in an established declining pattern; the price should be trading below the average of the closing prices. Each successive decline should bring the stock to new low territory as well as a short-term oversold condition. I said this in an earlier chapter, but I'll do it again. One of the major tenets of technical analysis is that "stocks trend." They do not go in one direction from top to bottom and up again. A contra rally will appear against the underlying direction and stocks will get oversold or overbought on a short-term basis, which are the forces of supply and demand struggling for dominance. In the case of a declining stock, a rally will develop and many times the moving average line will act as overhead resistance for the stock price or at least indicate the zone in which the stock has stopped in the past.

The whole idea is that the line itself is showing us the approximate level where prices have been turned back during the time span of the average you are running. This area is where supply and demand have come into balance before, and unless the stock is making a reversal, it should be turned back again. Here comes another Brooks's truism: "No market moves in a straight line." There are always zigzags or what they call contra rallies. These smaller rallies or selloffs are minor moves to relieve either an overbought or oversold short-term condition of a stock.

On the other side, if a stock or commodity is in an established uptrend and runs into a normal short selloff, then the MA will act as a support zone for the price. That average price line is the spot where demand has been seen in the past. This is the average price that the traders have been willing to pay for this instrument, but like everything in life, it sounds good on paper. Our task is in telling the difference between short-term corrective moves versus a major directional change. To that end, the moving average often gives us our first warnings.

Multiple Moving Averages

Another useful variation to the moving average is to run two separate lines of varying times to add punch to the analysis. Employing a few moving averages can help you in your efforts to use this tool successfully. The reasoning is straightforward. You select a time frame for the two averages that have some harmony to compare with each other. A 10-day MA (2 weeks), and a 20-day MA (4 weeks) would have a connection. The shorter time frame will be more sensitive to price movement and is called the fast line. The longer time period is slower to respond to current action because it is using more days in the average but will generate fewer signals. We can call that one the base line. What we are examining is the interaction of the two lines. The relationships of the two lines are all important. If we see the fast line cross above the base line, it will generate a buy signal from this tool. Why? Because forces of demand have been powerful enough, over the most recent time span, to push the price over the base line, which is the indication of growing strength.

If, however, we see the faster average fall below the base line, the implication is that the short-term picture is having problems. It should be assumed that the supply side of the equation is gaining, and weakness should be expected. Like all the averages, of course, the longer the time frame that you use in your averages, the slower the indicator and the fewer whipsaws will occur.

Just in case I haven't used that term already, a "whipsaw" is a false signal that reverses on you almost as soon as you take a position. You sell on a good signal and as soon as you do, it begins a rally. Or as soon as you buy, the bottom falls out. The best defense against whipsaws is studying your indicators before you act. Remember, if you get caught in a whipsaw, and you will sometime, do not wind up holding on to a loser because you are afraid to act. Also, having a good sense of humor can help. You'll need it. (See Figure 8-4.)

There are a few approaches that have worked over the years that you need to know about. I was going to use the words "rules that have worked," but to be honest with you there are very few hard-and-fast rules in technical analysis. Most of the tools that we use will adjust with the times, which is a good thing. As the markets change and new products are introduced, technical analysis has always changed with them. The approaches haven't changed, but changing of limits and extending them has been given a bit more leeway. When you look at any stock in today's market, you will see minor penetrations of the MA on a frequent basis.

FIGURE 8-4

Two MA–SLB. Courtesy of MetaStock.

If you made a trade every time a MA was penetrated, you'd need two stockbrokers just to handle your paperwork. Taking the example of Figure 8-5, we can see that the price had traded above the moving average in a number of spots and immediately turned back to its original direction. For the best results, you will want to use filters on your work to remove what is called "street noise."

Let's look at two criteria that I apply to crossovers.

1. The degree of the cross. The usual filter that I place on a penetration of a moving average line is about 3 percent. In order to maintain what I believe to be a good position, I am willing to give up 3 percent to avoid a whipsaw.

2. The second rule I will use on a trend line penetration is time itself. There are violations that occur that sometimes sit there with no movement at all. I have found over the years that if a stock has declined to a point below its MA and nobody cares about the discount they

FIGURE 8-5

A Stock with Minor Crossovers. Courtesy of MetaStock.

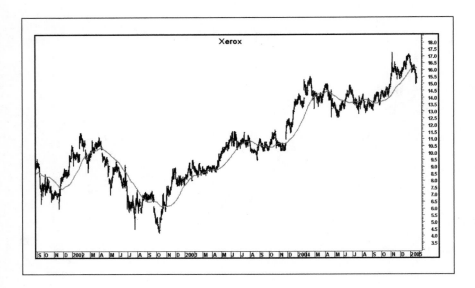

can take advantage of, then more times than not you are looking at a losing stock. My threshold of pain in a situation like that is 2 to 3 days as long as there is no meaningful movement and by movement I am referring to rule one, 3 percent and no more.

This type of elbow room is for accounts that have an intermediate to longer-term outlook. A short-term trader could never wait that long or give up that much profit/loss on a trade. Traders must take these two concepts and convert them to fit their schemes. Because a trader dose not have the luxury of either time or draw downs, I think the old method of one strike and you're out is the best approach. You will have whipsaws with that method, but you will keep your losses small and allow your winners to run. Most traders will tell you that the vast majority of your trades can be losses as long as they are minor. When a winner comes your way, you must be willing to let it run and keep moving up your stops.

THE DOWNSIDE TO MOVING AVERAGES

Short-term traders must employ a different screen in their work with moving averages. Because the one sure way for a trader to become an investor is for the trader to get caught in a losing position that was held too long. For their purposes the MA may not prove to be the best tool. The moving average is a trend-following tool, and very active traders might find it inappropriate for them. A slower trader (someone who wishes to trade on a weekly basis) might still want to employ this technique because of its basic values. In this case a close above or below the MA by the full day's action might be the answer. To register a signal we would want to see the high-low of a bar chart penetrate the line. Notice how I tried to give you an idea of the versatility of this tool and how you can make it fit *your* needs.

Don't forget that financial instruments not only go up and down in price but move into neutral patterns as well. These periods of trading ranges occur more times than you think. In neutral markets moving averages are not much help. The MA is a trend-following tool that is designed to keep you in a stock because after all, "The trend is your friend." When there is no trend, there is no friend.

WARNING SIGNS

A signal to watch for is when the moving average line flattens out after a long period in a trend. When we see the flat MA and criss-crossing of the price above and below the moving average, then we can say that we have a confirmed change in the price pattern from trending to flat. The question of this action signaling a top or a bottom will depend on a violation of the supports or resistance zones. Being forewarned by one of these red flags can and will make all the difference in the world in your performance.

As I mentioned earlier, you must know what you are trying to achieve and then find the appropriate tool to assist you in attaining your goals. A day trader would choose a very short term MA while a true investor could opt for the longer versions. Many people, myself included, use two or more of these moving averages in tandem. This tends to give added confirmation to the price action and will bring us to a discussion of crossovers and how to use them.

The crossover that I mention is a relatively simple concept. For example, let's say we are running two MAs, a 50-day moving average and a 100-day moving average. The 100-day gives us a longer-term, smoothed line of closing prices for that period. The shorter-term MA will be more sensitive, as we are dealing with fewer days to water down the swings. The theory is that if the sensitive/shorter MA crosses above the slower line, it is considered a positive signal. The reasoning is that the shorter moving average will reflect the most recent price action, and if the stock can rise above the slower average price line, then the current action is showing a pickup in overall demand. (See Figure 8-6.)

Like everything in technical analysis, the opposite calls for a warning flag. If the shorter MA fails to at least keep pace with the longer MA, then we are witnessing a loss of power, and the

FIGURE 8-6

150-Day Moving Average. Courtesy of MetaStock.

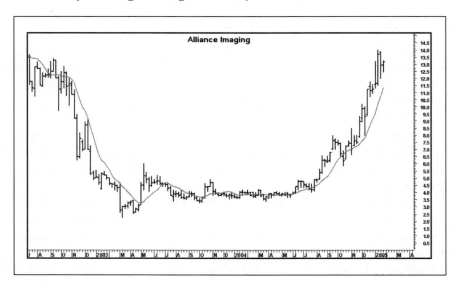

supply side of the trade is beginning to take hold. That's one approach with two moving averages, and there are those who will run many more MAs to place a sort of band around a stock. Thanks to the power of the PC, you can do as much creating as you like and let the computer do all the hard work. You might want to forget the idea of closing prices and run a MA of only the lows and another one of only the highs. What you will build is an envelope. The top band will be an average of highs over the given time and the lower band will be the average lows. You could, in theory, trade from the top of the envelope where you would be a seller, down to the lows of the envelope where you'd change to the buy side. Think of it as looking at the *averages* of supply and demand over a given period of time.

MOVING AVERAGE TYPES

Let's look at the types of moving averages and their pros and cons. We talked about the simple MA above when we showed how we add up the closing prices of a given number of days or weeks that you chose for your time span. I.e., for a 20-day MA you add up 20 days and divide by 20 to get your average. To move it ahead, the next day you subtract day 1, add day 21, divide by 20, and so on. This average is fine, but it does have its shortfalls. For one thing, all the data is treated equally. As a technician, I am more concerned with recent history than I am with data of 20 days ago. I know the importance of the past data, but current data is more germane to my day-to-day action. With a simple MA, every day carries the same weight as the next. If during the length of the moving average a major prices move occurs, for whatever reason, then we will have a bubble in the numbers that will eventually have to be removed from the average. It has an effect going in and has one coming out. Think about running a simple 50-day moving average line using the data from October of 1987.

On Friday, October 16th, the Dow Jones dropped 108 points, which at the time was the largest one-day fall ever for that index. Of course on Monday, Oct 19th, 1987 the Dow Jones declined another 500 points or so. The combination of these two days had a giant effect on the moving average. With a moving average that weights everything the same, you will not only have a major negative impact on the moving average as the event occurs, but when they drop off 50 days later the indicator will give a very strong reading. Their positive impact would be felt, and in the case of 1987, 48 days later, we might well see an unexpected strengthening of the MA because the data of the 16th and the 19th were being removed. I suppose we could leave a note for ourselves to remind us of the change, but it just isn't very practical. Besides, many of the outlying numbers that you will run into are not as dramatic as what I have put forward. Nonetheless, a single day on the downside or a large one-day rally can distort your numbers and possibly give you a false signal.

As past abnormal activity is removed, you will be replacing it with the current day's close. So if you use this type of moving average, you must always be on the lookout for large numbers that could generate a signal based on a bad assumption.

New approaches were taken to try to minimize some of these distortions. We have three general styles of moving averages.

Simple, Weighted, and Exponential

We have already talked about the simple moving average and we know all moving averages are trend-following by their nature. I would make one further point. As good as they are, MAs are late on turns because you are using average prices.

Another shortfall with moving averages is that they only really work well in trending markets. Moving averages are solid instruments in a trend, but once a market moves into a sideways pattern, it's best to lay that tool down for awhile. The stock markets spend a good deal of the time in nontrending phases. It is my experience that more than half the time we will find ourselves in a sideways market. So we have an indicator that is a lagging indicator, counts all the days as the same in the average, and only works in trending markets. This tool requires some work on our part.

Weighted Moving Averages

To address one of the failings of the simple average, analysts have come up with the weighted MA. Here we place more

importance on the most recent data points. There are many formulas for calculating a weighted moving average, and with today's computers they are standard with the technical services.
A 5-week moving average, for example, would multiply the oldest closing price by 1 and the most recent price by 5 for a total.
The divisor would be the total of the weighting, in this case 1 +
2 + 3 + 4 + 5 = 15. You have an average, but it has now become
more sensitive to current market action. Here's small example
of this approach.

Weekly Price	# of Weeks	Total
20	oldest 1	20
21	2	42
23	3	69
25	4	100
23	current 5	115
	TOTAL	346 divided by 15 gives a reading of 23.06.

Exponential Moving Averages

The exponential moving average is the next step up in the math-
ematical food chain, but basically you're still looking at a
weighted average. This approach will keep all the data in the
series in the equation. The interesting aspect of this approach
is that the most current day carries the greatest of the weighting in the average. The combination of the latest day and all
the other day's data must add up to 100 percent between the
two numbers. If you wanted a forward sensitive weighted average, you would place a heavier percentage for the current day,
thus making the recent data most important. If you assign a
small weighting to the current day's action, then you will get a
less sensitive moving average. It depends on what you are attempting to monitor.

PREVENTING WHIPSAWS

Outside of giving us the general direction of a stock action, the
moving average can act as a buy/sell signal. When the price
starts dropping below a MA, we see a warning that the forward momentum is slowing. The opposite is true for an upside

penetration of an MA in that it is signaling a "buy" because the
current price is above the average. That all sounds good on paper, but the truth is that it is very normal for the price action
to swing over and under the average during the course of a normal move. This approach will generate many whipsaws and false
starts and makes our job harder. To solve this concern, traders
sometime place filters on a penetration of a moving average line.
There are a few ways of trying to limit the number of whipsaws
in this type of analysis. One method is to say that the stock
must cross the threshold by some percentage point before it is

F I G U R E   8 - 7

An Envelope.

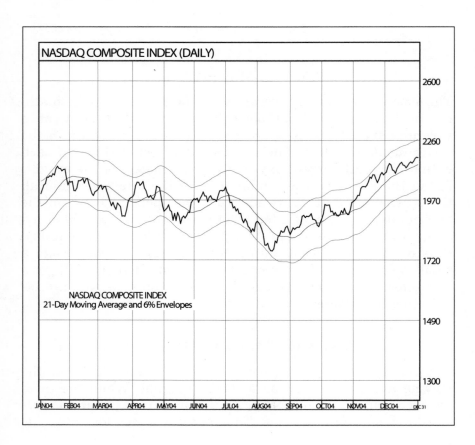

a valid signal. The most common amount seems to be about 3 percent. Traders also could place importance on the price being above or below an average for 2 or 3 days to assure themselves of no whipsaw. You will never avoid all mistakes, and every indicator can and will give false signals from time to time, but these extra requirements will save you money in the long run.

USING ENVELOPES IN MOVING AVERAGES

A great visual aide that I like to use when looking at averages is to construct an envelope around whatever I happen to be following. Let's use the NASDAQ Composite Index as an example. This approach can warn us if the series we are looking at has gotten overbought or oversold. If we use the theory that the price should not move too far afield from the average price, then we should be able to place a standard percentage filter on the single moving average. In this case study let's employ a 21-day moving average. From that moving average, if we create a 6 percent upper and lower band extended out from the average, then we have built our envelope around the center. When the S&P reaches the upper limit and shows any signs of waffling, we should be alerted to a possible change of direction. Likewise, when the lower limit is tested, our attention should be focused on a reversal to the upside. What we have done is to establish the upper and lower limits in a normal move. Once those limits have been met, then we must start to look for the signs of a turn in direction. (See Figure 8-7.)

Chapter 9

Money Flow

If price charts are the structure or skeleton of stocks, then money is surely its lifeblood. Without money available for the market, there isn't much chance that a healthy, strong market will survive for very long. An accommodative monetary policy and the accessibility of funds are keys for a positive market outlook. It is the examination of this piece of the puzzle that we will speak of in this chapter. To begin with any look at money flow, we must talk about the effects of interest rates on the markets. I am not going to give you a course in Economics 101, so rest easy, but I will point out a number of facts that cannot be ignored. There are very few theories in this business that work 100 percent of the time, and we can always find the exceptions to the rule. Now that I have gotten that hedge clause out of the way, let me give you another old expression from the Street, "Don't fight the Fed." Once rates start to move, the financial markets know that a) the cost of money will be affected, b) the bottom lines of corporations will either be improved or reduced, depending on the direction, c) a number of financial instruments will be affected that can influence the market's action as a whole.

If the Reserve starts on a course of easing rates, they are signaling that they wish to have a less restrictive strategy for money. This presupposes that rates were high and most likely beginning to cut off economic growth. In order to stimulate the economy, they will lower the Fed Funds. This particular interest rate is the most closely watched of all the rates because it is the beacon as to the intension of the Federal Reserve. This sets the charge that one bank must charge another bank for loans. Once the bank on our corner has funds to lend to the public, it will set the rate accordingly from what it had to pay to borrow. (See Figure 9-1.)

These lower interest rates can be a major factor for most people in deciding whether to make a purchase or not. Those purchases cover just about everything you can imagine. The money can go to building a new home, buying a new car, sending your children to college, or a million other reasons. Most of these expenditures help the economy grow and corporate

FIGURE 9-1

Interest Rates. Drawn by The ChartStore.com.

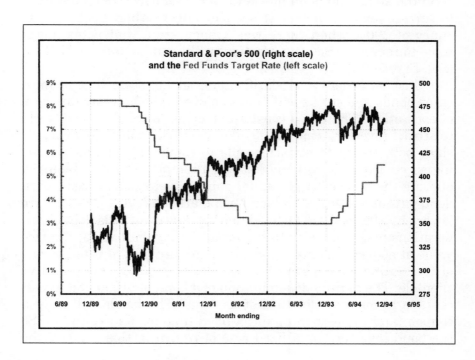

earnings to expand. Corporations also can borrow money at reasonable levels to build new factories or hire needed workers to meet current demands. As the economy expands and prosperity reaches to all areas, the stock prices begin to lift on the expectations of higher earnings. At least, so goes the theory.

CHANGING RATES

Why all the worry about changing rates? The change in interest rates will affect all levels of the market one way or another. What is at risk can be much more than just the fear of chocking off money to support stock prices. It can affect the general mood of the country towards investing or alter the spending plans of the largest corporations in the world. So a directional shift by the Fed can have long-term implications for the way we all deal with the financial markets. Once again we meet our old friends, fear and greed or supply and demand if you prefer. Usually, the mere mention that rates might change is enough to send the stock and bond markets on a wild ride. We do not have to turn to ancient history to see this effect either. Look at February of 2004, when there was a suggestion that rates might have to increase. See the reaction in the banks and the REITS. (See Figure 9-2.)

Just as a matter of clarification, let me state that in most cases bonds and stocks will tend to move in the opposite direction of each other. There is a constant struggle in the financial world to attract investor's capital. It's like two barkers at a carnival side show both trying to attract people to come on over and get the higher return. The stock market will attempt to draw investors by offering the hope of large capital gains plus in some cases a dividend payout. In periods of long-term market advances, that allure is very hard to resist. The bond market, however, sells debt of corporations to the public with the promise to pay it back at the face value at a specified date. Some bonds are tax free, or rated by one of the Rating Services AAA in quality to attract a conservative clientele. The normal denomination of a bond is $1000 and in percentage terms we refer to that as "par." The bonds will have a coupon (and interest rate) and a fixed time for its expiration. So the bond investor has a fixed rate of return in this bond. If the

FIGURE 9-2

Banks and REITS. Courtesy of MetaStock.

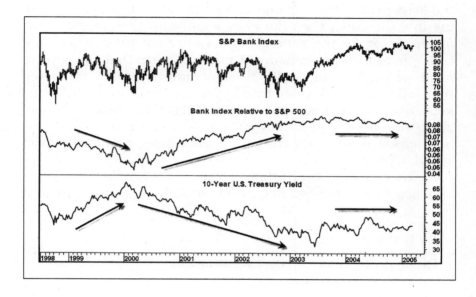

current interest rate goes higher or lower than that investor's already established rate of return, then the only way to attract buyers to that paper is for the price of the bond to rally or fall above or below "par." Contrary to popular belief, the bond market can have just as much volatility as the stock market. These two areas of the financial world are always struggling with each other for investor's money. If dividends and prices begin to rise in the stock market because rates fall in the bond market, then money that is earmarked for investing should flow to stocks. But if rates start to rise faster than prices, then the investing flow of cash will end up in the bond market. Again, try to think of the logic of it all.

Rates	Stocks	Bonds
Increase +	Lose ground	Attractive and gain
Decrease −	Attractive and gain	Lose ground

When I speak of an interest rate move, I am referring to a directional shift rather than a small adjustment because of some

minor event of the time. To have a rate shift that is meaningful, we must first have an existing long trend, either up or down,
to be reversed. Like most everything else in financial markets,
the longer the length of time those interest rates have been going in a direction, then the more significant the reversal. One
major reason for the Federal Reserve to raise rates is they are
trying to cool off an economy. A major concern that the government wishes to avoid is for the economy to get so overheated
that inflation starts going into hyperdrive and grinds the markets to a complete stop. During periods of runaway inflation,
prices are increasing far beyond wages, and it can stop a growing market dead in its tracks. People simply cannot afford to
spend. (See Figure 9-3.)

The Fed will lower interest rates if they believe the economy has slowed enough due to the existing high rates. At that

FIGURE 9-3

Rising Rates. Drawn by The ChartStore.com.

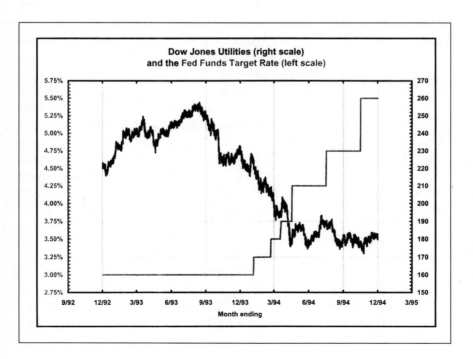

time they will wish to stimulate an economic expansion once again. Obviously, there are many other reasons for these adjustments by the Treasury Department. All I am trying to do is to make the point that if rates reverse, you need to know how to handle it. These adjustments not only influence markets but sectors and groups in the stock market. The bond market will be forced to adjust along with everyone else, and large pools of money will flow from one maturity to another trying to fit with the new paradigm.

The Yield Curve

The yield curve is a method of gauging the relationship between short-term interest rates and long-term interest rates. We can graph the path of two maturities and study their levels. When banks lend money, they usually will want a somewhat higher rate of return for longer time frames. So a 3-year loan will require more interest charge then a 3-month loan. Therefore the yield curve is considered normal if long rates are above the shorter rates. When the short rates move above the long, the curve is said to be inverted. This is a major signal that we are in a tight monetary atmosphere. There are many ways of measuring these two rates, and I am sure they can be constructed complicated enough to make a statistician sigh, but one basic way of watching rates is to divide long paper such as AAA corporate bonds with a short-term 3-month paper. (See Figure 9-4.)

Running this indicator on a 6-month basis and overlaying a moving average on top of those readings can give us a solid examination of the topic. This type of indicator is considered a leading market indicator and can signal the relationship of short versus long rates. An inverted yield curve often can give us a heads up as to a significant market top.

Three Steps and a Stumble

In the 1970s I had the pleasure of meeting Mr. Edson Gould, one of the truly great technicians of his time. His uncanny predictions of the stock markets have been categorized and restudied for years by many students of the market. When you have the chance you should learn a very interesting part of Wall

FIGURE 9-4

A Yield Curve with an Inverted Top. Courtesy of MetaStock.

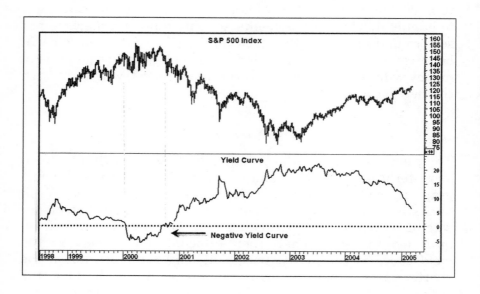

Street history by reading about Mr. Gould. One of the indicators he came up with was "The Three Step and Stumble Rule." This indicator stated that after the third rise in the discount rates, the stock market would stumble into a bear market. It referred to the discount rate only but later came to include margin requirements or reserve requirements.

Think of the logic of the rule for a minute. The Federal Reserve does not like to give the impression that they flip rates around any time they please. Therefore, a change on an important instrument like the discount rate is likely to be the law of the land for at least the intermediate term (3–6 months).These changes usually are announced at the Fed open market meeting every 3 months or so. By the time we get the third increase, the market will have been in a cautious mood already, so the third increase soon is considered a confirmation move. If we have a period where three increases occur, then we are speaking of a general tightening policy taking hold of the marketplace.

SECTORS AND GROUPS

With the financial markets so interlaced with the interest rate, it is imperative that you are aware of at least which sectors of the market will be helped or hurt by any movement in this area. As the Federal Reserve moves rates, the effect is felt on some groups very quickly and on others as a trickle-down reaction. Eventually most people, places, and things will be touched in one away or another. A rising rate environment is simply making it more expensive for the banks to borrow from each other, which means you and I will have to pay more in interest if we want to buy that new car or home, etc. So higher rates make people a little less in a hurry to borrow, and that can start a process of slowing, not stopping, an economy. Purchases that might have been made are deferred, waiting for better rates. Again this does not happen overnight but is an erosion effect rather then a sudden stop. If rates rise, think of the economy in terms of being on the Titanic. The guys playing the violins on the main deck did relatively better then the guys in the boiler rooms. The guys in the boiler room and the violinist ended up in the same place; one group got there first, that's all. In a period when rates are dropping, you have just the opposite effect. If money is free flowing and rates are low, then people are more willing to borrow and spend because they have been able to borrow money at lower rates. The sectors that rely very heavily on the availability of cash will be the first to react.

Utilities Sector

These groups will be affected almost immediately. Utilities are always borrowing money from the government and banks for the building of new sites and plants and upgrading the equipment they have in place. A perfect example of this need was the blackout that occurred in the northeastern United States in 2002. As a result, the utilities across the board have been sent back to their respective drawing boards to update their procedures and plants. We are talking about billions of dollars of borrowing for decades, perhaps forever for upgrading their businesses. This upgrading would have happened anyway; it's just that the blackout gave it somewhat of an emergency air about it. Regardless, even a half a point rate hike will affect the bottom line of these stocks greatly because of the added expense the corporations will incur. The more interest expense on their balance sheets, the less profits that they can report. More importantly, if the utilities make less money, they will pay lower dividends to their shareholders. One of the main reasons investors buy utilities is for the conservative nature of the group and the tendency to pay high dividends. (See Figure 9-5.)

Banks make their living out of lending money. Historically, short-term rates are below long-term interest rates. Because the institutions are lending money for a longer period of time, they must factor in uncertainties that can influence the risk to their lent money. The more risk, the more the reward. So when rates fall, the banking group will borrow short and lend long. If there is a shift in direction and rates start moving higher, the banks will have to adjust along with the policy. This shifting costs the

FIGURE 9-5

A Drop or Rally with Rates. Courtesy of MetaStock.

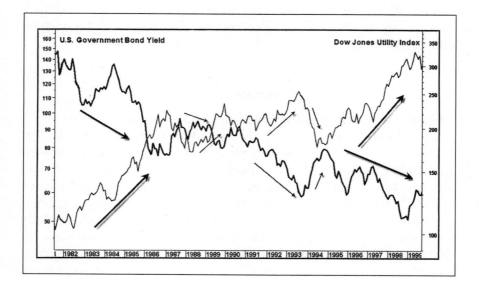

corporations lost revenues, and the less efficient banks can suffer greatly.

Industrials and Cyclic Issues

Industrials and cyclic companies will follow in short order. If the flow of money is being shut off or even slowed down, areas in the economy like car sales and new appliances, etc. will show signs of straining as the consumer finds it harder to buy goods. Sales slow, earnings drop, PEs rise, and stock prices fall. Of course, the exact opposite is also true for a period of lowering rates. That's the theory anyway, but what actually happens is that rates start going up and stock prices are already in a decline. The stock market is a leading economic indicator and should be treated as such. It's the technician's job to be well ahead of the action in the newspapers and concentrate our efforts in the action in the markets. The lesson here is that a move in rates will cause a move in major markets, which in turn will cause major moves in portfolios. The name of the game is to watch the money flow or you'll find that your own money has flowed away from you.

GOVERNMENT STATISTICS

We technicians follow money flows in order to help us in our overall view of the markets. Easy monetary policy from the Federal Reserve generally means a better atmosphere for stocks, while a tight policy would be viewed as being constrictive. To one degree or another, we all watch these numbers. No one place has more statistics on this subject than the government. The booklets and reams of paper that come from Washington are nothing less than staggering. The government can show net of money supply in the form of M1, M2, M3, L, and more to show exactly where the total money supply is at any given time. The information is well past overload, and no one would be expected to use or even read most of the numbers. But I will say that in our efforts to work through to a market opinion, some of these government statistics can be vital.

FED FUNDS RATE

One of the most closely followed numbers by all in the business world is the Fed Funds Rate. It is a window into the Federal Reserve's monetary policy. Basically this rate, set by the Treasury, is the rate at which one bank can borrow money from another. So by setting the lending rates between banks, the Fed can regulate availability of money to the system. There are many different ways that technicians have looked at this rate, and I will not go over all of them, as they all take you to the same answer. What we are looking for in the Fed Funds rates is change of direction and a shift in the monetary policy. Is the government making money plentiful or restrictive? A loose policy makes it a more positive atmosphere for investors, while a tight policy could cause disruptions for the markets. Many of the methods of looking at the funds rate require that in order to distinguish a reversal in policy from a short-term adjustment, we generally need a series of crossovers in the indicator chart. Possibly a rate of change (ROC) or a few moving averages. Perhaps even both.

GOVERNMENT NUMBERS

Knowing how much money is already invested in the market and what the public's tendencies towards equities are can be very revealing as to the health of the marketplace. The government runs many series that look at total financial assets in the country, and then finds the percentage that is already in the equity market. These series are very long term in nature and should be used only as an indication of the public's long-term position. They also run a series of the percentages of household ownership of stock. They look at the financial assets of the average family and check that number against their stock holdings. If the percentage is in a strong uptrend and growing, then the public is increasing their stake in stocks. No one can deny that this picture would offer an overall constructive attitude on the part of the public towards stocks and their perception of the economic future. A downturn, however, can be very negative for stock prices, as attitudes have changed to the sell side and the public is taking money out of equities. Also remember that these are long-term indicators that carry more weight in an overview opinion. Never try to use monthly or quarterly statistics in an attempt to reach a short-term opinion. It is amusing sometimes to see quarterly reports from the government announced and the traders run for cover or dive into the market.

CORPORATE CALENDAR REPORT

Each month the New York Stock Exchange makes a report available on the activities that will affect the general health of the markets. By showing us how many deals in the form of Initial Public Offerings and/or secondary offerings plus any bond deals are scheduled to come to market in the near future can influence opinions greatly. When a new company is just being listed or will be offering new stock to the public, overall it is a signal of a healthy market. Activity in this area is simply a reflection of a strong economy that has stimulated new business growth. There are times, however, that too many of these initial public offerings, or secondary offerings, can drain off money from normal day-to-day business. It's the old story of too much of a good thing is bad for you. As the business cycle matures and corporations begin to worry if the expansion can last, they will tend to rush to the market in the hopes of catching the upward wave of bullishness, and we will see the deal calendar explode with activity. If the economy slows, then we run the danger of being left with the supply of new stock at a time when there is no increase on the demand side. This places pressure on the market and can sometimes cause tops in the marketplace.

INTERNATIONAL VIEWPOINT

Just like the mutual fund numbers and the percentage of equities in the hands of the public, the government also measures the amount of foreign buying and selling that is going on in the markets. In bonds, many foreign countries are very heavy participants indeed. Many countries do not have their own bond markets or in many cases their government bonds are yielding less than in the United States. For example, in the late 1990s when the Japanese markets were down below the 10000-yen mark and their government bonds were yielding less than 4 percent, on their way down to less than ½ percent, there was a great inflow of Japanese money into the U.S. bond market. The Japanese have been a large buyer of U.S. government bonds, but their participation during that period was above and beyond normal. As their equity market worsened, we kept getting reports of how Japan would have to be net sellers of our bond market just to meet expenses at home stemming from the losses in their equity accounts. Make no mistake about it, at the time when these stories of Japanese bond liquidations were taking place, our short-term equity equity market suffered.

The number of purchases and sales by foreigners are recorded and reported each month by the government. A steady flow of international money into our market is always a welcome sign. Seeing foreign buyers enter our market means that the world investment professionals are pleased with the outlook for the United States and wish to participate in a winning economy with a strong growth potential.

Obviously, a low reading has a negative implication to it. The fact that foreigners are not buying our market might be caused by a period of recession in this country or perhaps overvaluation. The biggest reason might be that their own country is having its own period of prosperity and there is no need for them to look for ideas abroad. By keeping an eye on these numbers, you can get a general feel for how others view our prospects.

It is an interesting contrary observation, but a very high level of foreign buying has tended in the past to sound the death knell for our markets. It might be because of the time delay between countries or might be the fact that people get information a bit slower outside the United States. It seems to me over the years that spike periods of foreign buying have been a harbinger of a top, as foreign accounts do seem to be the last to join in the party. I was in Paris and talking to a few good fellow technicians from AFTAA (Association Francaise des Analysles Techniques). Claude Mattern in the International Federation of Technical Analysis explained it the best to me. In today's global market, it is not likely that one country will have a major bull market while everyone else is sleeping. The locals are all too busy with their own markets to worry about the United States. The advantage the United States has is our depth of business. Our markets are huge compared to some other nations, and we tend to have many other alternatives in forms of investments. As the advance matures for all markets, investors tend to look elsewhere for more ideas. The United States is the largest and best capitalized market in the world, so naturally money flows this way. In reality what has happened is that the global expansion has had its run to the upside, and foreign money coming here in excessive amounts is simply the indication of the end of the cycle.

MUTUAL FUNDS PERCENT OF CASH

If you have ever seen any of the financial news programs, you could not miss hearing talk about "flows." There are a few areas covered when speaking about flows in general. One is mutual fund cash numbers and the other is the flow of funds in and out of the specific sectors.

Let's look at mutual cash numbers first, as this is of major importance for everyone. The mutual fund industry publishes a monthly total of assets in these funds, and again it doesn't take a rocket scientist or a technical analyst to figure out that as the total grows the implications are positive. The mutual fund industry is charged to invest this money given to them. One of the faults that I find with the funds is that regardless of market conditions, they are paid to invest the money. If I've heard it once I've heard it a million times. "They are not paid to hold cash." As a result, the vast majority of the total asset value of the industry is committed. There is of course a percentage of the total that they keep in reserves in case of redemptions for whatever reason. This percentage will swing, however, depending on market conditions. It is an excellent number to follow, as it gives us a temperature reading of how the funds are looking at the market.

When they look at the cash positions, they are showing us a few items all within one number.

1. A rising cash position means that the funds are getting more defensive and are trying to build up as much cash as they are allowed.

2. A falling cash position is saying that the market and demand for stocks are favorable and the funds are using up the new cash they bring into the funds as fast as they can.

3. A flat reading indicates status quo.

A sharp reversal of these numbers in either direction will call for a reshuffling of portfolios, as a major shift in market thinking might be at hand. Flows can also mean following volume of the floor of the exchange itself to see where the daily flow of funds is going. Tracking volume flow in and out of the various groups is a great pastime. The activity is more than just a way of killing time. We have already spoken about the value of watching sectors and groups based on relative strength and gauging interest movement. Well, the same importance is placed on volume. One thing is for sure: Volume leads price. If you can spot a sharp increase in volume in a particular group, you might well get advance warning of a move.

Chapter 10

Sentiment

There is an old saw on Wall Street that you should keep in your memory for future use: "Investors make bottoms; traders make tops." I referred to this before when I told you that bottoms take time to form and a top can happen like a clap of thunder. Investors' attitudes towards the market can change quickly for any of a million reasons. These shifts in their emotions rather than their reason are called sentiments. We technicians try to keep our eyes on changes in investor psychology because it is important to a solid market opinion, but at all times you will find that the investor attitude is very elusive. There are plenty of sentiment indicators to aid in this task, and all serve to examine different portions and players that make up the stock market. We look at the individual investors, professionals on the floors, traders on the upstairs trading desk, international investors, etc., all in hopes of getting a sense of how the investors are acting towards the market. These are tools that you need not spend an inordinate amount of time poring over, but it is an area that you need to be aware of at all times. Trying to get a sense of the mood of the investors, as we approach a support zone or an overhead resistance area, sometimes can be the key difference in reaching a correct market opinion. There are many occasions when the tape can have almost everything going in its favor on the surface when in fact the sentiment indicators were flashing a warning signal. Perhaps there are too many shorts in a stock or a high put/call opinion ratio, which will give us a sense of investors' feelings. Sentiment indicators were developed to give us a gauge of how both the investors and the traders are feeling or how they are likely to react in any given market situation. These tools help us in taking the market's internal readings. Is the market pulse racing and therefore nervous, or is it steady and ready for whatever lies ahead? The sentiment indicators can help us measure the condition of the investor, and they play an important part in market analysis.

THE ADVISORY SENTIMENT INDEX

This sentiment index tries to give us a look into the world of market letter writers. It shows the results of a weekly survey of roughly 100 market letter writers as to their current opinion and is reported through a publication/Web site called Investors Intelligence. They have been reporting these numbers since the early 1960s and are widely followed by the investing community. What is actually reported are three sets of numbers that are very helpful in our sentiment work. These numbers express what the current opinion of the "professional market letter writers" are in percentage terms. The groups are:

% BULLS—how many writers believe the stock market is going to rally or continue its current advance.

% BEARS—how many of these professionals believe that the market is in a falling trend and is likely to remain in a decline.

% CORRECTION—how many believe that although the market direction remains to the plus side, we should have a temporary correction to relieve any short-term overbought state.

Because the sentiment numbers are used to show what the professional market letter writers are thinking as a whole, they can be used as a barometer of market thinking. If we could measure "when" market opinion is too one-sided, then we could potentially spot turns. An overbought/oversold band can be constructed on the index with the lower band at 35 percent and an upper band at 55 percent. These numbers are used as a contrary indicator because advisory service tends to be wrong en masse at market extremes. A reading of higher than 55 percent is considered too bullish and would be a warning sign. If the market letter writers did their jobs, well then the people who buy these letters have already spent their money on buying stocks. Once all of the investors' money is *in* the market, there is only one way for the market to go, and that's down. If, however, the number of bulls drops to below the 35 percent range, then possibly we should start looking for a low. These numbers are quite volatile, so many technicians run a 3- or 4-week moving average to smooth out the gyrations. Like most of our indicators, just because we have reached one of the limits of showing too many bulls or too many bears, that does not give us a signal by itself. We need to see other indicators combined with these readings to give us something to act upon. Simply looking at a number and reacting to it can be a great misuse of a good tool. Many times the market is clearly bullish or bearish, and few people have an argument with the outlook. Therefore these numbers can reflect a correct outlook for a long stretch.

The concept of contrary opinion was introduced by a gentleman by the name of Humphrey Neil in his book *The Art of Contrary Thinking*. This philosophy states that whenever a majority is in agreement on a central point, then the odds favor that they're wrong. Traders keep their eyes on the investors' intelligence numbers in an effort not to get caught with the crowd. There are so many examples of the investors getting crushed in a market turn because they were *all* convinced the market was going to act one particular way or another. Remember that these numbers are not to be used as buy and sell signals. These are indications that you must factor into your opinions. When you find yourself in a market where everyone, and that must include yourself, is starting to think and act in the same way towards the market, be on your guard.

Here's another Brooks Truism: "Stay out of crowds if you don't want to be trampled."

SHORT SELLING

Short selling could be an entire book all unto itself. Some technicians still follow the numbers generated by short sellers, but these folks have committed themselves to the study of that side of the market almost to the exclusion of the other tools. I prefer to use an assortment of tools that will give me a boarder look at the market.

A short seller is someone who, for whatever reason, has decided to sell a stock or a stock index futures or some other product in an attempt to capitalize on the downward movement of the market. If a trader feels that a fall is coming she may chose to sell short in the hope that she can buy the shares back at a lower price. I have spent a fair amount of time on trading desks and have been short as a matter of doing business. Maybe it doesn't make sense from an analytical standpoint, but the emotions are dramatically different than a long position. For one thing, you are selling something that you do not own and it will have to be bought back at some future date. For another, short sellers are usually near-term traders by nature, which means they want to see the downdraft and instant gratification of their positions. The pressure can be quite powerful. That pressure and how the traders react to it can be helpful information in building our market outlook.

The short-selling statistics try to cover many areas in the marketplace. I will just mention them and their purposes briefly.

Specialist Short Sales

The specialists on the floor of the New York Stock Exchange are required to maintain an orderly market during the course of the day's trading. This forces them to place their own money at risk in order to facilitate the completion of some trades. As a result they are considered to be very perceptive traders and tend not to get exposed for too long to the wrong side of the market. The actual amount of short selling done by the specialist is a matter of public record and is reported by the NYSE on a weekly basis. The Specialist Short Sale Index is computed by dividing the total specialist short sales by the total of all the shorts that occurred that week. That ratio can then offer us a look at how the professional trader is really feeling about the short-term market. A low reading for this indicator is considered to be positive for the market because the specialists are saying that they do not wish to carry large short positions. A high ratio reading is showing their willingness to be on the negative side. Remember, "shorts" must be repurchased at some future date. If the general market begins a rally, your short positions might likely run against you.

Public Shorts Interest Ratio

This indicator measures the total amount of outright shorts that have been executed by the public on the NYSE. It is then turned into a ratio against the average trading volume for the month on the exchange. The rule has been a ratio of over 2.0 was considered bullish. A reading that high means that the short sellers are at a high risk in their positions. The theory goes that if for some unknown reason from whatever source they found reasons to cover their shorts and turn bullish on the news and cause all the shorts to cover their positions, it would take 2 full days of average trading volume to completely close out those shorts. When you consider that "short positions" can only be covered on an uptick in price, you begin to see the possibilities. What I am suggesting could be a potential explosion to the upside. The totals are reported at the end of the month and offer further insight into our market outlook.

Member Short Ratio

The member's short sale ratio is a simple reading of the level of the positive and negative outlook for the members of the New York Stock Exchange. Each week the exchange reports the total number of shorts placed by their members. If we divide that total by the total of all short sales, we find the percentage of members to the total of shorts. The members are considered better traders than most, and therefore this indicator is read on face value. A high level of shorts means they are expecting a drop in the market. A low reading can be very positive.

AMERICAN ASSOCIATION OF
INDIVIDUAL INVESTORS

The AAII surveys its investment clubs on a daily basis to get a
sentiment reading from John Q. Public. This indicator is interpreted from a contrary opinion stance, as the public, rightfully
or wrongfully, is considered less informed then the professionals. With the information overkill and the Internet, I'm not quite
sure if it's fair to say the average investor is totally uninformed.
Those types of statements are not as true as they once might
have been. Notice in Figure 10-1 that we are using a 3-week

FIGURE   10-1

AAII Sentiment Survey.

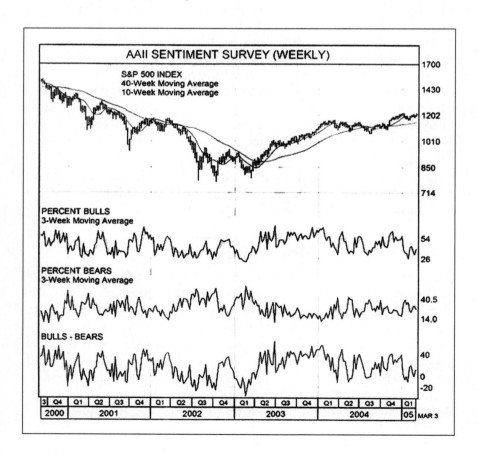

moving average of % Bulls, Bears, and Bulls minus Bears. For the sake of avoiding whipsaw from these sensitive series, many technical analysts will smooth the numbers out for a more accurate picture.

VIX INDEX

The CBOE (Chicago Board of Options Exchange) Volatility Index (VIX) measures volatility in the price of a basket of options on the S&P 100 Index. (See Figure 10-2.) Traders can gauge the

FIGURE 10-2

Volatility Index.

market sentiment by the rise and fall in the implied option volatility. A high level of volatility has often accompanied market declines. The increase in the VIX is a direct reflection of mounting fears of a market decline. Because fear is a prime element in most major bottoms, the VIX can serve as a powerful tool and is very useful in pinpointing important market bottoms. Confirmation of a major low would usually be a large increase in daily total volume. A low VIX reading would be considered positive but often is not as useful at tops as we find at lowpoints. The lows in the market tend to be quite a bit more emotional, which lends itself to an indicator like the VIX.

EQUITY PUT/CALL

Usually the put/call data is derived from the CBOE daily activity. This market sentiment indicator is simply calculated by dividing the daily volume of puts by the daily volume of calls. Remember that a call option gives you the right to buy a stock or bond or commodities at a given "strike price." The put option is the right to sell at a "strike price." This indicator works best at extremes in the marketplace. Investors usually get caught up in the emotion of the market in both directions. At major tops or bottoms it can feel like you are about to retire to your own island in the Caribbean or lose every nickel you ever earned. The put/call ratio's purpose is to express that feeling of the public towards the market. Because the public is considered to be incorrect at these extremes, the indicator is interpreted from a contrary basis like many of these sentiment indicators.

As a result, when we see a high level of put buying compared to calls, it is suggesting that the public is thinking that the market is about to decline. If the market drops, they will be able to cover their puts at a profit and start looking for that island in the sun. What it really means is that everyone is too bearish and most likely wrong. On the other side, a low reading of put buying means that most people are expecting a rising market, and we would give that a bearish reading.

Many years ago I would go fishing on the party boats out of Sheepshead Bay in Brooklyn. Every time someone would catch a fish, you'd get 30 guys coming on that side of the boat thinking that's where all the fish are biting. It's the same thing. If you have too many people on one side or the other, you are going to topple the boat.

FOREIGN: THE "TED SPREAD"

To gauge how the foreign investors feel about the U.S. markets, there is an indicator call the TED Spread. It compares the Eurodollar futures yield to the T-bill futures yield. The Eurodollar yield is the interest rate paid on 90-day dollar deposits in foreign banks, while the Treasury bill interest rate is the yield paid for short-term 90-day paper in the United States. The T-bill is backed by the full faith and credit of the United States, while the Eurodollar is not backed by a government. Therefore the Euro always has needed more yield to attract investors' dollars. If we divide the Euro dollar by the T-bills, we come up with a spread between the two rates. The theory is that a narrow spread between the two rates means that investors believe that all is well in the marketplace and that generally the interest rate picture is stable and world politics are reasonable. However, if the spread widens, then it is signaling a loss of confidence in the markets and requires the protection and safer yield afforded by the T-bills. Watching this indicator can give us insight into investors' feelings towards interest rates and world pressures.

NEWS

There is another tool that we use that has no format or structure except the use of simple common sense. One characteristic that I believe exists in good technical analysts is that they usually will have great deal of common sense. I have said before that technical analysis is part art form, and this is one of the areas where the concept most applies. This tool observes how the general market reacts to news. It can be any kind of news that could influence the marketplace. Earnings, wars, economic data, etc., but it's how the market handles the events that should concern us.

If the market is very high and good news has no effect on its price, then we are looking at a situation that is saying the price has discounted everything, and the next important move could be down. On the other hand, after a major selloff if further negative news fails to push a market or stocks any lower, then we most likely have seen the worst of the bear market and we should prepare for an upward turn. The market would be considered sold out.

I was in Russia a few years back the week that Boris Yeltsin had his heart attack and was undergoing surgery. I happened to be giving a speech to the Banking Group in Moscow when someone in the audience asked me for a technical reading on the Russian Stock Index. I called up the (RSI) Russian Stock Index on the screen for everyone to see and we all saw a pattern that appeared to be bottoming. In fact, for two weeks prior to my coming to Russia, their market had been in a rally despite the fact that the world headlines read that their leader was about to undergo some serious medical problems. It was clear to me that their market had already discounted the trouble and was down low enough to attract demand for stocks, regardless of the news. The supply side was washed out and a new trend was beginning. Information from the media is fine and an important part of the business, but always keep your eyes on the marketplace and how it reacts to news because that's where the real story is to be found. By the way, the Russian Stock Index rallied from around 100 to well past 200 during the next 6 months. Within 3 years the RTS was above 700.

MUTUAL CASH

In today's market the institutional accounts make up approximately 85–90 percent of the total volume every day. It would therefore be quite helpful to have a reading of where mutual fund cash levels are at any give time. The Investment Company Institute collects data from the mutual funds and reports their findings on a monthly basis. They take the total assets of all the funds and divide that by the level of cash and equivalents held by the funds.

This cash ratio, like other sentiment indicators, is read from a contrary point of view. A high cash level would indicate that mutual funds as a group are expecting lower prices and therefore wish to hold as much cash as allowed. It is considered bullish. On the other hand, a low reading for the ratio would suggest that they were very willing to commit as much as possible to capitalize on the market's rally potential. It is considered bearish.

The other way of viewing this ratio is by simply looking at the numbers for what they are representing. High cash means that there is money to eventually be invested in the market, a bullish sign. Low cash means that the cash has already been invested and is considered bearish. With the advent of large numbers of hedge funds, roughly 8000 in today's market, the cash ratio numbers have taken somewhat of a second-place standing, but they are still very important for an overview of buying power. Not so long ago the mutual cash was one of the few numbers investors could look at for a sense of cash on hand. With the popularity of the hedge funds today, we can see swings in the billions of dollars almost at a moment's notice based on a program trade. This new element to the market has diminished the importance of the mutual fund numbers somewhat because the hedge funds do not report their cash numbers. It is impossible to get a real handle on "cash on hand" readings.

INSIDE/OUTSIDE DAYS

I could have placed these two items in Chapter 3, Pattern Recognition, but in my view these are more connected to a sentiment shift rather then an actual pattern. The "outside day" is seen when a stock's price exceeds both the high and the low of yesterday's stock price. It makes no difference if we are looking at an uptrend or downtrend. When an outside day occurs, there is an indication that a reversal could be taking place. The logic in this pattern is that at least for a part of the day the existing trend had the upper hand, but later the opposite forces took control. This is a true example of the supply/demand battle ceding victory one to the other.

An "inside day" is just the reverse; that is when today's high and low prices are contained within the range of yesterday's high and low. These sessions suggest a lack of conviction on everyone's part, which more times then not causes lower prices.

In both cases what we have is reversal of the dominance of the powers of supply and demand. The stock's direction will determine which side is taking control. On the outside day on the upside you have a strong new high, but during the day's trading the stock manages to reach a low point below yesterday's low, a clear loss of forward momentum and a shift in sentiment. Of course these are warning flags and by themselves are not actionable, but once the warnings are given, then a break of a support or resistance point will take on more significance. An inside day has the same connotations except here we have a chart that fails to exceed either yesterday's high or yesterday's low. It is inside yesterday's range and is suggesting by its action that whatever direction the chart was in at the time, the forces of supply and demand were about to switch roles.

VALUATION

The word valuation in the world of technical analysis has little use. A technician doesn't try to judge a market or stock's value. It is very true that we assign targets to everything that has a bid and ask connected to it, but answering the question of value is someone else's job. We do, however, recognize past levels that have proven to represent value zones. For example, we know that the long-term growth rate of the U.S. stock market runs on an historical basis at around 9 percent. We also are aware that an average PE ratio for common stocks over the last 100 years has been around 15 times earnings. These are some facts that should be known, so when we find ourselves in a market that is 30 times earnings and running at a 40 percent growth rate, some *very* large red flags should start to fly overhead. Conversely, if after a long bear market we find ourselves selling below these norms, then we have reasons for preparing for a low and "waiting" for confirmations. However, neither situation of overvalued or undervalued has much relevance in the chart world except for the obvious connotations. The market spent many years in the 1960s and 1970s in an undervalued state, while in the 1990s most of the time was spent in a constant state of overvaluation. So other than a reference point, the concept of valuation has only a minor value.

MARGIN DEBT

The Federal Reserve sets the margin requirements for the banks and brokerage houses. (See Figure 10-3.) The margin debt itself is the money that you can borrow from these institutions using stocks in your account as collateral. By following the total amount of margin debt in the system, we gain insight into two areas of the market.

    a. The level of margin debt can give us good longer-term readings as to the investing public's attitudes. As a new bull market commences, the debt levels are traditionally low because most of the excesses of the last bear cycle have been erased. As the market picks up momentum to the upside, investors become more

FIGURE 10-3

Margin Debt. Drawn by The ChartStore.com.

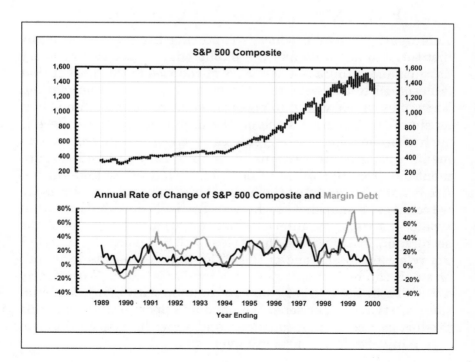

assured of their actions and pour back into the market. Many will leverage themselves by going to their margin account for extra purchasing power. This expansion is very positive, as it is a direct indication of investors' belief in the market's trend and increases the flow of funds into the market in general. Obviously, by the time we are ending a bull cycle, this debt level is extremely high, as once again we run into our old buddy *greed*.

b. Once the margin debt begins to fall, it acts as a negative force in the market. The reason is that all margin accounts must maintain a ratio of cash to stock in their accounts at all times. As the value of their portfolios drops, the need for cash in the accounts becomes more important, or the trader can choose to sell stock instead of adding cash. In a bear market the traders will not add cash, but rather they will choose to sell stock.

EXCHANGE TRADED FUNDS (ETFs)

This relatively new product is capturing the interest of many institutional accounts and the public alike. It seems like every day just about there is a new ETF introduced to the market that is designed to concentrate on a particular area of the market. They offer an easy way to enter a sector or country fund. It is as simple as buying a stock on the exchange. Because there is such a broad selection of vehicles to choose from and instruments that are offered to us, it is quite easy to build a sentiment tool from this one new product. If we were to take the entire list of ETFs and sort them in order of their relative strength, we could get a snapshot of where money is flowing and into what type of instruments: international investments, any one of the sectors, or possibly even the styles of their choice. By a style I am referring to any one of the ETFs that represents large cap or small cap or technology versus industrials, etc. With nearly 170 ETFs in the market, you can come up with many combinations of style comparisons. We have an opportunity to use this product as a sentiment indicator, and all we have to do is to run a ranking of relative strength over it.

Chapter 11

Relative Strength Analysis

If Nome, Alaska, were showing a temperature reading of minus 20 and Billings, Montana, were 0, we could say that Billings had a relatively warmer climate than Nome. After living below the Mason-Dixon line for more than 30 years, I can't say that conditions in either place thrill me enough to cause me to move, but one is relatively better than the other. All we are doing is comparing one data point to other in an attempt to find the stronger or the weaker of the two. In this case Billings wins hands down.

In the stock market, relative strength analysis does the same thing by trying to find the best place to invest your capital. Relative strength is probably the most used and widely accepted indicator in the world of technical analysis. Almost everyone I have ever come in contact with in the financial world recognizes the value of this comparative tool. A relative strength line is simply building a ratio between two market values. This technique works across all markets, commodities, stocks, bonds, international markets, and currencies. To build a relative strength ratio, you simply take the price of one entity and divide it into the price of another. Although it is a very old approach, it is a very effective way of finding the current power in the stock market and staying with that power until new leadership shows itself.

The traditional approach to this work is to compare a stock to a market index. What you want to know is how the instrument that you are thinking of buying is acting in comparison to the overall market. (See Figure 11-1.) If the ratio line is declining, then the denominator is indicated as having the power. A rising line is indicating the numerator has the strength. This ratio is usually plotted at the bottom of the chart and is interpreted as a straightforward indicator, similar to others we have already covered in past chapters. The interpretation follows along normal lines. A rising line is positive for your stock and a declining line says the index is where the better power is to be found. It also suggests that there are other stocks in that comparative index that would be better buys.

A major value with this tool is that any two items can be compared. The most common use of R/S is to show the strength or weakness between a stock and an index. If you wanted to run an R/S line of say General Electric compared to the Dow Jones

FIGURE   11-1

GE and S&P 500. Courtesy of MetaStock.

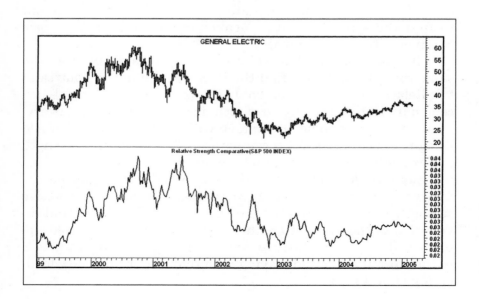

Industrial Average, it would be an easy enough task. All you need is to have the data for the closing prices of the GE and the closing prices for the Dow and divide one into the other. Today you will find that many computer systems have built-in relative strength programs, and most use the Standard and Poors 500 Index as the benchmark. As you might know, the Standard and Poor's 500 is the benchmark that most portfolio managers measure against.

HOW WE USE IT IN OUR WORK

The R/S line can take on many different variations in its calculation, but the bottom-line interpretation will always be the same. You are not interested in the actual number of a relative strength line, but rather the direction the line is taking. That directional information is the key. One major quality of the relative strength indicator is that it can be a very flexible tool; we can use in on a daily, weekly, or monthly basis with no shift in how we read the chart. This method is a great way of staying ahead of the market, and by following the road maps, hopefully you will do relatively better than your competition. Using the R/S tool can provide us with a look into the market's power points, which in turn can keep us ahead of the averages.

When a market is in an uptrend and the R/S for a stock is strong, we would consider that it is a fully in-gear market and there are no warning signs present. The stock you are measuring is keeping pace with the index that you are using and therefore there is no need to act. Let's take the same two items, but this time we see a market that is strong and making new highs while the relative strength of your holding is falling off. Although your stock might still be moving ahead, it is lagging behind the indexes. We are witnessing the loss of power, or put another way, the loss of demand. (See Figure 11-2.)

A divergence like that is telling us one of three things:

a. The financial series you are studying is showing weakness outright. The reasons for this are too many to cover. It might be expensive compared to the market or perhaps ran into bad news or just a normal cycle

FIGURE 11-2

Negative R/S.

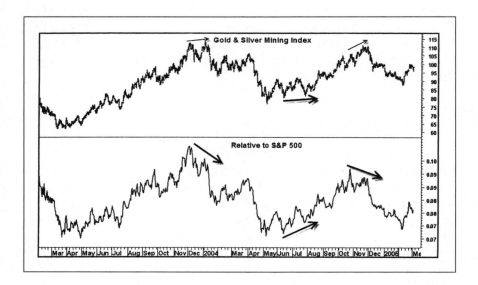

top. But for whatever reason, it is in fact lagging the
index.

b. There are better opportunities to choose in the market. There might not be anything wrong with the
stock that you own at all, except that other stocks
might be more attractive than yours.

c. The index that you are comparing to is doing better
than your holding. You could be holding a midcap issue in the S&P 500 that had been performing quit
well and suddenly there is a shift in leadership for the
general market into large-cap issues.

Keep in mind that we are dealing with relative strength,
with the optimum word being "relative." A drop in relative
strength is never a sell signal, nor is an upturn a signal to buy.
What it is telling us is that a signal is being flashed and you
need to pay attention. Like so many technical indicators, they
are best used in conjunction with other tools.

SPOTTING NEW AREAS

There are other useful applications for this tool. Many investors like to use relative strength to find the areas that are attracting the new money flow. In Figure 11-3 we compare a Big Cap Index to a Small Cap Index. Within the equity market there are many subdivisions that you need to explore for opportunities. Another wonderful benefit of the PC is how it has given us the power to compare these various "styles" of investments. As far as I am aware, there is no limit to what you can study. For example, say we compare any stock on the New York Stock Exchange versus NASDAQ.

FIGURE 11-3

Lowry's Report Style.

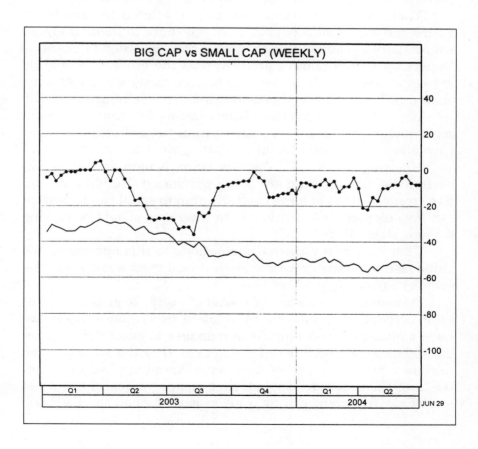

Besides trying to find which exchange is stronger than the other, what else are we accomplishing? In making this comparison, we are discovering the current aggressiveness of the investing public. We know that the Dow Jones represents the largest capitalization blue chip issues that are considered conservative in nature. We also know that the NASDAQ often is the standard bearer for more aggressive trading vehicles. By taking a relative strength reading of one to the other, we can surmise what the risk tolerance of investors currently is. Obviously, if the NASDQ is showing better strength than the DJIA, then investors' confidence levels are high and the overall feeling is positive. If investors were worried about the future and the uncertainly were prevalent, then the more conservative issues would be gaining the power. In times of uncertainty, investors seek safe havens for protection.

There are many styles that can be related to each other with a certain amount of predictive relevance to them. Suppose we compared commodities to stock prices in order to examine leadership in one market arena versus the other. It would be extremely relevant to know if gold and metal should be purchased rather then say Microsoft (MSFT) or Halliburton (HAL).

If we compared stocks to bonds in this R/S chart, we could see a picture of the Street's expectation toward interest rates. How about one international market against another?

Knowing the "type" of equity being bought is just as important as "where" they are being purchased. Building a relative strength chart of large capitalization to small capitalization can give us more information as to where we should be looking for new stock ideas.

There are many more combinations to this approach, like value issues versus growth or high-priced versus low-priced issues, etc. (See Figure 11-4.)

It is sometimes a strange concept to come to grips with, but most accounts live and die by relative performance. Here we have a situation that requires a manager to outperform an index, let's say the S&P 500. I did not say that the manager had to show a profit, but rather that her performance had to be better than the index. In English that means you can have a net loss of say 5 percent during a given period when the S&P 500

FIGURE 11-4

Relative Strength.

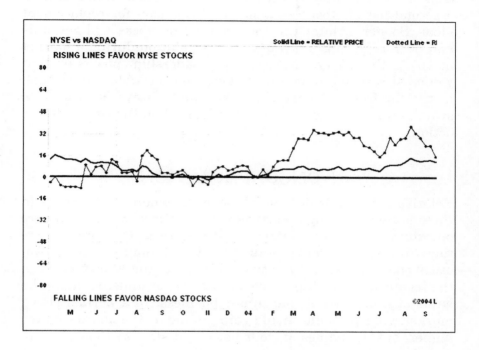

is down 6 percent and show a positive relative performance by beating your benchmark. Your portfolio, in other words, did better than the overall market. So many institutional accounts abide by R/S almost as a religion. The theory is that the strongest issue out in front of the pack is likely to be the winner. In using relative strength in your portfolio, therefore, what you need to do is to constantly update your stocks and make sure you are holding the best.

As a portfolio manager, you could take your stocks that you are currently holding and compare the entire list to an index. It is important to always compare apples to apples in this task. In other words, if I am an aggressive PM and my typical stock is low priced and high multiple issues, then I should be using, as my denominator, an aggressive index rather then the Dow Jones.

Once that R/S ranking has been accomplished, all you need to know are the names of the top-ranked issues for new purchases. I have found that it is always a smart idea to maintain a second list of stocks as a sort of farm team for replacement ideas. Sooner or later your original list of stocks will get stale and need replacing. It's a question of rotation during a market move. As the market matures, new leadership springs up that you must respond to in order to keep your portfolio current and in the forefront of leadership. We must always be willing to switch into new groups and new stocks when the time calls for action.

NONCONFIRMATION

Relative strength is designed to show us where the power is in the market. By using a particular benchmark, we can compare our stock selection to determine if we are in the correct positions to maximize our profits. That is only half the story. Another characteristic of relative strength is the ability to warn the technician of a shift in leadership. Never underestimate the value of a negative signal in our business. In a normal rising market, your portfolio should gain ground as the market moves higher, but the names on your list might start to show signs of a slowing R/S line, maybe even a declining pattern. Your stocks might be either moving into a top, or possibly the general market is gaining strength and leaving your issues behind. Regardless of which, you are being warned of a shift. Whether or not you take action will depend on a few things.

1. Has any trend line or support zone been violated?
2. Can you determine if the R/S weakness is due to increased strength in the index or loss of power in your stock?
3. If it is an increase push in the index itself, then you have to decide if you want to disturb your existing holdings in favor of a stock that is tied to that index. Many times that choice can be made only after you have studied your tools like the trends, volume, chart patterns, and moving averages.

A MAJOR BEAR MARKET TOOL

Relative strength is also very handy to have in bear markets. During a prolonged bear market, R/S is to be used to make sure you are in the best of the best stocks. In hard times you need to run your portfolios with a very stern hand. In a general retreat, stocks are going to decline and there is nothing we can do about that at all. But in that decline there are going to be issues that decline less than the pack, and those are the names we are looking to purchase. By running an ongoing review of a large portfolio of stocks against the S&P 500, we can continually upgrade and protect our capital the best we can. Many times you can come out of a market low ahead of the game. The simple task of letting go of positions that fail to maintain their relative strength can improve your performance greatly.

You also will find that as we approach a major low in the market, the stocks that show the strongest resistance to the decline can quite often become the leadership on a turn, and that is where you want your money to be invested. Think about what is occurring at a major low. Investors that have been holding on to stocks are finally giving up and throwing in the towel on their stocks. Volume should be increasing as fear builds and stocks move from weak hands (supply side) to stronger hands (demand side). In the early stages of a low, not every issue is attractive. In fact, only a relatively small number of stocks might find themselves on a wanted list. A key way of determining the leaders is by employing a relative strength analysis. As we approach a trough in the market, we will begin to see some issues' R/S lines begin to turn from a decline pattern to flat. As buyers step into the stock, the price drop slows. I didn't say reverses. I said slows, showing that it is resisting the general retrenchment. These types of stocks are usually among the issues that emerge as the leaders of the next rally phase.

These nonconfirmations are great ways of keeping on top of your portfolio, and it is a great graphic way of determining if a move is gaining or losing power. However, like many indicators in technical analysis, we should not use this one indicator by itself as our only buy/sell decision maker. Using relative strength in conjunction with other indicators is the smartest approach. Because relative strength tends to swing more than price, it will often lead, but, as I said, we don't use this as a buy or sell signal. The best approach is to use more traditional tools like a price trend line violation in the same direction as the relative strength readings.

A TOP-DOWN TOOL

If we think of a major market cycle as having four distinct periods (a basing phase, a rally phase, a declining phase, and finally a bottoming phase), we can perhaps demonstrate how useful relative strength can be in all facets of our work. Figure 11-5 shows General Electric and a relative strength line against the S&P 500. You will notice that during the basing period the R/S begins to increase ahead of the price breakout (A). During the rally phase the indicator (B) is running fully in gear with the S&P 500. Now in the declining phase we first notice a loss, (C)

FIGURE   11-5

Phases of Relative Strength. Courtesy of MetaStock.

of forward momentum and the R/S turns down. Without a doubt here is where supply finally comes into balance with demand and the sellers take the upper hand. In the final bottoming phase, relative strength is trying to find the strength again. Once it does find the strength the cycle begins anew. Hopefully this shows that R/S can be used in almost all parts of technical analysis.

SECTORS AND GROUPS

Perhaps one of the great uses of R/S is as a time saver, as it works particularly well in comparing sectors or groups of stocks. This approach can allow you to go through a small amount of charts in your search for strong areas within the market. Instead of spending hours of your time looking at thousands of chart patterns, you can scan the sectors and find the strongest sectors against the market. Again, follow the thinking at this juncture. If a sector or group demonstrates it is weak, then there is no reason to be going through that group of stocks. The vast majority of time, you will find that if the group has lost power, then the stocks that make up that group will lose also. In the beginning of a downturn, there will be a few issues in all the groups that will still be attractive, but buying strong stocks in a weakening group is truly rearranging chairs on the Titanic. From that small list of bullish sector charts, you can then go to the groups that make up those sectors to find the power. In this fashion we can cull a massive amount of charts down to a few. When you are finished you can clearly see the areas of the market that are attracting the new money. Remember, strength is a function of demand, and weakness is a function of supply. By selecting the top relative strength sectors and groups, you can find yourself with a short list of the demand in the marketplace. Finding the best relative performer in a few groups is quite simple and will save you many hours of hard work. Once your stocks or indexes have been picked based upon their relative strength, then the use of the other technical tools like support and resistance, moving averages, volume, etc., should be added to your analysis.

NEW PRODUCTS

In today's market one of the fastest ways of putting large sums of money to work quickly is by using instruments like ETFs (Exchange Traded Funds) or tradable funds like the Rydex or Pro Funds as entry vehicles. As of the writing of this book, there were approximately 170 ETFs and about 50 tradable Funds available. By using some benchmark, whatever is to your liking, you can run all the vehicles at once on a relative strength basis and come up with your best sector investment, all with just a few keystrokes.

You could also take all 150-plus ETFs and compare their strengths to each other. Imagine looking at ETFs as a portfolio unto itself. By comparing the domestic, international, sectors, and bonds ETFs, you would be looking at a relative strength ranking of the world of Exchange Traded Funds. These funds are becoming more popular in the financial business daily, as can be seen in the increasing volume figures for this asset class.

By using a time-tested approach like relative strength and applying our analysis to the ETFs, we can build a new way of looking at the markets.

BE CREATIVE WITH THIS TOOL

Use the power that you have at your disposal to your advantage. The personal computer and the data that is available to you make it a very attainable goal to compare all sorts of interesting items to each other. Who cares if 95 percent of the comparisons are worthless and a waste of time? It must be considered R&D in your education. Make lots of mistakes and go down lots of rabbit holes. You'll get mad and tired, but it's the best way I know to tell you to use your brains. The mistakes are between you and your computer, and I'm fairly sure the PC won't tell anyone. Then again with all the innovations in the technology these days, maybe it can rat on you. Take the chance.

It's easy enough to look at large areas like the Dow Jones Industrial Average versus one of the more aggressive indexes such as Value Line. The Dow Jones is a large-cap, conservative NYSE index, while the Value Line represents smaller, less capitalized issues and higher risk. Here we can see which group is attracting investors' capital—low-priced stocks or large, conservative names. When you are trying to determine what *you* should buy, these types of questions become very important.

But those are the relationships that are simple to explain and are obvious. You should learn how to play with the figures and the numbers that are before you. Try many experiments and do all the back testing your computer will allow. Take a look at the relationships that exist in our markets. Find out on your own the relationship between interest rates and housing starts. Possibly there is a relationship between a bumper crop of wheat and the food sector chart, crude oil and inflation, bonds versus stocks, U.S. dollar and multinational companies. But keep in mind that what you are doing is making a comparison of two items to see where the strength is to be found. At the same time you're trying to understand relationships that are found in financial data.

CLOSING POINTS

Relative strength is going to be one of your best utility tools that you must carry with you at all times. It is a very old indicator for only one reason. It works. So learn well how to work with it. Keep in mind that that R/S is a leading indicator and as such should be watched for divergence. Having an edge on a potential move can save and/or make you extra profits. When we look at this tool, we can use all the typical technical indicators in its analysis, like drawing trend lines and spotting support and resistance areas.

This type of indicator is showing us where our stocks are in relation to the other issues we could buy. Try to keep your portfolio in a strong relative position and you'll be fine. You need not be in the number-one stocks all the time, but rather you want to be in the top 10–15 percent of a list. Relative strength is not to be used as a sell/buy signal for every move. No stock will hold a top slot all the time. There is nothing wrong with a stock taking a breather once in awhile. But by watching the trend line and supports and resistance points, we can stay ahead of the performance game.

Chapter 12

Building Your Own Toolbox

There is no right or wrong answer as to what tools you select as your base arsenal that you will be employing to study the stock market. You will have to gather your own set of indicators that you wish to use as your primary tools. I strongly suggest, however, that you make sure you have a mixture of long-term, intermediate-term, and short-term indicators that you can call your basic daily working routine. The long-term indicators should be able to assist you in building the market overview that will be needed in order to function. You will want to know if you are working in a generally rising market or declining atmosphere. You will be amazed how many people never take into account the general market direction when they invest. I also find it helpful to have an understanding of the "Street's" feelings about the economy and the markets. This gives you the framework for your day.

The intermediate-term tools are the ones that you will find yourself using the most, and therefore they are the ones you must master in order to deal with current market behavior. Understanding the indicators and what they are telling you is vital. Trend lines and oscillators and sentiment work will all become second nature to you after awhile. But it will be pattern recognition as a visual depiction of supply and demand that will be one of your most powerful items.

Finally, your short-term tools can aid you as to where and when to place your orders. It might sound a little trite at the moment, but knowing if you should be selling the rallies or buying the dips is what this business is all about. Building a handful of tools that help you in that choice can mean the difference between a winning and/or a losing trade.

TOP-DOWN ANALYSIS

There are some fine services and technicians that function very well by looking at stocks or bonds or commodities one item at a time and coming up with higher-than-average returns. I, however, am not one that can do this job looking through a tube. I find that I am squarely in the top-down analysis camp. I find I want that longer-term perspective for developing my plan of attack.

Of course, the last thing I want *you* to believe is that I am an economist or a fundamentalist, but I am not closed minded enough to think that these areas should be ignored. I do want to know the general facts and current stats about the market that I am attempting to trade. Therefore, being aware of earnings or valuation levels as well as the Street's overall outlook for the market and economy is always factored into and is a part of my opinions. Looking at price alone is one-dimensional for me and it tells only a part of the story. I enjoy knowing the strong sectors and the strong groups and using many of the technical tools I've been writing about. Put it this way. If the general stock market is in a full retreat because of economic news or world events, I would not think of buying a stock just because it has a good chart pattern with good volume and favorable moving averages. Rather I would factor in the events around my market and then add it to my decision process. Here comes another Brooks truism. "Fighting the tape is like having screen doors on a submarine; it's not a useful idea."

LONG-TERM TOOLS
Key Groups

Key groups can help to form an overall opinion. Using a relatively small number of groups, a technical analyst can make a

reasonable general market assumption. Knowing the health of
the financials and the energy and technology groups can answer
many questions for you quickly. Financials can give you a general overview of interest rates. Rates can affect money flow, and
money flow can affect stock prices. It is hard to have a bull market if interest rates are choking off the supply of money to the
system. Therefore, one of the elements for a bull market should
be an improving financial sector. Energy and commodities prices
can help in assessing the level of inflation. If prices of commodities are flat, there is no concern for the market's inflation
picture, but if we have runaway rising prices showing up on the
commodities charts and the price of, for example, home heating
oil and gasoline are rising, you can assume that some amount
of the public's funds are going to be diverted away from stocks
and toward paying for these items. Regardless if it is true or
not, rising commodities bring back memories of the 1960s when
hyperinflation crippled the U.S. economy. Today, some say that
the new economic formulas have changed since the 1960s and
that oil doesn't have the same impact on markets as it once did.
I will tell you this: In today's computer-driven market and fast-
paced action brought on by instant dissemination of news
events, all you have to hear is Alan Greenspan say something
about inflation and half the traders on *all* the exchanges start
reaching for their nitroglycerin pills. So pay attention and do
not listen to people who will tell you that this time it's different. It's not. Figure 12-1 shows a sharp decline in the price of
the Real Estate Investment Trust (REIT) group chart in the beginning of the second quarter of 2004. The catalyst for that move
was a comment from the Federal Reserve that some increase in
interest rates may be needed.

Finally, technology issues represent a very good gauge of
investors and traders' feelings about the future of the market.
As a general rule, tech stocks trade at higher multiples than
most other areas. These issues represent innovation and research and many times just plain taking a chance with a concept. Many people believe that technology represents some of
the best long-term power of America. The new ideas and dis-
coveries in the Bio Tech area alone are amazing, and you can
understand why people believe that the NASDAQ is where the

FIGURE 12-1

REITs after Greenspan.

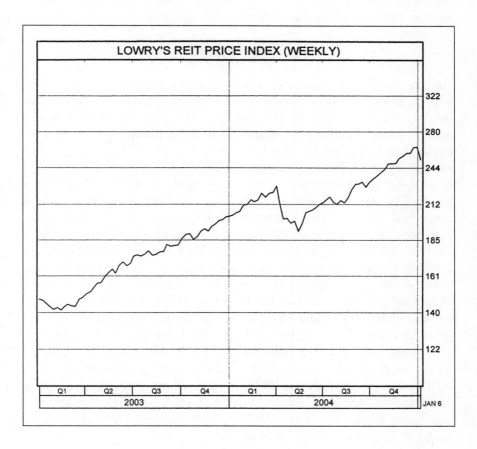

new ideas for our future are born. Of course, taking a chance on the future is also where the most risk is taken. As a result, the P/Es on these issues are often very high, and only the belief that the general market will be rising would make someone take a risk with these stocks. Ergo: A rising technology group suggests that investors are positive about the outlook for the market.

So by looking at only three key groups, we can determine if interest rates are or are not a problem; if inflation and therefore money flow is a problem; and finally how investors see the economy and therefore the market, at least for the immediate future. These are just three concepts in a marketplace where dozens of comparisons can be made and contrasted.

CYCLES

An excellent way of keeping the long-term market outlook folded into your overview is to maintain a running tally of a few of the long cycles that exist in the market. Many of these we'll speak about in the next chapter. Earlier we spoke about the 4–4-½ year cycle that is found for the Dow Jones Industrial Averages. Let me give you an idea of their use. The last few 4-year cycle lows have been in 1990, 1994, 1998, and again in 2002. If we really wanted to get technical about it, the low actually was a reverse head and shoulder pattern with the left shoulder in July of 2002, the head in October of 2003, and the right shoulder finally in March of 2003. But who's counting? This would suggest that according to this one cycle, a new low might be found sometime in 2006. Just as a ballpark estimate. If we can have a general idea of "when" a long-term low might occur in the market, as a model we can start to make more precise plans as that time frame approaches. But this is to be used only for your long-term thinking.

Also, knowing the seasonal factors in the markets is a must as far as building your outlook. I have no way of knowing what will occur in 2005 or in 2015, but it is interesting that since 1885 to the present, every year that ends in the number five has been a winning year. Will it work again? I could not say, and yet it is something to consider.

It is smart to know about what to expect in a presidential cycle. If by studying the past we can learn about the future then we should invest at least a little time. You might need to know the year that is most advantageous to buy or sell. As a rule, the first year of a president's term in office is somewhat positive for the market. With the passing of time, some policy that people might not enjoy can cause the middle years to show a mixed picture. Finally, in an attempt to be reelected, the last year can be bullish for stock prices. Where the longer cycles are positioned can be a major consideration in your outlook. You need not act upon any of these bits of information, but added together, they can be part of your thinking. The other traders out there who will be trading against you are aware of these numbers, and they will be using every tool they have, so you better be alert to their existence.

Finally, when we are selecting our monthly tools, we must include the monthly bar charts of the major indexes as well as the monthly group work. Following a monthly MACD and stochastic is always a wise choice. In all of these charts, we will want to draw in our long-term trend lines and make sure we know where the violations and the overhead resistances are found at all times.

SOME WEEKLY TOOLS

The percent of stocks trading above their 10- and 30-week moving averages was a concept developed by Joseph Granville back in the early 1960s. The theory is that a stock that is able to trade above a 10-week average of its own closing price is showing very solid intermediate-term strength. Likewise, any stock that can trade above its 30-week average of its closing price must, by definition, be a powerful stock indeed. So if we were to look at the total percent number of all the stocks on the NYSE that are trading above these two levels, then we should be able to make a generalization as to the strength or weakness of the market. Like everything in technical analysis, the other side of the equation is very valuable in our thinking. If we have low readings of the amount of issues above their average closing prices, then we have a weak market picture. You must also keep a keen eye on the overbought /oversold levels. Using this indicator to identify extremes is very helpful. A market that is showing a percent number above 80 percent or below 20 percent is clearly stretched out too far in one direction, and it would suggest that a reversal could be anticipated. (See Figure 12-2.)

Correct A/D Figures

Many years ago someone was asked if you were on a dessert island and you wanted only one indicator to tell you what was

F I G U R E   1 2 - 2

Thirty-Week Moving Average.

going on in the market, what would it be? The answer was the
advance/decline line for the New York Stock Exchange. That
was my answer as well, but over the last 15 years or so the
NYSE has been listing new products on the exchange that have
corrupted the meaning of the original indicator. The original in-
tent of this indicator was to show the direction of the overall
stock market. It takes the net of the stocks that are up versus
the stocks that are down so we can graphically see general stock
movement. However, with the introduction of ADRs, closed-end
funds, bond funds, and even preferred stocks, etc., the numbers

aren't what they were. Today, 53 percent of the issues that are included in the NYSE Adv/Dec figures are not operating companies at all. Here we have more than half the data for an indicator really related to interest rates rather then equities. Despite the fact that the advance/decline is a still the indicator used by many and therefore still of value, at times it is not giving us a true look at operating companies. These numbers can mask a move in the market by suggesting more strength or weakness than really is present.

Lowry's Reports does carry in its arsenal the OCO index, which is an index of Operating Companies Only as well as the advance/decline line that goes with it. From an index that has removed nonoperating companies from the calculations, we can get a much clearer picture of what is really happening, as the original indicator had meant. Figure 12-3 shows the Dow Jones Industrial Average and the "OCO" Adv/Dec Line for 2004. Notice the nonconfirmation move in August. The DJIA made a new low in August–September, while the "OCO" does not confirm.

Pattern Recognition

As a card-carrying technical analyst of both the International Federation of Technical Analysts (IFTA) and the Society of Technical Analysts, UK (STA), and the American Association of Professional Technical Analysts (AAPTA), pattern recognition is mother's milk to me. I could have a dozen indicators telling one thing, but before I spend any of my money either long or short, I have to see a chart. To me this is where the rubber meets the road. There are many types of patterns, and we have tried to cover the basics in Chapter 3. Like everything in technical analysis, we get used to patterns that make us money on a consistent basis, and we tend to stay with those.

After I have done my top-down analysis and after I feel I know what sectors and what groups I wish to invest in, I will then look at the charts and try to find that pattern or at least that pattern's look-alike. What is that pattern, you ask? For me it's a stock with strong R/S, breaking out of an extended base pattern on increasing volume. That low inside pitch, which we call a saucer formation is the one I seek out all the time. *But,*

FIGURE   12-3

The OCO A/D.

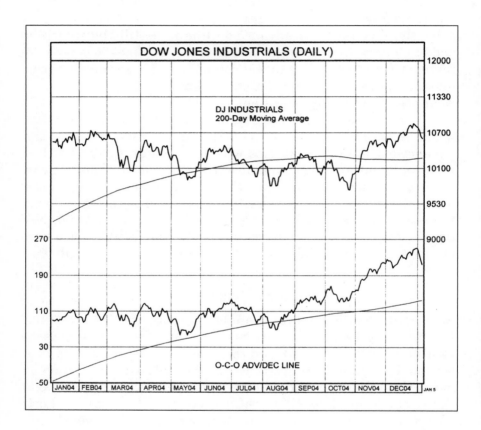

and here is another Brooks truism, "Your choice of pattern is a product of the type of market you're in."

I believe that every market I have ever been in has its own fingerprint to it. It is the characteristic of the current market. At times saucer formations are the rage, and then in a wink of an eye the characteristics of the charts change. We might find that high-momentum stock patterns work best. If you look at the late 1990s, high technology issues were just about the only thing that was in demand. There are times the darlings might prove to be low-priced issues or stocks that have rolled over and are short candidates. So we must always observe what the pattern is that is attracting the most interest and work with the type that is attracting the investors.

But remember, we can all have an idea of the perfect pattern. Some people like momentum stocks making new all-time highs and would never think of buying anything but a stock on the new high list. Some look for value in low P/E with strong technical internals. Yet, in Japan investors look upon low-P/E issues as stocks that nobody wants and have been overlooking them on purpose. What your task has to be is to find the type of configuration that fits your temperament. If anyone tells you he has the perfect pattern, hold on to your wallet and run.

New Highs/New Lows Indicator

The New High/New Low Index might be one of the oldest indicators in the business, but it is still one that carries a strong message. This tool is used to measure the overall health of the market and is usually recorded on daily or weekly basis. All that is done to configure this indicator is to tally up the number of issues that have reached a new 52-week high or have declined to a 52-week new low. The technician will then run two totals above and below a zero line. The new highs are usually posted above the zero line, while the new lows are posted below. The point here is obvious, but I guess I should run through it once. As the new highs list expands, it is an indication that the broad-based market is in a bull phase and is growing. In a bear market, or declining market, the new lows list grows as a indication that we are seeing many stocks breaking support areas and extending their losses into new low territory. One point we must add here as a disclaimer. I mentioned earlier in this chapter that the New York Stock Exchange has added many new types of issues on its exchange. This diluting of the numbers can give misleading signals from time to time. The new high/new low has the same problem. When we see the numbers, we should give a glance to the names on the list before jumping to conclusions. Not very long ago, May 10, 2004, the daily new low list jumped to 845 lows, which, under normal conditions would have had a very negative connotation for the equity market. The simple fact that nearly a third of the stocks on the NYSE were on a low suggest a market that is falling apart.

The real story, however, was that of the 845 issues that were registering new lows, the vast majority were not operating companies but rather preferred issues and closed-end funds. As you can see from Figure 12-4, the move represented a substantial increase in the negative side. Closer examination of the numbers, however, revealed that there were only 36 companies on that new low list that were actual operating companies. Again, the numbers were correct from the stock exchange, but

FIGURE   12-4

The NH/NL.

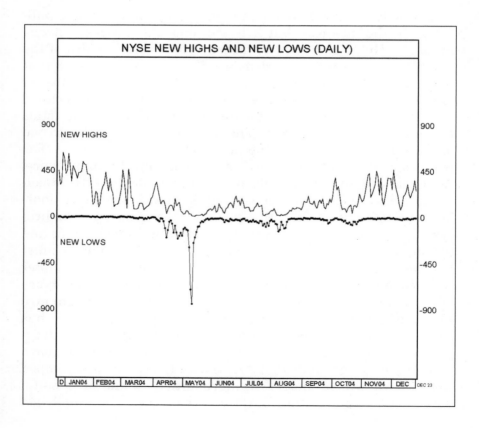

the question that must be asked is, were those numbers telling a correct story? It is my feeling that a list of lows on the New York *Stock* exchange should reflect stocks and not closed-end funds.

Relative Strength

Most charting services these days have built into them a relative strength function for all their data, and the normal readings, as we have mentioned in a past chapter, still apply for them and are still useful to me. A twist on this theme, however, is to run as many comparisons between indexes and groups as you can. The results of these "style" comparisons can open your eyes to different slants to the marketplace. For example, comparing low-capitalization issues to large-capitalization issues can tip you off on "where" you should be investing. Too many times we have all seen people get the market opinion correct just to see their stock selections stand still. Relative strength of the different styles is useful in your overall performance.

More of the indictors that we should work with would be a weekly MACD, in which I use a 26-week and a 12-week exponential moving average, and then the 9-week smoothing of those two lines. The weekly stochastic gives us a feel for the shorter-term extremes of the trading swings.

And, of course, part of my weekend reading will be all the sentiment surveys of *aii* and investors' intelligence numbers.

Lowry's 90 Percent Days

Lowry's Reports, Inc. has a very well known indicator called the 90 percent day signal. From time to time a market will trade to the extremes because of the current conditions. On occasions, at the end of the trading day we will see a 90 percent day registered in the ending data. I say "ending data" because very often during a session, markets can reach emotional extremes, but it is very difficult to maintain that pressure into the close of the day. Lowry's considers that a true 90 percent day shows that the total prices of all stocks traded on the New York Stock Exchange are 90 percent in one direction. They also feel that the volume for the same day must also register a 90 percent plurality in the same direction as the price in order to be a true extreme. What is sought here is a sign of an emotional top or bottom. For example, a 90 percent down day followed by a 90 percent up reversal day would be a traditional signal that a market has sold out, and then buyers have rushed in to scoop up bargains. What they are gauging here is supply and demand boundaries.

Trend Analysis Weekly Charts

The procedures here are easy, and after a short while they become second nature to you. As part of your analysis, you should spend time each week drawing trend lines and trend channels for key areas of the market. When we draw these lines, they act as limits or guidelines for our opinions. Drawing and adjusting your lines for such major indexes as the Dow Jones Industrials, the S&P 500, the NASDAQ, and a few others is quite helpful in grounding your outlook. If we draw a trend line for a small-cap index, say the Russell 2000, you can watch its performance against another larger-cap index like the S&P 500, which will allow you to compare one to the other. If we see a violation of a trend of one and not the other, we can make some assumptions as to where the power in the overall market is to be found. You will also want to make sure you have your trend drawn for stocks that you are holding and the stocks you are thinking of buying.

Upside/Downside Point Change

By studying the total of upside points and downside points each day, we can build an indicator that shows levels of aggressiveness in the market. The process here is to count up every fractional price movement for all the stocks on the New York Stock Exchange. You add up all the gains and then you add all the losses to reach a total for the day. Many of the same theories that apply to upside and downside volume apply here. But the points demonstrate how urgent the investors are becoming. A large volume spike with very little point movement can be trouble, but if you have an equivalent number of points accompanying the volume, then the confirmation is made and a stronger opinion can be formed.

Upside/Downside Volume

To compliment the above price calculation, you should also study the volume. This indicator, instead of looking at total volume, splits the volume into two categories. The stocks that have traded that day on the positive side are segmented and the total volume in those stocks is added together to give us the reading of upside volume. The same is performed for the issues that sold off, and that total will show us the downside volume. The interpretation of the numbers is clear. If we have "upside volume" trading above the downside volume, then we are dealing with a market where the majority of the daily volume is found in rising issues. That should bode well for the market. When the downside volume is dominant over the upside, then weakness should be anticipated. This is about as simple an example of supply/demand that we can follow. (See Figure 12-5.)

McClellan Oscillator

The McClellan Oscillator is a market breadth indicator developed by Sherman McClellan. It is the difference of two exponential moving averages of advance and decline numbers on the New York Stock Exchange. The length of time McClellan uses in his calculations is a 19-day and a 39-day exponential MA. The oscillator is run on a daily basis and moves above or below a zero line. The market is considered overbought when it reaches +100 and oversold at −100. Of course, the crossing above or below zero is usually a signal as well.

DAILY INDICATORS
Percent of Stocks above Their 10-day MA

A good friend of mine and a first-rate technician, Richard A. Ramsey, took Joe Granville's basic idea one step further and

FIGURE 12-5

Lowry's Up/Down Volume and Points.

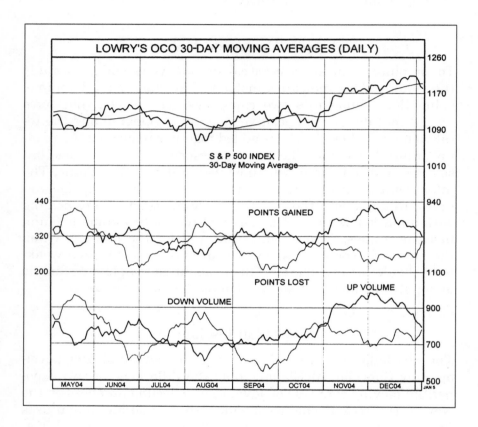

built an indicator based on a 10-day moving average. This indicator is *very* sensitive to say the least, but Ramsey discovered that this short-term indicator turned out to be a great tool for spotting bottoms and tops in the market. When the percent of stocks above their 10-day MA falls below the 10 percent level, it has signaled a general tradable market rally. Likewise, when this indicator reaches an excess of 90 percent, the market could be in for a decline. Like many things in life, the simple things are the best. Anytime we have a market condition that is in an extreme state, you can have a high degree of conviction that a reversal is close at hand.

10-Day ROC

Keeping your eyes on a simple 10-day rate of change can be the easiest way to view short-term market momentum. By taking today's price and dividing it into an index's price 10 days ago, we can construct an oscillator. A rising ROC indicates a positive tone to the short-term picture, while a falling reading is a sign of correction or possibly a worsening condition. Either way, a 10-day ROC is an excellent way to alert you to a turn in the market's direction. Most computer systems allow you to run this simple calculation.

30-Day Average of Upside/Downside Volume

These two measures of upside and downside activity help us trace the path of the supply and demand equation. It is a sensitive indicator and often leads the major indices. Following this volume indicator can help in your execution strategy. The volume picture can show us the quality of the trends. It answers the question of whether the momentum of the price is as strong as the volume. It can identify between churning and real power. Finally, volume indicators can give us insight into the validity of tops and bottoms.

Short-Term Trends Analysis

Watching groups and indexes from a short-term basis is always a must. Constructing short-term trend lines by using the chart pattern for the last 30 days as the basis for your trends and channels will serve you well. A breakdown or breakout of your near-term trends will force you to look at the intermediate picture.

GET INTO A ROUTINE

Let's take a look at my typical activities as I go into a normal day. Being in this business as long as I have been, I'm not sure if I know what normal is, but here goes one approach that might help.

I first run through the *Wall Street Journal* to glean all the statistical facts from the Market Lineup. It's the information from yesterday and always helps as an eye opener. I watch the morning financial shows from my treadmill just like everyone else, but you would be amazed at some of the intricate pieces the TV shows can miss or simply don't have time to cover.

I have a glance at the news of the day, and then after that I see if the market opinion I am carrying needs to be altered because of the day's input. One thing I am sure of: Your market opinion needs constant updating. A while ago a buddy of mine asked me for a funny opening line concerning market opinions for a speech he was giving. I said that "Market opinions are like socks; most people have two, and if you don't want to offend anyone, they need to change on a regular basis." I see no reason to alter that opinion.

Once the overview is done and I'm comfortable that I'm on the right track, its time to get down to real work. The overview part should last no longer than a cup of coffee because theoretically all we are doing is refreshing and updating.

I said before that I am an enormous believer in top-down analysis. Therefore the next tool I run for is my sectors. I have already divided the stock market into 10 sectors that I trust. Many years ago I started out with the traditional Standard and Poor's sectors and added and subtracted issues where I saw fit. I have set up my computer to sort the groups by relative strength to show me where the interest is to be to found in the market. The next step is not easy to understand, so let's spend some time with the concept.

Market Positioning

I have just talked about running a list of relative strength charts on my 10 sectors to see where I should be working. On paper that sounds simple and not very complex and believe me, I am the last person on the planet that wishes to make anything complex, but here I have to draw the line. In our read out of the top to the bottom of the list of sectors, we *must* take into deliberation where the general stock market is in relation to our selections. For example, if the market was just completing a major low and a new bull market was starting, we could be a little fast and loose with many of the tools. Often when the market is making a new major low, you'll find that the most oversold/ forgotten stocks in the early stages will make the most money. That phenomenon doesn't last long, and once the oversold quality has been removed and the easy money has been made, they tend to head back down where they belong.

As the market rally broadens out, I would want to stay with the groups that have the wind at their backs. In other words, I would want to invest in the high-momentum issues, groups, and sectors that are showing the best relative strength and positive price patterns as possible.

The hard part to this picture is in the late stages of a move. Anyone can be a genius in the runaway bull market; the trick is to still be standing after the market is back down at the bottom. As the market starts to show signs of age and loss of momentum, you must shift your portfolio. This is when a more conservative approach has to be taken.

Let's paint a picture of a market that has been generally rising for more than two years. The atmosphere is positive but the price action has given more than a few negative warnings. Please remember, I'm only trying to make a point here. At this phase of the market you do not need to be buying the *most* aggressive groups and stocks in an attempt to beat the market. Sometimes you'll find that singles and doubles win ballgames too. In other words, you don't always have to choose to be the lead sled dog. The view isn't as good, but it can be safer. Towards the end of a market rally, you choose to take a much more conservative approach, or more importantly a more defensive view. Setting stops and limits on your stocks' sectors can save more then I can tell you. Relative strength works both ways, you know, and if the market turns down, R/S is just as useful on the downside as it can be on the upside.

REWARD/RISK

Before you start with real money, simply set limits for yourself as far as what you are willing to risk against what you are expecting as a reward. There were a few times that I hit major home runs in my stock selection, but I never had set a target or placed a stop order. My thinking, like most greedy, egotistical, blinded-sided, crazy people, was that I'm correct, therefore the stock will go up forever. Stocks don't, and in some cases I walked away with much less than I should have netted.

The solution to this problem is easy. Know your support levels and take your loss if those levels are violated. That's your risk. Therefore, if a stock has already rallied far away from a support point and is higher then you are willing to risk, don't trade. Wait for a pullback to support or just figure you missed it and go on with other ideas. There is always another bus coming along. Don't chase stocks up unless you can handle the downside retrenchments.

On the flip side you must identify the resistance and once reached move your support up in line with your risk tolerance. Trend lines are helpful at this point.

What I have written might sound detailed and very involved. That's because it is, but after a relatively short time, it will become part of the things you do in the morning and you'll think nothing more about it.

Think about almost anything in your daily life like commuting to work. When we write it down, it can sound complicated when in reality it isn't. This is like the answer to a tourist's question of how to get to Carnegie Hall. The cab driver said, "Practice, practice practice."

Chapter 13

Cycles

If you look back through history, you will find that most periods of growth have been noted by events other than business. There was no mention or even an attempt to explain a historic period in any other way but extraordinary events. The Black Plague and Irish Potato Famine were biggies in their day, and of course the ever-popular war that would pop up from time to time helped shape the world on all levels, including business. There was nothing like a long war to turn an agricultural economy to a wartime machine and stimulate the old economy. A major upheaval like the Irish Potato Famine was an important event for bringing a new labor force to New York City, stimulating the U.S. economy, helping in its expansion. These shifts of people and materials because of fate's twists and turns not only cause great disruption in lives but also open up great opportunities in ways few could have ever imagined. The idea, however, that something of the ilk of an economic or a business cycle could influence growth was not even a notion worthy of consideration.

As cultures and nations grew, so did the study of economic data and business activity, and for the first time these records were kept. It wasn't until the early 1800s that people began to study these statistics in an effort to understand business for business' sake. For hundreds of years there was not much more than just the gathering of information and really no formal work done at all on the "business cycle."

The advent of the Industrial Revolution between the late eighteenth century and early nineteenth century found economies around the world bustling, and the "business of business" was becoming a topic of conversation and a new field of study in its own right. Having the desire to study business cycles was one thing, but having reliable statistical data was not an easy commodity to come across. The data needed to accomplish this task was available in England and the United States at first, and by the late 1800s a number of other countries were gathering economic data as well. It did not take long for students of this new phenomenon to spot and categorize repeating patterns that could be tracked and used as forecasting tools. At the time, the concept of actually having a repeating pattern to the mercantile structure seemed strange. Once they had proper records to study, the work could commence in earnest. The only repeating cycle that could be recognized was from the agricultural field, where the power of supply and demand was understood and respected.

As we go through this chapter, you will see that much of the major work that has been done was based on fundamental or economic statistics. Once the idea of recurring cycles in business was accepted, it then was a short jump to reengineering tools to look at the stock market and then stocks. Still it is interesting that the starting point for cycle analysis is based in economics.

Technicians use cycles to add the element of "time" into their analysis, which can be very interesting indeed. The mainstay book that I would recommend to anyone whether or not they intend to use cycles is *The Mysterious Forces That Trigger Events* by Edward R Dewey. Dewey himself is a remarkable man. The volume of work this man has put together on the subject of cycles is nothing less then mind-boggling. In Dewey's studies, he found amazing facts that after awhile just can't be ignored. After examining a countless variety of occurrences, he found that many unrelated phenomena seem to group together and that there seems to be a force in nature that pulls many of these events into a rhythm with each other. In his book he looks at thousands of cycles from troughs and peaks and troughs again of totally unrelated occurrences, and he showed that they reside in the same time cycles. For example, the flood stages of the Nile from 641–1451, Real Estate Activity between 1851–1954, and Java Tree Rings 1514–1929 all had an 18.2 cycle to them. His studies eventually lead to the stock market.

CYCLE BASICS

A working definition of a "cycle" would be a time frame where events can be expected to recur. Cycles are around us in almost every walk of our lives. A day is a cycle with the sun rising in the east at dawn and setting in the west at dusk. A year is one cycle, and within that year we have seasonal cycles of spring, summer, fall, and winter. We can predict that summer will be warmer than winter, which can help us in many ways just by recognizing the recurring events. This is a perfect example of one cycle within another cycle. We live with cycles in our daily lives, but most of the time we fail to recognize them for what they are.

There are a few basics that must be touched on before you can begin to understand cycles. First, all cycles are counted from the lows. These lows are called troughs, and when we speak of the time of a cycle, it's the distance between these troughs that we are usually counting. This is called "the periodicity" of the cycle. If we can find the period of a stock's cycle, it can give us a framework for our studies. For argument's sake, let's say we know that a stock usually completes its move in 30 days. That means if we go from a trough to a top and back again to the next trough within that time span, then we can "guess-ti-mate" that around the fifteenth day we may see a temporary top in this stock.

There is no sense in looking at cycles and the stock market without pulling price into the conversation. Within a cycle period, we have to take into account the magnitude of a cycle. This means trying to gauge the height or the depth of a stock's move. If a stocks has the power to rally 10 points in its cycle, then the "amplitude" is 10, or 10 dollars. We have therefore measured a stock's amplitude from the trough to the crest of the move. So now we have two pieces of information: 1. The period =

30 days with a half-life of 15 days and 2. The magnitude = 10 points.

And finally, there is "phase," which is nothing more than the time between two waves. It allows the cycle analysis to look at the length of two cycles at the same time. There are always cycles within cycles, and the longer the length of the cycle, the more the dominance.

We can look at the three major trends in a cycle: primary cycle, intermediate cycle, and short-term cycle.

The primary cycle is usually 4 to 4-½ years and is the result of investors' long-term views of the economy and the market.

The intermediate cycle is measured somewhere in the 4- to 6-month range and is often the most active cycle used by investors.

The short term is contained mostly with a 2-month span, 60 days or so. These three time frames make up a time rhythm in the market that is a generally accepted beat for most markets. We do find that the currency markets tend to have about a half-life to the equity rhythm.

You don't have to be in the business long before you will hear people say that they like a stock long term, but it has gotten ahead of itself on a short- to intermediate-term basis and needs to pull back before they can buy. Having a group or a stock out of order with an overall market is not that uncommon. These people are talking about two cycles coming together, hopefully to create a solid zone to purchase—an idea that they have already decided is a good one.

I was privileged to have studied cycle analysis with one of the best on the subject, Ian Notley. Up until I started with Ian I was a 100 percent pencil-pushing, trend-line- drawing, support and resistance technician and still am to a degree. The cycles, however, brought a new dimension to the charts, and I consider them a facet to TA that everyone should look at and make up their own minds as to their use. I find that when people turn away from cycles, it's because they are expecting too much from them. They have never made a form of analysis that can pinpoint an exact date or price for anything to turn up or top out. I don't care what type of investment approach you are using. But what cycles do is to give us an estimate of when a market might be expected to reverse or pick up. Up until now I have been speaking about cycles in general. For example, a day is a cycle that has 24 hours, a midpoint, and a decline. The "year" is a cycle as we run around the sun: spring is a season to start anew; summer is the growing time; fall is for gathering; and winter is for rebuilding. Seasonality is a feature of cycle analysis.

There are few principles that we should highlight:

The Principle of Harmonics states that there are cycles within each other and there is usually a relationship between them. In other words, there can be a harmony among a long cycle of say 50 weeks, and within that time frame we may recognize an intermediate-term cycle of approximately half the time as the dominant cycle.

The Principle of Synchronicity points out that cycles have an inclination to bottom together, even through they are various lengths of time. The fact is that when we see a few cycles cluster in a bottom together, called "nesting," the move that follows tends to have extra power behind it because all the forces of the short, intermediate, and long-term cycles are working together in essence, adding their own power to a coordinated move.

The Principle of Summation states that price is the total of all current cycles. When we have "nesting cycles" at a bottom, the upcoming move is usually very powerful. However, when we reach a turning point and one of the cycles is out of step with the rest, the magnitude move is reduced. Say the long and short-term cycles are at a low but the intermediate cycle has not bottomed yet. The resulting rally will have some of its power subtracted from its potential advance. Consider that one cycle as an anchor that retards the overall move.

The Principle of Commonality means those cycles of like lengths exist in all markets and securities. If a 4-year cycle exists for one market, it exits for all markets, stocks, commodities, and even international markets. The corollary to this concept is variation.

The Principle of Variation states that all the above principles exist, however they can vary in their timing. In another words, we must use these principles as simple guidelines and not absolutes. Variation can be looked upon as the escape clause for commonality. All the cycles are similar, but they will all have different magnitudes and lengths because of the economic condition and the condition of each stock and index as it relates to the current market. For example, Ian Notley points out that if we were to look at an ideal 4-year business cycle from the theoretical first day of the cycle to the theoretical last day, we could lay out a road map of how the market should respond given a new economic advance.

One of the main motivators of a new recovery is usually a reduction in interest rates in an effort to stimulate a sluggish economy. In an ideal pattern, the interest-sensitive issues would be the first to benefit from an improving economy. As the buildup in strength takes hold, the expansion migrates into other areas of the market and the cyclic, consumer, and industrials stocks would emerge as new market leaders and we would see the picked-up forward momentum. Finally, in the cycle's last months, some 3 years later, gold and basis material stocks would become the new leaders of the parade, along with other commodities that reflect an economic need for goods to meet current demands, as well as some inflationary pressures that generally follow long bull markets. The key here is that this pattern doesn't have to happen exactly the same way each time. It's the variations that make cycle analysis interesting. We can have the same cycle with a different time beat.

Proportionality simply says that the longer the time of the cycle, the higher the height of a rally or drop for the stock or an index. There is a proportion between length of time and amplitude. One principle that cycle analysis utilizes is that the longer-term cycle dominates the shorter cycle. A 4-year cycle has dominance over a 1-year cycle. Dominance means that the price direction of the 4-year cycle will have more influence on the price action than a shorter-term cycle.

LEFT AND RIGHT SKEW

We have mentioned that the longer the length of the cycle, the more dominance it will exert on shorter cycles. Let's look at the concept of secular versus cyclical movements. A secular trend is a combination of a number of 4-year cycles. Secular patterns are considered a generational move and can last anywhere from 10 to 20 years, depending on the underlying power of the economy and world events. These long secular rising backdrops gave the shorter market down cycles a generally benign character, as was felt in the 1950s and part of the 1960s.

The 1980s and 1990s saw normal cyclic pullback as respites rather than severe bear market corrections. Periods of declining secular backdrops, however, which were experienced between 1929 and 1942 and again in the late 1960s to the early 1970s, gave the down cycles a more severe tone. These declining periods tend to be longer in length and could last up to three 4-year cycles and on rare occasions possibly a fourth (12 to 16 years).

Taking this into consideration, let's look at a normal 4–4-½ year cycle. The shape of this cycle should be usually 3 years up and 1 year down with, of course, intermediate rallies and declines, along the way. For example, IBM might run from 50 to 100 over the course of 3 years and decline to 75 before a new 4-year cycle would begin again. This tendency to spend more time on the upside then the down is one of the reasons there is a long-term growth rate in the stock market of about 9 percent. However, a market that is held in a secular decline will tend to shift the balances more to an even distribution in time. Now we see a cyclical market that will last only two up and two down because the long-term negative forces of the secular decline is pushing prices lower.

I have just given you a very brief look at some of the principles and building blocks of cycles. Like a few other topics in technical analysis, we could fill up a library on the subject, but for our purpose I would like to hit some of the highlights in an effort to whet your appetite to look for more information on the topic.

Now let's apply this topic to the stock market and look at how cycles might help us. This is the point where we leave the Java Tree Rings behind and start looking at stocks and indexes.

Cycle analysis believes that when you measure a cycle, it is best to count from trough to trough.

There are a few bottom-line characteristics about cycles that we need to explain. A cycle has three traits that are common to all cycles.

A. They have amplitude (magnitude).

B. They have the length of time between troughs periodicity.

C. And they have position (phase).

Amplitude

Height of a cycle means that there is a repeatable rhythm that a stock will swing within. Once a cycle has been observed and identified, then we can set the limits in dollars and cents on a chart for a particular issue or index. One stock might have a normal 10 range that it moves within, while another could have a much larger swing to it. When we look back at a stock chart, we can determine from past troughs in the stock how high a move is likely to be from the stocks history.

Periodicity

The length of a cycle is simple enough, as it measures the days, weeks, or months between troughs. Remember, cycles are measured from low points. Lows are clearer to spot and pinpoint, while tops can drag on and be less definite. Knowing the length of time from one trough to another can give you a time target for the next cycle. We can view the stock's history in the chart to give us a time frame.

Phase

Position is concerned with dealing with two cycles of differing lengths and measuring the time between the troughs of the two cycles. Once we see the time between cycle lows, it can help in spotting the next bottom, assuming the cycle remains fairly firm.

MAJOR CYCLES TO STUDY

In an attempt to follow the general belief that the longer the cycle length, the more dominant the cycle will be on all other cycles, I will lay out the highlights of a few studies that have been done in order of their cycle dominance.

Kondratieff Wave 54-Year Cycle

In any talk of cycles, you will always have someone start off with a discussion of the K wave. Nikolai D. Kondratieff was a

Russian economist who found a 50–54 year cycle in the business of the United States. A problem with his study was that it only covered two observations, and the statistical relevance is very questionable. It is an interesting aside, however, that Professor Stanley Jevons, an English economist, found a similar cycle for the British economy between 1271–1954.

Kondratieff's wanted to show that a *long wave* did exist within the capitalist process. He believed that there was about a 20-year upward move in an economy when an economy would expand. Eventually, as inflationary pressure took hold, the economy would have a flatting plateau period of 7–10 years followed by a 20-year decline. Kondratieff felt that this wave was a direct refection of a country's social fabric. The country would go from strong growth and good times to social unrest and war.

His theory stated that out of depression, an economy would be the beneficiary of cheap money and cheap labor. These periods of low economic activity meant that interest rates were very low as well. The money that business could borrow at these low rates helped in the refitting of plants and equipment. These elements laid the building blocks for a long period of economic growth. Also, as the economy emerged from depressed levels, business would use the current-day technology to improve business productivity. Innovations, by the way, can be very hard on businesses that fail to innovate. By very hard I mean they fail.

Kondratieff, after studying pig iron prices, gold, coal, interest rates, and stock prices from around the world, said that the long business cycle is a self-correcting cycle. This is one of the oldest theories of them all when we go from fear to greed and back to fear again.

Remember, he was an economist under Joseph Stalin, and Stalin wanted to hear that capitalism was doomed to fail because of its evil nature. He was not interested in a system that was self-correcting. The concept that capitalism might work for whatever reasons was enough to gain Stalin's displeasure. As a result of his reports and theories, Kondratieff was sent to Siberia and died there in the 1930s. That makes him the only economist that actually went to jail for his theories.

Juglar 9.2-Year Cycle

Clemant Juglar postulated that economies moved from one extreme to another in a 9.2-year cycle. After his study of pig iron prices, interest rates, loan figures, patents issued, and many more economic functions, he reached his conclusions. His is the theory of prosperity and liquidation, which is based on an economy going from boom to bust, one being the offshoot of the other. This cycle repeated itself 16 times between 1834 and 1966. Now, there is/was a theory of Random Walk that stated that stock prices act in a random fashion and therefore you cannot predict stock prices. No cycles exist except by chance. In Dewey's book, he mentions that according to Bartels test probability, a 9.2-year cycle could not occur by chance more than once in 5000 times. If that's not enough proof that cycles exist, then I guess you should move on to the next chapter. I would also point out that this study covers a period from the 2 years before the invention of the first refrigeration unit in 1836 to the introduction of the computer mouse in 1965. That's quite a span in time.

Kitchin 4- to 4-½-Year Cycle

In Chapter 4 we showed in some detail the four-year cycle from the 1940s to the present, so we need not go there again. In 1923 Professor Crum from Harvard showed his work on commercial paper rates. His study covered approximately 60 years and showed that there was a recurring 40-month cycle in the rates. This study was the stepping-stone for additional papers on the subject, as it showed that an economic series could show a regular and predictable rhythm. Professor Joseph Kitchin, also of Harvard, found the 4-year cycle in Great Britain and the United States from 1890 to 1922. He used interest rates, bank clearing numbers, and the like. It must be pointed out that in 1946 the cycle inverted for no apparent reason and the cycle clock was restarted into today's pattern. This shows that nothing is infallible, and you must always confirm any tool that is used. Since 1950, however, that cycle has been one of the most reliable cycles we can find. Most people believe it is the business cycle that is showing itself to be the heartbeat of capitalism that accounts for this cycle.

"Schumpeter" Model

Another Harvard economist by the name of Joseph Schumpeter authored an exhaustive study entitled *Business Cycles: A Theoretical and Statistical Analysis of the Capitalist Process.* This is the clearest example of the Principle of Summation that I can find. We mentioned before that summation is the combination of the total of all the active cycles. If we could add them together and come up with one picture, we could build a road map. Keep in mind that many of these cycles are not exactly the same length. Cycles can fluctuate within their time frames, but by and large Schumpeter felt that a general picture of business conditions could be gleaned from his model.

Schumpeter started with the Kondratieff wave to create the overall background shell in his model. The 54-year cycle, which began in the 1840s, is the longest cycle in this series and therefore the most dominant of all. As we have stated already, the longer the cycle the more influence it will have on neighboring cycles. The next cycle used in his model was the Juglar 9.2-year cycle, which can be found at the midpoint of Figure 13-1. Finally, the Kitchin 4-year cycle was added to the mix to come up with the Schumpeter Model of a smoothed line for economic activity. He is using the two shorter-term cycles, Juglar's 9.2 years and Kitchin's 4 to 4-½ year cycles as brakes and accelerators for the K-Wave. The result was the Schumpeter Model. If you examine Figure 13-1, you will see that during times when all of the cycles are in agreement with each other, the moves that follow usually represent some of the most powerful moves in the markets. A great example is the market in the late 1950s.

On the other hand, when we get a divergence and one cycle is fighting another, you tend to have less fruitful moves. If we look at the late 1960s and early 1970s, you can see how the K wave was still in a strong upward pattern, while the other two cycles were pulling in the opposite direction. (See Figure 13-1.)

SEASONAL FACTORS

The fact that the calendar can have effects on the stock market should not come to anyone as a big surprise. If we look at all of

FIGURE 13-1

Schumpter's Model.

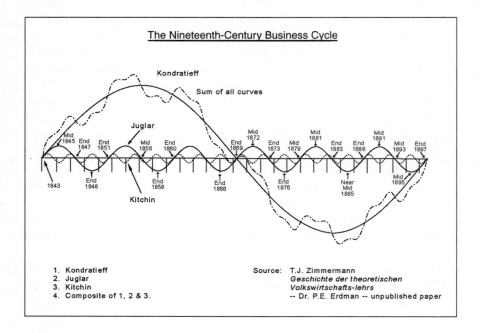

the stock markets as an extension of human emotion, then why shouldn't it respond to something as simple as seasonal factors? It is, after all, human emotions that cause the prices to rise and fall because of fear and greed. The chart patterns are simply a reflection of supply and demand. I'm beginning to sound like the cat that ate the rat that ate the cheese, etc.

But it is true. There is a seasonal trend in the market as a whole. Any price pattern that repeats itself in a year time after time is considered a seasonal cycle. The commodities markets are filled with seasonal patterns that repeat based on planting and harvesting times. I come from Brooklyn and never really spent too much time on a farm, but even I know that at harvest time the supply of "whatever" commodity you're trading is going to be at its greatest level and the price of that commodity is likely to be under pressure. On the other end, we will have the smallest amount of supply at planting time, when prices could experience highs in trading. The question is how we capitalize on that information and when the proper time is in each commodity cycle.

This is an example of how you use common sense and the forces of supply and demand to assist you in the commodity markets. For every market there are a number of seasonal cycles that come into play.

Retail stocks perk up during and right after Christmas. We all know that, but when you look at Figure 13-2, showing retail issues over the last 12 years, you can see that the retailers tend to bottom out in February, and they run until midyear. (See Figure 13-2.)

FIGURE 13-2

Composite Chart of Retailers for the Last 12 Years.

There is a positive price pattern for the October to March time frame. Here we have some recent misinformation on Wall Street that the month of October is the worst time of the year because of a few selloffs in the past. The newspapers just love to bring up the ghost of October 1987, and every year we have to hear the grim stories all over again. The truth is, however, that October is a *bear killer* more than anything else, and it is an excellent time to buy stocks. The months of May and June, on the other hand, are the worst months to buy. Why? Could be because people have just had a talk with the Internal Revenue Service and are feeling low or maybe because the summer is starting and families are busy with other activities. The reason it is true counts very little in the grand scheme of things. What is important is that it has proven to be true in the past, and unless there is a good reason to expect a change in the pattern, there is no reason to think May–June will act any differently.

I have taught many classes on cycles over the years, and a question that always is asked is why a student should know about these seasonal cycles. The answer is that your competition knows about them and will be happy to be on the other side of a trade if you choose to ignore the seasonal patterns. You do not need to be a cycle analyst, but being unaware of their potential can leave you blinded on one side.

There is an excellent publication that should be on all desks for easy reading and some very solid market knowledge. The name is *Stock Traders Almanac*, Hirsch Organization. Yale Hirsch and son Jeffrey Hirsch have compiled an exhaustive amount of market statistics and seasonal information on a month-by-month calendar basis. The Almanac is filled with Wall Street history and data. Get a copy and keep it handy.

Presidential Cycle

The presidential cycle is another excellent example of a seasonal cycle. It is a pattern that has reoccurred every 4 years and starts in January after the presidential election in November. In *The Stock Traders Almanac*, Yale Hirsch shows that in 43 administrations since 1833, the last 2 years of a term of office produced a stock market gain of 717.5 percent compared to 227.6 percent gains for the first 2 years in office. Seems as if the president is going to do things that are unpopular with the public, they tend to do it early in their administration rather then waiting for re-election time to be harsh.

As I said, you don't have to live your lives as a cycle analyst, but it pays in the long run to know the stock market's rhythm. It is helpful to know that November–December–January is the best 3-month span in the year, or that August and September are the 2 worst months of the year. As your time in the business grows, you will notice that most areas of the market do take on a seasonal pattern. There are statistics on the best time of the month, the week, the day, the hour, and yes even the half-hour to buy a stock. Do I follow the market that closely? As a rule, no. Yet if I had a large trade that needed to a little extra help, I might rely on these points. You might not even be aware of it at the time, but the pulse of the market is there.

Chapter 14

What to Look at in the Market

I mentioned this much earlier in this book, but I started on Wall Street in 1964, and one of the reasons they gave me a job at the early age of 17 was that the daily volume had expanded all the way up to about 5 million shares a day. Think of it, 5 million shares a day and the Street couldn't keep up with the avalanche of business. Today, the New York Stock Exchange does that amount on Sunday. (Just kidding.) The point is that over the years, the level of activity has grown at a breakneck pace, and many of the ways of the technicians have changed right along with this trend.

There was a time when a wire inquiry would come from a broker and it would have taken a half a day to respond to that person's question. You needed to update the chart first of all with the current price, and back then many times that required going to another office or making a phone call to find out where that stock was trading. Then you had the process of going through all the tools you had at your command and reaching a conclusion.

Today the answers need to be off your desk 30 seconds before *now*. You might ask if things have gotten harder and I would say no, just faster. To help cope with the speed, we have those great computers that fill in many of the gaps. In fact, it's the advent of the computer that has allowed for much of the volume expansion.

I talked about posting 4000 P&F charts every morning. Well, not every chart needed to be posted every day. When the exchange is trading only 5 million shares a day, it's easier to update those amounts of charts. If we were to try that today, with the level of activity we have and the high volatility, you would have to be posting charts 24/7, and you still might not get the job finished.

Take a look at Figure 14-1, a chart of the Dow Jones Industrials and look at the volume patterns. Increasing volume is just a fact of life in our business and is something that we will always have to factor into our thinking. The rules that applied 20 years ago as to size have very little to do with today's market. You should flip through some chart books sometime and give yourself an historic view of trading levels. I believe it was

FIGURE 14-1

Daily Volume. Drawn by The Chartstore.com.

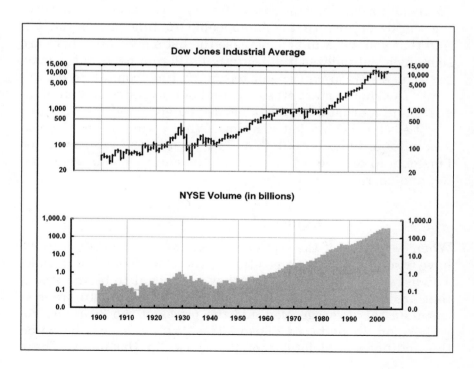

well into the 1980s before we traded 100 million shares in one day and 500-million-share days were not seen for several years after that high level was reached. The point is that every time we break an old level of volume, we tend to maintain that level going forward and build from there. When we reached 1 billion shares in a day, it felt like my head was going to explode. Of course it didn't and we are now doing 2 billion a day on a regular basis. So be willing to adjust your indicators when needed to keep pace with volatility.

WHAT TO FOLLOW

Now that you have gotten this far and you are ready to venture into the real world, the next question that has to be answered is what indexes you should follow that will give you a firm view of the market but not overwhelm you. When you look at an area, you want to try to cover the waterfront without having to flip through tons of paper, which in this business is quite easy to do. By following a few indexes at first, you can construct a working market opinion that is manageable. As time passes you will find that you will want to increase the list a good bit. There are so many great indexes that represent different parts of the market that a person can spend too much time coming to an answer. You should start off slowly and build your collection of indexes and market overview tools as you go.

Let's try one market at a time. What I will do is to give you a handful of indexes that should be used in the various areas. I'm going to confine my remarks to the equity, bonds, commodity, and currencies markets.

Equity Market Indexes

When we speak of the equity market, we must make sure we have a solid hold on the position of the Dow Jones Industrials. The list is only 30 names, but they are meant to be the stocks that are the best of the best in the United States. In order to calculate this average, you add the prices of the 30 issues together and divide by its divisor. The Dow's divisor is based on the additions or deletions of the stocks in the index. These changes occur in order to keep the index current with the times. The divisor is also affected by splits and dividends, and this number is reported each day in the *Wall Street Journal* and many other places. It is true that there are many issues that are just as respected in the national market, and many issues have more liquidity, but these 30 names are still the group that most people ask about when they want to know how "the market is doing." For comparison, you should also work with the Dow Transportation and Dow Utilities Averages. All three, theoretically, represent the quality in the stock market. There is, after all, something in a name.

You also must have a working knowledge of the Standard and Poor's 500, as this is the index that most institutional portfolio manager's performance is measured against. It is a listing of the 500 largest capitalized stocks on the New York Stock Exchange. Although these indexes are important, we are still dealing with a relatively small number of stocks compared to the total. I should mention that this index is capitalization weighted, and because we are dealing with the biggest 500 names on the NYSE, we are also looking at an index that accounts for roughly 80–85 percent of the exchange's capitalization value. So it is important to keep your eyes on it at all times. (See Figure 14-2.)

Staying with the study of the NYSE, we must include a few broad-based indexes like the Russell 2000, which is an index of low-priced stocks. Possibly the last index would be the NYSE Composite Index, which tallies up all the issues on the NYSE.

What I have suggested is to follow the Dow Jones' three major averages, the S&P 500 for additional depth in the large-cap arena, and two broad-based indexes like the Russell 2000 and the NYSE Composite. Using this combination of indexes can offer a broad look into the market, and it also gives us a chance to spy for divergences. Watching the large-cap stock indexes rally ahead while the rank-and-file issues are falling can be a classic sell signal. It is usually referred to as having the generals in your army attacking a position, while your soldiers remain in their foxholes. Not a smart idea. (See Figure 14-3.)

NASDAQ will require a similar array of indexes that should help you to reach your goals. Like the New York, the over the counter has many indexes that allow us to break down the

F I G U R E   1 4 - 2

The S&P 500.

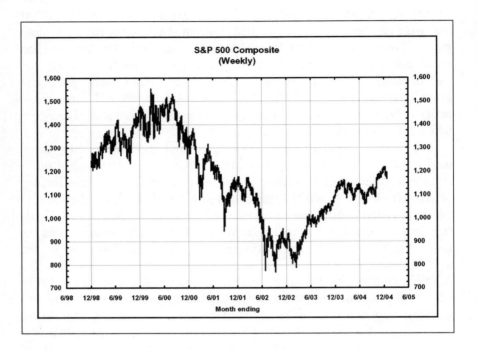

market. The main index for this area is the NASDAQ Composite, which has in its mix more than 5000 plus issues of all types. These names not only show the movement of that market very well, but also show us the level of aggressiveness for equities in general. The NASDAQ can be sliced and diced in many different ways.

NASDAQ 100 INDEX

One index that has been developed is the unweighted NASDAQ 100 Index. Here the large-capitalization, high-technology issues are examined and in many cases can give you a forward look into the exchanges moves. Many of the major sectors on this exchange, like the biotech and the financials, are available, but it

FIGURE   14-3

NYSE. Courtesy of MetaStock.

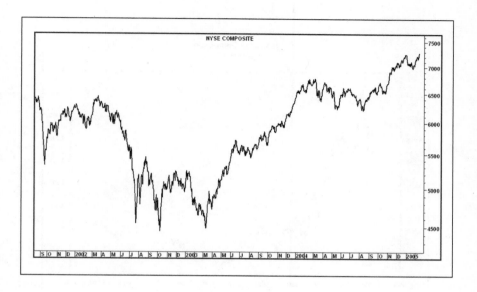

does seem that the Unweighted National Market Index is one of the main tools that should be mastered, as the questions about this one are unending. These questions are most active when there is a divergence between the action in the Composite and the Unweighted, for again we are dealing with an index that looks at stocks as equals versus the Composite, which is cap weighted and therefore heavily influenced by the largest issues.

I could go on with the many market indexes that can be followed, but I wanted to give you a reasonable number to work around. (See Figure 14-4.)

BOND MARKETS

There is no way of coming to grips with the bond market without a complete study of the interest rate picture and the economic forecast. To accomplish this we must have a few indexes that will follow the U.S. 30-day Fed Funds rates and the

FIGURE 14-4

NASDAQ. Drawn by The Chartstore.com.

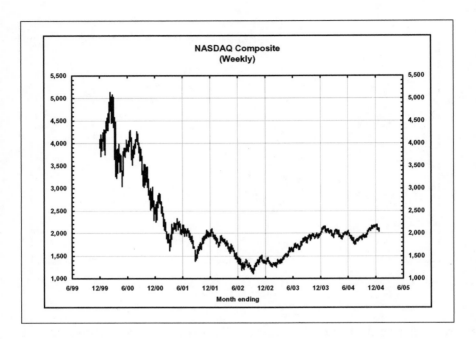

3-month T-bills. These should give us the picture for the short-term interest rates. There are many other indexes that can be followed, but these will work as a start.

With the short end covered, we must now look to the Long Bonds for contrast. To accomplish this you can use the Bond Buyer Index and the bond Buyer Municipal Index for comparison. (See Figure 14-5.)

What we want here is to be able to compare high-quality bonds with lesser-quality bonds to give us a sense of rates and stock prices. There is a great little index called the Barrons Confidence Index that Joe Granville is credited with that appears each week in *Barron's* magazine. It takes the average of high-grade bond yields and divides them by lower-grade bond yields. What we get in the Confidence Index is an indication of the

F I G U R E   1 4 - 5

Bond Chart, 10 Year.

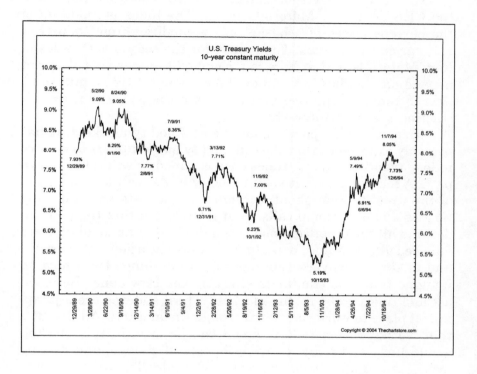

willingness of bond buyers to take a risk and buy low-quality bonds in order to lock in higher yields. Or are they worried about the outlook for the economy and wish to go down a more conservative path with higher-quality names. This should be used as a guidepost and not as a buy or sell indicator.

COMMODITIES

The commodity market, like the equity market, has it own hierarchy of indexes. In this area it the Commodity Research Bureau and its various subgroups that most traders will watch. The CRB index is made up of a mix of industrial and agricultural commodities to give you a broad-based overview. There are

21 different commodities that make up this group, but there is a heavy influence from the grain in this mixture.

There are subcategories like the CRB Spot Cash Index and the CRB Spot Raw Materials Index. The index is made up of the current prices of a basket of commodities from industrial and agricultural areas. The reason for the second spot index of Raw Materials is that here is a commodity index that does not depend on weather but rather the economy. It is helpful to be able to compare the two indexes to see the zones that are attracting the most interest.

Here is a side point about the commodity markets. It has been my experience that the commodity market tends to be very independent, and many times each commodity will take its own path. A conversation with a commodity trader will wind up, most of the time, talking about a number of markets with differing targets and directional calls. So it is my belief that the CRB index and all the other commodities indexes that are available are followed as a reference point to simply give us a general overview and to start a conversation more then anything else. I have to imagine that it is similar to studying the Dow Jones Industrials and talking about "the market." These indexes are a jumping off place to work your way through the markets. All the tools that we have been talking about can be used in this market. Trend lines and relative strength, rate of change, and moving averages are all extremely useful when dealing with so many diverse markets. Every imaginable commodity has a chart of its own, from aluminum to zinc. Many are influenced a great deal by the calendar and the rest by the economy. They are all influenced by supply and demand. (See Figure 14-6.)

FOREIGN MARKETS

The foreign markets are very important from the standpoint of knowing how the rest of the world in doing in relation to the United States. In today's world of finance, most of the markets are connected to each other. Sometimes these connections are very straightforward as to their possible impact on our markets, and sometime they are more subtle, but its hard to hide the

F I G U R E   1 4 - 6

A Commodity. Drawn by The Chartstore.com.

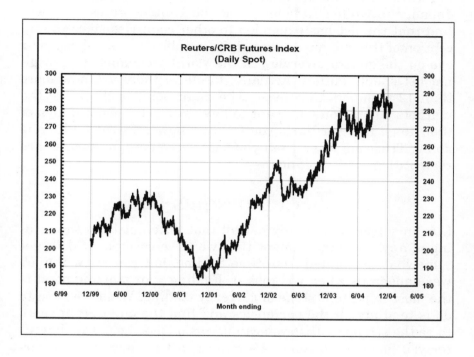

world markets' condition when you look at the charts. I am not trying to say that if the New Zealand 30 Gross Index were to top out and start a bear market, then lower Manhattan better watch out. However, if all the major market indexes began rolling over at the same time, then I would start to worry about our own prospects here at home. There are goods and services that are sold overseas and imported into our country. If economic times are going to get hard, then those harder times could very easily start knocking at our doors. Remember, stock markets are leading economic indicators, and if the world starts responding to poor economic times across the board, then we should factor that information into our outlook. As to indexes, I would choose the G-7 for starters, as they will give you the backbone picture of the world markets and the international feelings toward the economic prospects for their respective communities. Those countries are Canada, France, Germany, Italy, Japan, the United Kingdom, and the United States. You will find that the list has expanded to other countries since the inception of this committee, but since our objective is to keep your eye on the general overview of the world economies, this original list should suffice. Actually, I believe there are now more than 12 members that meet. The main point is these are the markets where you will want to have at least a general idea of their tone. It never hurts you to know how your competition is doing. Trust me when I tell you that these foreign markets are competition for U.S. funds.

CURRENCIES

Currency trading is really not all that different than the trading of any other instrument that we have covered. It does get somewhat convoluted from time to time, but you knew the job was dangerous when you took it. Finding your starting point is the most important stage of currency trading. What we need to do is to study all the currencies and find the one that appears to be the strongest that you can use as a base. Let's say that after you have run a relative strength sort against the key currencies, you decide on one. We would then make a choice among the remaining list that we feel our selection would best be matched against. There are a few things that must be remembered about the currency markets. There are no official volume numbers to this market, so obviously all of the volume indicators are of no use. Also, the currencies have no official opening and closing because it's a 24-hour global market. The caveat to these points are that a sharp increase in activity will always be spotted and noted as levels are penetrated or broken. These points are usually at existing reversal points. As to the opening and closing, they are based on world change of the day.

All other technical indicators that deal with price are used in trading in this arena. Trend lines, channels, MACD, STOC, and simple support and resistance are all fair tools in this very active market.

EXCHANGE TRADED FUNDS (ETFs)

ETFs have been around since 1993, when they first started trading on the New York Stock Exchange. The first of these new fund types was called "Spyders," which was a fund that represented the Standard and Poor's 500. Because it was a new product and an experiment at the time, the interest in this new item was by no means a barnburner. But the SPYs lasted and soon were joined by another ETF called the Nasdaq 100 Index, named the Qs. Its symbol is **QQQ** and most recently has moved to the NASDAQ and come up with the very innovative symbol of QQQQ. (See Figure 14-7.)

In the late 1990s, the major upward force in the stock market in the United States was technology stocks. That sector of stocks traded in a powerful uptrend almost to the exclusion of the rest of the market and was the powerhouse behind the our country's growth. The Nasdaq exchange has always been the exchange that represents technology issues and smaller

FIGURE 14-7

The QQQQ. Courtesy of MetaStock.

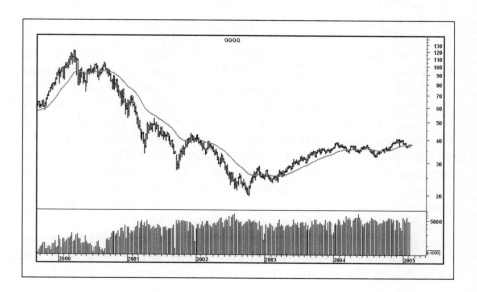

corporations in their beginning stages of growth. When the Qs were introduced, it was like putting gasoline on a fire. The best thing you could do is to just stand back and watch it grow.

Once the SPYs, which represented a basket of large-cap issues on the NYSE, were combined with the QQQs, which represented a basket of over-the-counter technology issues, the fate of the ETFs as a lasting product was assured.

Even today these two ETFs still represent the lion's share of daily activity.

This new product now allows anyone to trade in and out of the markets quickly. This product line is especially helpful to the professional money managers, as it offers a method of injecting large pools of money in and out of the marketplace without sacrificing liquidity. Also unlike traditional open-ended funds, you can trade the Exchange Traded Funds either from the long side (buy) or the short side (sell). You no longer have to wait until the end of the day to execute orders, as ETFs trade just like common stock.

If there is a problem with this product, it is that the overall interest is still concentrated in just a handful of the largest ETFs. The fear is that a daily volume in the majority of ETFs is quite low and people are worried about getting caught in a product that has low liquidity. The truth, however, is that new shares of any of the ETFs can be credited at any time by the street, thus reducing the fear of illiquidity.

I would say from the growing acceptance of this product, however, that in the future the daily volume of many of these funds should expand as investors become more and more familiar with their value and tax advantages. Almost every day we hear or read about ETFs and their uses. They now have funds for sectors, groups, type of equities, international, and commodities. An investor, either large or small, can take advantage of the market just by buying one instrument. If news came out on healthcare sectors that was overall positive and you wanted to invest in it, you only need to make a decision on XLVs or the IYHs.

These ETFs have made it possible to invest in the very indexes that I have mentioned above. Instead of looking at the Dow Jones Industrial Averages and then coming up with the correct stock to invest in, we can now use these tools to shot-gun the category in one blow. By purchasing the Diamond (DIA) we can buy an ETF and own the Dow Jones Index equivalent that will shadow that index. The same can be said for the NASDAQ. Simply by purchasing the QQQQ we can participate in the action in that exchange, and the SPYs represent the Standard and Poor's 500. If we are set on participating in the Russell 2000 Growth index, we need go no further then to look at the IWOs, which represent the ishares Russell 2000. There are many other ETF types that can be employed, but I believe you have the picture. All of these can be purchased the same as buying stock on any exchange. It is my opinion that as investors become aware of these tools, their acceptance will do nothing but grow.

Chapter 15

Sectors and Groups

TAKING A LONG VIEW

From the standpoint of how people study the stock markets, there are two major categories in the financial markets, top-down analysis versus bottoms up. Although neither term fully describes them perfectly, it does capture their general approach. There is nothing wrong with either form of analysis; it is simply a matter of technique. The top-down folks like to look at the broad economic overview and make a determination as to the health of the overall economy before taking the first step in investing. After calculating the risks and rewards that the market offers, they try to deduce the best way of taking advantage of those conclusions. Once they are finished with the overview, their next step is to weight the types of investments that will fit best in their scenario, i.e., small cap, large cap, growth or value, domestic or international, etc. Finally, after they have gone over all these points, they will begin to look at the stock market. Their work will bring them to look at sectors of the market that should benefit from the current atmosphere. Usually the next step in this process is to find the groups within those favorable sectors that would fit in the overall investment scenario. As an example of this type of search, let's look at the consumer/noncyclical sector.

Within this sector you will find the following groups: alcohol and tobacco, consumer products, health products, food, drugs, and retail–food. After studying the groups, it is a short step to the selection process of choosing the stock that matches the strong power of the group. By employing a few of the tools that we have already mentioned, like relative strength, moving averages, trend analysis, etc., all of the filtering steps can be done with a limited amount of effort. All in all this approach makes the most sense to me because it starts from the macro and goes down to the particular. If I were going to buy a house, I would naturally take into consideration the economy, the health of my own finances, the housing market, and finally a good neighborhood and the right house that matches my needs. This top-down approach has been the method that I have employed since the day I started.

The bottoms-up analysts also have a legitimate approach to the markets as they look to companies to stand on their own, regardless of these other factors. A solid stock is a solid stock. Some of these people have niches carved out that allow them to stay within a clearly defined area of expertise and never stray very far from their chosen areas. Someone who is a specialist on the floor or on a trading desk on one of the exchanges who maintains an orderly market for 30 or so stocks would have little reason to study many stocks outside of that book of business. Perhaps he is a research analyst that covers only a limited number of stocks for a brokerage house, or a money manager that only invests in one area because of the charter limitations on her fund, like a Biotech Specialty Fund. If they have to invest in only one area, there is little reason for them to study too many other sectors except for their own general information. But if every morning you are faced with the problem of investing in any market on the planet and in any financial instrument, then a broader approach is a must in my opinion. I used the word "problem" above because sometimes having too many choices can be overwhelming and can result in no action. So being disciplined in a top-down filtering approach can be very valuable.

STRENGTH IN GROUPS

Many professional investors tend to pick stocks based on their individual merits, like strong earnings, new management or perhaps just a plain old "good story." But the pressures of their industry groups also heavily influence individual stocks. We have all seen cases in the recent past in which the stock of a company with strong fundamentals has been dragged down because of bad news about the industry group. We have also seen many cases in which the stock of a mediocre company has far exceeded price expectations due to the strength of its industry group. The dynamics of the industry group can have a very important influence on the performance of an individual stock.

The following study shows that concentrating stock purchases within the industry groups reflecting the strongest investor buying enthusiasm can dramatically improve overall performance.

Lowry's Reports, Inc., from North Palm Beach, Florida, had such a study that showed the results over a 3-year period of how your performance can greatly be improved by buying strong groups. An assumption is that the groups that are strong are also in strong sectors. A further assumption is that each week an investor bought equal dollar amounts of the industry groups that were in Lowry's industry groups that were showing strong power ratings. Of course, we must also assume that an investor bought stocks in the weakest industry groups to have a fair comparison. Figure 15-1 shows the results.

These rankings are based on an established system that examines the trend of the current power rating, the relationship of the current power rating to its 30-week moving average, the position of the relative strength histogram above or below the zero line, and the position of the current price to its 30-week moving average.

What they have done is to combine a number of the general tools that we have been speaking about into a workable product that attempts to keep investors in the strong sectors, the strong groups, and the strong stocks. It's hard to swim upstream for very long.

There are a few points that should be made here that are very important for overall results and bring a bit of the real world into the picture. When the trend of the general market turns down, even the strongest industry group will find it hard to buck the trend. It is often referred to as rearranging the deck chairs on the Titanic. In these cases it is best for an investor to

FIGURE 15·1

The Industry Groups.

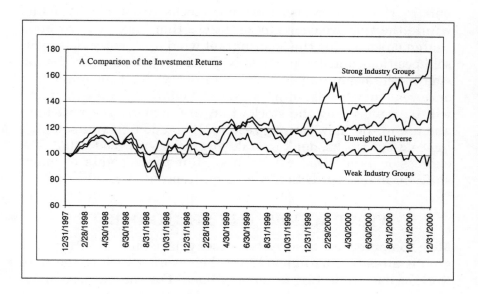

A Comparison of the Investment Returns

Strong Industry Groups

Unweighted Universe

Weak Industry Groups

hold off purchases or at least reduce the size of new commitments until the primary trend turns back up.

Another trap that should be avoided is finding a sector or group that is showing power, but when you examine the stocks that make up that group, you might find that one or two issues are dominating the index. For example, if we were to look at the S&P tobacco group we would find that Altria, a.k.a. Phillip Morris, is by far the heaviest weight in that group's numbers. So the question must be are we looking at an index that represents tobacco or are we looking at one company that's in the tobacco field? Perhaps a group has gone through a period of mergers, which has left one of the components of the group much larger than the rest and therefore could distort the story a group chart is showing us. The point is that when using these charts, make sure you have a solid grasp of what is entailed in the data.

There are times when industry group analysis does not work as well as it usually does. Again we have to always consider the market's position at all times as part of our decision process. Indicators, patterns, volume levels, groups, etc. will act differently during different stages of a market cycle.

Take, for instance, in the very early stages of a new major bull market, the best-performing stocks are typically found within the very weakest stocks. Issues that have been severely beaten down during the bear market wind up in extremely oversold positions and can prove to be percentage leaders on the upside in the beginning stage of a recovery. Keep in mind that once real "new leadership" is established, these sold-out stocks will be replaced by the stocks that are actually the best buys and are in the "new" strong sectors. If you do find yourself buying sold-out stocks, don't mistake oversold with good value. The expression is a "dead cat bounce." But these points of major shifts in market direction can be quite profitable.

WHAT MAKES THE SECTORS RUN

Most computer technical systems today have built-in sectors and groups already programmed into their work. Much of the hard work of data collecting is already done. For the purpose of explanation, let's look at the groups and try to show the "why" behind group moves and what the forces of supply and demand might be trying to tell us. Groups and sectors are subject to the same influences as indivual stocks, except in these cases we sometimes can glean much more information then just a buy/sell. Certain group movements often give the analyst clues as to major shifts in the market, and you need to know these signs.

There is no holy grail as to the exact number of sectors, but the following grouping has all the necessary bases covered and works quite well. The 10 basic sectors that are generally accepted in the marketplace are in alphabetical order: basic materials, conglomerates, consumers-cyclic, consumers/noncyclic, energy, financials, industrials, technology, transportations, and finally, utilities.

Each one of the sectors has its own part to play in the general movement in a market. While it's true that a rising tide lifts all boats, it's also true that not all the boats lift at the same time, nor do they all reach the same heights. Some of those boats have holes in their hulls.

I am going to try to paint an idealistic picture of a market cycle where the sectors act perfectly in the order that they should move. Of course you realize that nothing is perfect: this, however, should give you an understanding of what leads and lags and how that can enhance your pocketbook. We'll divide the sectors into three basic business zones, which are variation on a theme that was taught to me by another mentor, Ian Notley.

When a new cycle commences, the first areas to watch for improvement are bonds, utilities, and financial, as the shift in the Federal Reserve policy would start to take hold. As time progresses and we move into the middle of a cycle, issues that reflect the results of those rate cuts take on a leadership role in the marketplace, such as consumers, technology, and industrials. Finally, as the cycle matures and some overheating takes place, the issues that could benefit from the economy's strength, such as cyclical, energy, and precious metals, see power.

LEADING SECTORS

Whenever we look at a business cycle, it is often hard to pinpoint the beginning and the end because all the cycles are different, yet they have some characteristics that are similar. For our purposes, let's say that a stock market has been in a recession and stock prices have been in a decline for a long while. One of the elements that are present in a bear market is either high or rising interest rates. Usually, the sequence of events that sets a bear market in motion is the Federal Reverse tightening of key interest rates in an effort to slow an economy that has overheated. This is not a valuation question about the stock market but rather a judgment based on growth rates and their consequences later on. One item that the Federal Reserve seems to worry about more then most others is hyperinflation and it's effect on J.Q. Public. When this cutting off of money has had its desired results, the Fed then starts a series of rate cuts to start the process all over again. Now before you all get crazy, let me say that the market is not that simple or easy. Many times the Fed can act and there is no apparent effect on the markets. But by keeping an eye on the sectors and the groups that should be affected directly by an interest rate move, you can spot the required signals that would separate a simple interest rate adjustment from a major policy shift. It is those policy shifts that can eat you alive if you're not observant. Ignoring the actions taken by the Federal Reserve is usually not a very smart move. These sectors listed below will show you what the market thinks about Fed action fairly quickly.

Leading Groups

Financial, major banks, regional banks, bonds prices, utilities, insurance, and brokerage groups are usually considered leading groups, as they will lead the market in a new cycle.

All of these groups will be affected as interest rates take on a new direction. In a new business cycle that has been initiated by the belief that interest rates will be declining over a long period, we should see the financial and bonds areas respond quickly. If there is no reaction in these areas, then the outlook for rates might be in question. But you will find that the market will make adjustments to the new rate picture rather quickly. The question as to whether or not an interest rate shift is major will manifest itself in the individual chart patterns. This is another excellent reason for drawing those trend lines and keeping your eyes on support and resistance levels. By watching short-term tools you can gauge long-term implications.

Coincident Sectors

Conglomerates, industrial, technology, and consumers, in a normal business cycle, will tend to take over leadership as the general conditions of the economy become more apparent. We see a large improvement in stocks and groups that begin to reap the benefits of the rising economic strength. These groups will gain power in their earnings and attract buyers coincident with the business growth. Sometimes this part of the cycle can last a very long period, as this is where the economy shows its power, and many companies are included in this area.

Lagging Sectors

These groups are usually the last to benefit from a rising economy and a strong bull market. They are basic materials, energy, cyclic resources, precious metals, and commodities.

As the economic cycle extends and begins to get long in tooth, we begin to see many of the back-end-of-the-cycle issues respond. One of the side effects to a rallying market in its third year or so of an advance is investors will begin to worry about inflation and overvaluations. In an attempt to protect what they have gained or protect against a serious pullback, investors and traders will begin to hedge their bets in these back-end sectors. These areas are the last beneficiaries of the cycle from an earnings standpoint and should continue to show earnings growth well past the top in the general market.

Now let's put the reasons behind this order into some kind of a sensible road map. The basic materials sector is usually made up of anything from gold and copper to materials used in building such as steel or aluminum as well as papers and chemicals.

Conglomerates are exactly what they sound like. They are companies that have many facets to them, and placing them in any one sector would be misleading.

When we refer to the consumer/noncyclic sector, we are speaking of alcohol and tobacco, consumer products, health services, food, retail food, and drugs. These are the names that tend to grow with the economy and are usually sought by investors after the economic improvement has become evident. These names tend to enjoy the sweet spot in the business cycle. They are coincidental winners along with the expansion.

Consumer/cyclic: Here we have one of the broadest sectors in the marketplace. The groups that make this sector are hotel/motel, restaurants, recreation, building resident, retail department stores, publishing, automotive, housewares, textile/apparel, retail, and entertainment. By any standard this sector must be considered a very large area indeed. You can see by the names of the groups that an economic expansion would help all these areas and their stock components simply by a general increase in the business cycle. These groups are coincidental to an economic expansion.

Energy: Here we are dealing with a product that touches every person. The groups are gas pipelines, oil refining and manufacturing, and oil and gas production. Most people that drive cars to work, haul goods over roads or in the air, use any kind of chemical product, or just would like to visit grandma on Sunday are affected by the price of oil.

Financials are the best area to try to get a handle on the interest picture. Why is that so important? The ease and tightness of interest rates has always had a major effect on the stock markets. Perhaps no other news item is as second-guessed and overanalyzed than rates. If the Federal Reserve, which regulates interest rates, were to cut off money to the markets by raising rates sharply, stocks would tumble. Conversely, an easy monetary policy offers a positive atmosphere for stocks. (See Figure 15-2.)

Industrials: This sector is another coincidental market participant. The depth of this area goes to machinery, both light and

FIGURE 15-2

Financials. Drawn by The Chartstore.com.

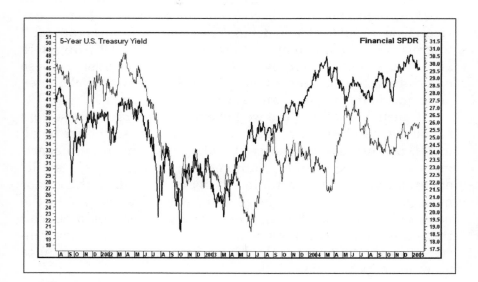

heavy, precision instruments, building materials, business services, environment, electrical equipment, and commercial building. These are the issues that come to life as the view of the economy becomes clear and people wish to join in the advance.

Technology is the hottest part of the new economy and gives
us a clear view of corporate spending plans and improvement
in productivity. Also, this group represents investor's willingness to speculate on the future. A healthy technology group usually says that investors are hopeful about the economy. They
are willing to take a chance on tomorrow.

Transportation: The groups that make up this sector are
railroads, truckers, and airlines, and although the magnitude
of their importance has changed over the years compared to the
days when the Dow Theory was first introduced; they still do
move goods and merchandise across the country. (You cannot
deliver a sofa or a container of milk over the Internet.) Their
activity is an indication of economic activity. (See Figure 15-3.)

FIGURE 15-3

Transportation. Courtesy of MetaStock.

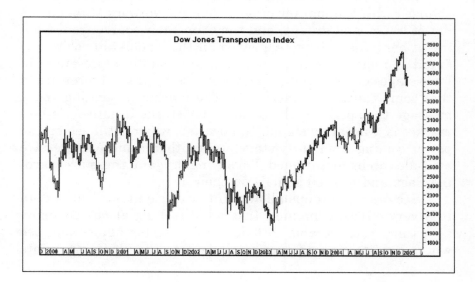

Utilities are conservative investments that are usually played for their yields. From time to time there are sea changes in the group, but as a rule this group is an excellent indicator for interest rates.

GROUP ROTATION

The concept of group rotation is one of the cornerstones of market analysis. It is true that in bull markets the majority of stocks will lift along with the averages. That is after all one definition of a bull market, more stocks going up than going down. But it comes down to how to get the best performance within all of these rising stocks. If we were to run a relative strength comparison of all the sectors to the S&P 500 and run those numbers on a weekly basis, we could be kept up-to-date on where investors and traders were concentrating their efforts and stay in the middle of the action from the beginning of the new bull market. For the investor who is holding long term, you might choose to run the same relative strength charts on a monthly basis. The long-term look at the sectors can give you a much clearer snapshot of a market and a perspective of how far along the market cycle had progressed.

Let's look at the logic for a minute. The leadership role changes with the market progression. As we work through the list of issues and groups, and they run their course from trading at bargains to being expensive, if the leadership position is found one day to be in groups that are usually represented in later stages of a recovery, then we should be at least forewarned that some caution is warranted. The market is sending you a message that perhaps the demand for stocks in late-cycle bull market is a negative signal. If, however, we are still seeing the power coming from early-stage stocks, then a more aggressive attitude can be maintained. I'm saying it again; these are warning flags and not sell signals on their own.

Sectors and groups allow you to cover a great deal of data in a very efficient manner. Instead of looking at one company at a time, you are able to follow a few sector names and see where investors are gathering. It is not difficult to move into the groups that make up those strong sectors. Simply by using the other tools in technical analysis like trend lines and moving averages, etc., you then can move to stock selections. This is not an impossible chore that I am talking about. Your computers will do most of the heavy toil. What is required more than anything else is the discipline to follow the guidelines. Do your top-down analysis, find where in the cycle we are, check your sectors and groups, and finally, use the tools at your disposal for your stock selections.

Chapter 16

Individual Stock Selection

By using the concepts that have been covered in this book, you should begin to understand that stock selection should be based on the combining of tools from a number of different angles. Simply going into a chart book or a computer service that maintains charts is not acceptable as far as performing all that is necessary to succeed in this business. It has always amazed me how people can have a tremendous amount of knowledge about the financial markets and never seem to bring it to bear when it comes to buying stocks. Let's try to make a few general observations that should assist you in winning in any of the financial markets.

Fundamentals and technical analysis are the two main disciplines that will help you attain your goals. We know that fundamentals tell us "what" to buy and that technical analysis tells us "when" to buy it. You need not be a rocket scientist to reach the conclusion that if we had access to an analytically solid research list of fundamental favorable ideas and could cross-reference our technical studies with that list of buys, we would surely increase the odds that our decisions were more likely to be profitable.

Finding a source of solid fundamentals that you can trust is a job you will have to perform yourself. That takes time and requires you to ask the right questions. The scandals of the late

1990s have left many investors with not too kind a feeling towards Wall Street analysts and their firms. The truth is that getting caught up in the greed of the 1990s, which is what you're really looking at, should not completely turn you off on research. A number of prominent people and corporations got blinded to their professions by money and made the whole industry look very bad. A plug for my side—I didn't see any technicians get arrested in that mess.

Your job, as far as the fundamental side is concerned, is before you open an account, ask some questions about backup for your account. Not only is their research available to you, but you should ask for records of past recommendations. Just because someone is called an analyst doesn't prove anything. Another piece of advice is to ask around about the quality and satisfaction of a brokerage house. People are more than pleased to let you know how their experiences have been with a firm. I personally would be very open and willing to tell someone if they were about to make a mistake. There are rating services on the Internet as well that can give a rundown of services offered by the brokerages to the public.

If you are going to go with a discount house or online order taker, there are a few rules that should be followed. The commissions charged for a trade have come down to a point nowadays that allows for very minimal, razor-edge profits. One of the great truths that I learned early on growing up in Brooklyn was "you get nothing for nothing." So expect nothing and keep your eyes open. One thing that these firms offer is a great way of accessing various other tools and the ability to execute an order very efficiently, but in the long run you will need more tools. There is nothing wrong with getting the lowest rates possible and paying for additional research help. In fact you can always change these outside research sources easily enough. But the selection of what is right for you will, in the end, be your personal choice.

All I am suggesting to you is to use both disciplines in your stock selections. It is my belief that the technical side is the most important element in the equation, as it is the action side. Buying correctly and more importantly selling when needed is the function of the technical tools, and they can be the difference between winning or losing money in the market. Of course, I realize that I might get a different opinion on the subject at an AMIR convention, but that's what makes a horse race, now isn't it?

BASIC PLAN OF ATTACK

Simply waking up one morning and deciding to buy a stock is the fastest way I know of throwing your money away. You might hear something at a party, or a news item catches your ear, and all of a sudden you have mastered this business and are ready to enter the wonderful world of investing. Wrong. What you need to do is first take your time and construct an investment plan that fits your goals. You must decide on a few major points right from day one. Some people even commit these plans to paper in a more formal style just to keep a record of what their objectives are in the beginning.

Are you going to be a trader or an investor?
Are you doing this part time or as a career?
How much of my net worth am I going use in the markets?
Which markets am I going to work within?

If you were starting a new business as a corner grocery store, you would first write out a business plan for your banker or a lawyer. Deciding to enter the stock market is no different. You will be risking your money, on a daily basis, alongside the best minds in the world, and none of them are your long lost buddies. The financial markets are hard, fast, tough, mind-boggling, gut wrenching, and the most wonderful business you'll ever get into. But like feeding an alligator, you have to stay alert.

Once the general questions are covered, you might want to decide on your risk tolerance and how much pressure you will accept. They say "Every prize fighter has a plan until he gets hit in the ring. Then it's just a fight." With investing you can take all the correct steps before acting by finding a solid stock with a great technical background in a market that is rising, just to find you've run into a stone wall. Mistakes happen. What you must decide is how much of a loss are you willing to accept before you cut bait and run for cover. You might read many books on the subject, but it seems to me that over the years the 8 percent level for investors and roughly 2–3 percent for short-term futures traders are the usual limits employed. This, of course, is left strictly up to you. Also consider the daily pressure you will be placing on yourself before diving into the market. It is very common for some day traders to have 200 to 300 trades a day in active markets. They will trade for one-fourths and one-halves and feel right at home in doing that type of trading. I'd prefer an easier, softer path to travel. But to each his own. In your decision-making plans, take into consideration the type of markets you want to trade. Commodities and futures trading can be very demanding and require a certain amount of ice in your blood. The more traditional markets like stocks and bonds can offer slower action but are easier on the nerves. Again we have another one of those choices that only you can make.

It is never wise to be too rigid as to your approach to the market. You should stagger your investment styles and set realistic goals for your account. So we must make as part of our financial plan a predetermined percentage of how much capital we will direct for trading and how much for investment. What this does is to set boundaries for your portfolio and stop you from comingling your funds.

Why is that bad, you ask? The main reason is that the only reason a person robs from Peter to pay Paul is to cover up a mistake. There is nothing like averaging down on a position to make a bad trade worse. Hopes and wishes are not market tools. It might even be a good rule for me to say that you must not double down a bad position for at least the first 5 years you're in the business. After that, if you want to throw your money away, it's not my concern. Just remember that the reason the stock is down is not to help you buy at a better price. It's down because no other investor is willing to buy it. Hope might spring eternal, but not in this business. Floundering about in the financial world without a plan is like going to sea without a rudder. Set high expectations for yourself and do your homework. What will happen is that your chances of being successful will be greatly enhanced.

MARKET DIRECTION

Most of the next few items will become apart of your ongoing practice in a relatively short period of time. Regardless of whether you plan to become an analyst or a private investor, you need to develop a working market opinion. At this stage of the process, it need not be formal and detailed but should be constructed on the facts and data you can piece together to answer the question as to market direction.

Rising markets are not the only times you profit. Declining markets where supply side is clearly in control can be just as profitable as any rising market. In fact, it is my experience that long-term declining markets are in many ways easier to navigate. The main reason is that as the bear market signature becomes more dominant, the more the total volume will decrease because traders and investors leave the market in masses. This tends to remove mom and pop from the crowds, which in turn leaves the playing field to the professionals. The counterrallies tend to be less emotional and therefore it is easier to make money. If that sounds a little crass, that because it's meant to be. A long-term market decline occurs when the economic, fundamentals, or geopolitical atmosphere has turned negative. These bear markets are not going to end on a whim. A major low will only occur after the last bull has tossed in the towel and liquidates whatever it has been holding. Once that occurs and time is spent rebuilding, the demand side of the market must regain its footing enough to overpower the sellers. This can only be done with a great deal of power and aggressiveness on the part of the new buyers. The professionals are aware of what is needed to signal a true bottom, so they wait for the novice to throw good money after bad in the hope of a bottom, and then they short right into those hopes. Their misplaced loyalties can be used in your favor. There was an old trader friend of mine who would yell across the trading room to me and say, "The red tickets can make you as much as the black tickets." Because most of us haven't seen a ticket in years, let me explain that the red tickets were the sells orders and the black tickets were buy orders.

I know that someone out there will tell you that you can only make a limited amount of return on the short side (95 percent–100 percent) while the sky is the limit with the long side. *Horsefeathers*. For a statement like that, you would need to be a college professor, a research director, or possibly a lawyer. Their math is correct but the truth is that during a bear market, which is what we are talking about, you really have two choices: A) get out, B) get short. A bear market will in the long run eat you alive and requires a good deal of respect. Some people will tell you to play the long term and hold your positions and average down as time passes. The problem with that advice is, who's to say that the stocks you are holding onto are going to be the leaders of the next major bull advance? You can find yourself holding your positions during a bear market decline just to find that once the general market reverses to the upside, you are holding out-of-favor issues. Recognize what the powers of supply and demand are telling you and go with the flow.

So knowing the correct side of the market to be on is, in my opinion, imperative as your first step in building your portfolio. You can start right now as you are reading this book. I have no idea what the current date is, but it doesn't matter. Stop and ask yourself some overview questions about the current market.

A. Is the Federal Reserve raising or lowering the interest rate? Are rates generally high or low?

B. What is the general outlook for the economy? Your sources can be Wall Street firms—don't get me started on that one. Government statistics are published on the Internet, ad nauseam. Even your own observation from readings papers and magazines like the *Wall Street Journal*, *Barrons* or *Fortune*, etc.

C. Are P/Es historically high or low? You need not be exact on this one. All you need to realize is that a very high peak for P/E has been around 30 times earnings, while the lows reached somewhere below 8 times. In that overview, where is the current market trading?

D. Are earnings in general expected to rise or fall?

Once you have satisfied yourself with these questions, then you need to get to work with some hard-and-fast tools. Fundamentals and technicals can be used in concert with each other, and when they agree we find some very powerful moves indeed. The problem often is that they do not dovetail.

All the questions I have suggested asking yourself are simply to determine the direction of the market. They will not aid you at turning a point; that's what the technical factors do best.

Tops will be made when the fundamentals are at their best, the earnings outlooks are wonderful, and of course the economy is humming along. Under those conditions, if you find that price cannot perform well and supply seems to be taking over and gaining the upper hand, then you must begin to worry. Bottoms in the market are formed out of the worst of the news and the darkest of times. Yet with all the negatives around, you will see prices begin to gain ground despite the fundamental developments. Remember the stock market is a *leading* indicator and responds to investors expectations.

One thing you have to master is the ability to analyze the news and reports against actual price data and volume. Supply and demand will tell you so much more then simply listening to news. The answer is in how the market reacts to the news.

USING TRENDS

Using the techniques described in Chapter 5, you should begin drawing trend lines and channels on both an intermediate- and long-term basis for a few market indexes. My choices would be the Dow Jones Industrials Average in order to keep an eye on the large-cap names that are on the NYSE, and the S&P 500 for a broader view of that same market. Next I'd include the NASDAQ for a look at the more aggressive stocks. As long as we are looking, let's add to the list the Russell 2000 and the Lowry's OCO for good measure. The Lowry indicator has already been discussed as a pure index of operating companies only on the NYSE.

To construct the intermediate trends, you should use weekly charts. Find a recent significant low and extend the line to the next likely higher low. Remember, to be a confirmed trend we need to have three points on the line that are respected. Now do the same method for the longer term by using monthly charts.

Note on Figure 16-1 that the violation of an uptrend and later the presentation of a declining trend line in mid-2003 did not pinpoint the tops or bottoms exactly, but they would have saved an account loads of cash.

What you have done by completing this task is to define the market direction and at the same time zero in on a reward/risk ratio for your opinion. By drawing these lines, you will have set an upper and lower limit in the form of a trend channel. These potential support and resistance areas have set a few targets for you to use.

Think about what I've just asked of you. I have asked you to check the economy and the fundamental from whatever sources you select. After that, however, all I've suggested is to draw 10 lines. Five on the intermediate charts and five lines on the long-term charts. If the news background and the charts are in opposition to each other, then you have a problem. If news is

FIGURE 16-1

Intermediate Trend. Courtesy of MetaStock.

good and the charts are not, then you are looking at a possible negative divergence. If both sides are in agreement, then you go with that direction. From my vantage point, the charts tell the real story.

Technical indicators will lead the way. They are the tools that will give you the advance warning you need to deal with the market. Never get yourself into a situation of trading the market based on long-term data. If you are going to trade, then use trading information for your decisions. Long-term data is for the long-term questions.

After going through that exercise, we need to bring the process down one more step and look at the sector and groups we want to work. We need to look at all the sectors and not just the positive ones.

Many times watching the sectors that are declining can give us just as much information about a market as the positive one can. Spotting a major breakdown in a group like the financial area can be quite enlightening as to the direction of the overall market. Strength in basic material and gold and oils could suggest a hike in inflationary pressures. So don't be myopic towards data. All the numbers are telling us something; we just have to learn to listen.

Let's say that we have determined that we should invest in the market from the long side, as we have looked at the evidence and have said the picture is bright. After analyzing the sectors and groups, we have chosen a particular area. Going to the stock ideas is simple enough, as most computer services have the stocks that make up the various groups. Now that we have narrowed the field quite a bit, we can get down to cases.

The Toolbox

To me, a chart pattern is one of the most important elements that you can rely upon, but by no means does it tell the whole story. It would be like buying a new home. You can pull into the driveway and like the looks of it, but until you find out more information you cannot make a good decision.

Where are the trend lines? Can we determine what the supply/demand picture is suggesting? Look at the tools that *you* have selected, such as volume patterns, moving averages, perhaps an on-balance volume chart, RSI, etc. Check the oscillators and supports and resistance points. Keep your head and don't get caught up in the moment.

Many years ago Mr. Humphrey B. Neal authored a book entitled *The Art of Contrary Thinking*. Mr. Neal has written many books and articles over the years, but I guess this is the book that stuck with me the most, as it speaks to the subject of using your head and not your emotions in the stock market. I'd like to quote a passage from his work that I think fits what I've been trying to convey in my work.

Ten Ways to Lose Money in Wall Street
By
The Market Cynic

1. Put your trust in board room gossip.
2. Believe everything you hear, especially tips.
3. If you don't know, guess.
4. Follow the public.
5. Be impatient.
6. Greedily hang on for the top eighth.
7. Trade on thin margin.
8. Hold to your opinion, right or wrong.
9. Never stay out of the market.
10. Accept small profits and large losses.

These are words to live by. *Not*! But taking the opposite approach will save you more money than you can believe.

All of Mr. Neal's points, funny as they are, can be deadly serious. You will find that once you have your own money at risk in the market, you can start to act a bit foolish and very emotional. It's part of the pressure that goes with the territory. There is an entire field of study called behavioral finance that deals with investor's activities and why we do what we do.

Mr. Neal's ninth point, "Never stay out of the market," is worth an extra comment. You will find there are times when you cannot seem to reach a sensible conclusion based on the facts you have handy. Just know that you do not need to be in the market at all times. Here comes another Brooksism: "When

in doubt, stay out." Many times investors get into trouble because the indicators are neutral but the investors feel they
should be in the market. Do me a favor before you start using
words like "feel." Get a number of years under your belt first.
Guesswork will never help your positions. Know your tools and
your facts and act.

MARKET DIRECTION

Let's say that you have now decided on the path that you feel
best fits your own personality. And just to make life easy, let's
say that you have decided your accounts should be set up with
a split of your capital into 50 percent investing and 50 percent
trading. With that done, we can now proceed to the next logical steps. First, take your time before you jump into the market. Nothing is running away from you, and there is always another day to invest. Never buy or sell something because this
will be your last chance to act. If that were the case, then we
are all in a lot of trouble. Do your homework by studying as
much as you can and make sure your "I's" are dotted and "T's"
are crossed.

In a strong, solid market, you want to stay with the winners, which means you want to be invested in the top relative
strength issues and you want those issues to maintain the patterns and indications that suggest that demand is still actively
moving them ahead. Also, make no mistake about it; a long-
term bear market will take no prisoners.

Chapter 17

Bits and Pieces

One of the purposes of reading a book like this is to gain some insight into the workings of the business from someone who's been around the block a few times. This chapter is dedicated to items that are part of the rich tapestry of the market and must be part of your overall market knowledge. Hopefully you will absorb a few pointers that can help in your education. One of the bits of information that might accomplish this task is to learn about facets of the market that can sometimes fall between the cracks. Many of the items I wish to talk about are very important, but they simply are not broad enough to be considered a stand-alone subject.

I've decided to call them bits and pieces because that's what they are in the day-to-day life of a technical analyst. If I know these points, then I would strongly suggest that you know them as well. You'll find that being the only person in the game that doesn't understand all the rules of engagement will make you the loser. It's something akin to playing video games with my two boys, John and Peter. Only after I lost miserably and the game was over did they tell me the function of the "X" button.

For example, years that end in 9 tend to be strong years. I have absoluly no idea why that is so, but there you are. In the last 10 occasions from 1909 to 1999, there have been only three years showing a loss and one of those years was 1929. This will not make you a millionaire but, like learning Algebra in high school, someday it just might save the day, possibly in 2009, not tomorrow. I don't want you to do a thing with that information except be aware of it.

THE SEASONAL INFLUENCE

Most people, places, and things are affected by seasonal factors. The stock market is no exception, and as part of our working knowledge of the financial markets you should be aware of these pulls and drags. Some of the items are more important than others, but because you never know when one of these might pop up, I chose no particular order for them to appear.

Here's an item that could help in a few of your decisions. Did you know that November, December, and January are considered the best 3-month period to expect positive returns during the year. Additionally, from November to the end of April is the strongest 6-month period in the market. This time span is so pronounced as a strong period that the Street has even made up a saying. The expression is "Sell in May and go away." Of course this is not to say that the rest of the year is negative and that the November to April time is the only period to earn returns. All the statistic is saying is that this time of year has shown to be the most profitable slot for investors. Now you don't want to be out of the market for half the year because of this information. The way this information can help you is when you have a choice to make about one of your positions, is will be helpful in your decision process to know if you have the wind at your back or you are swimming upstream. And remember, it says nothing about the other part of the year being negative.

Commodity Markets

Commodities are all affected by seasonal factors. The agricultural commodities are the most directly affected by the calendar and have seasonal patterns unto themselves. The farmers plant a crop at a certain time each year, and then they must harvest the crop. During the time of harvest, when supply is the greatest, we will see the lows established in many of these commodities. These patterns are determined by weather and consumption, which of course is demand side for commodities, etc. Notice on Figure 17-1, a spot chart of soybeans, how the lows tends to be found in the fourth quarter of the year while the second quarter tends to be a high point. The interesting point is that everything in the commodity markets seems to trade in a rhythm of its own. We even find these patterns in the metals market, which as far as I know doesn't have a planting season, unless you are trying to "salt" a gold mine. I have never traded in metals myself, but I am aware that many metals find a low in the fourth quarter, and around midyear they run into trouble.

Another fine technical analyst, Tony Dwyer, who was studying market cycles for oil, published a report showing that

F I G U R E   1 7 - 1

A Commodity Chart. Drawn by The Chartstore.com.

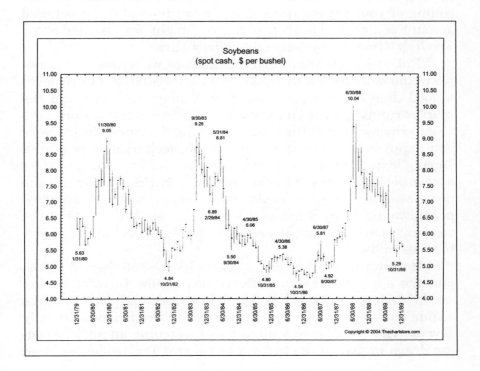

oil has the tendency to underperform in the market between October and February. When we remember that the market is a
discounting function, then selling oil in the wintertime when demand has driven the prices high is nothing more than taking
advantage of the typical cold weather patterns. High demand
will create the best prices for any product. Selling this commodity into potential short-term power on the demand side is
simply taking advantage of a good opportunity. This is normal
behavior, and if you don't believe me ask the shopper in your
family if prices for bathing suits are cheaper at the beginning
of the summer season or around Christmas. Keep in mind that
these thoughts are not meant to pinpoint highs and lows but
rather to give you a sense of your surroundings.

PATTERNS DURING THE DAY

I am not talking about day trading but rather the beat of the
day's trading that can sometimes be a great deal of help in your
timing of your transactions. For a more in-depth and detailed
account of a normal day's trading, you might wish to read *Stock
Trader's Almanac* by Yale and Jeffrey Hirsh.

Did you know that during periods of weakness, for example in the mid-1960s and most of the 1970s, Mondays were never
a good time for new purchases and Fridays seldom found the
market running away on the upside. Traders and investors were
so gun shy because of the constant selling that most people were
just happy to go home at the end of the week with no positions.
During lean times there aren't many people that want to start
a new position going into the weekend on Friday because the
news over the weekend could easily be negative. On Monday,
people would delay purchases waiting to see the effects of the
weekend news. If things were fairly stable we would see opportunities midweek.

However, in ripping bull markets like the 1980s and 1990s,
just the opposite was true. Every day a new wave of buying
would rush into the market and investors and traders alike
couldn't get enough. When Friday rolled around, we actually
saw activity build. It was almost like watching an addict hord-
ing drugs in fear of not getting any more. The traders wanted

to take stocks home over the weekend in the anticipations that good news would drive their stocks higher on Monday.

When you trade, look for the current pattern of the tape and learn from it. If expectations are bullish Fridays and Mondays, hold little to fear. If traders are cautious, there is no reason to buy on the close of the week. You most likely can buy it cheaper on Monday.

Another simple point but semi-important is that the amateur trades during the first and the last half hours of the day, while the professionals trade during the session. Pros would rather get a look at the first half hour at least before committing themselves. If you are in a situation where you must jump in on the opening or make a move at the close, you are probably dealing with high emotions, and the odds are you are going to be reacting to events instead of making a clear-headed decision.

The Noon Balloon

Buying stocks at noon before you go out to lunch is not a wise thing to do. The lunch hour, when people are typically away from their desks for an hour or so, allows the tape to sometimes be influenced by a small crowd. A market, however, that is trading on a limited amount of volume can be manipulated. Most of the professional traders know this, and they tend to stay away unless they can take advantage of a dip or a rally. Most of the time, moves during lunch are set right again after 2:00 o'clock. Again, this is not in granite, but it pays to know where the lion traps are set before you go into the jungle.

End-of-the-Day Orders

Once you have completed your analysis and you are convinced that you have reached the correct conclusion, then be prepared to act. There are many people who delay a sale or a purchase to a point that nothing gets done on a timely basis. Reaching a conclusion that you should be a seller or a buyer is not going to become "more correct" by waiting until the next day. If you are in a strong market, there is little reason to wait for the morning, and if you need to sell, surely waiting will only make matters worse. If there is action to be taken and you have done your homework, then you must move. Being frozen in the headlights will only get you run over in the end.

HOLIDAY PATTERNS
Thanksgiving

Thanksgiving is an interesting time. We have a few things going our way on this holiday. Most importantly, the market is in the early stages of the best 3-month and 6-month period for the market. The seasonal cycle should be the strongest at that point. Also, many feel it's the beginning of the holidays in this country and we tend to lighten up a bit and feel somewhat better. I think it might be true. Who knows? But that's as good a reason as some. What is known is that between Tuesday and the following Monday, the market has a better than three-to-one chance of trading higher in that span. Is that a guarantee in itself of profits? No. But if you are in the middle of a trade and you know that a seasonal effect is going to hurt or help you, it sometimes is just enough added information to save the day.

Santa Claus

Christmas time has a seasonal flavor to it also. A rally is usually seen right after Christmas and will last about two days into January. Why? It could be that traders and trading desks are evening up their books for the accounting departments, or perhaps no one really is willing to initiate new positions until the new year starts and we can see a clearer picture. Christmas week is a great time to catch up with paperwork for year end and to formalize your plan of action going into the next year. It also could be that many players are away from the market, home for the holidays as it were, and the accounts that are active don't want to be drawn into a market that is thin. Many times if the closing year was powerful, people will delay selling for tax reasons. For me, I'll say it's the spirit of Christmas and be done with it.

January Barometer

This piece of folklore has been around forever. It has changed a few times since I've been around, but what I know calls for the action in the S&P 500 over the first 5 days of the year to reflect the general direction of the market for the year. The thinking behind this barometer it is clear enough. If we come into the new year with a sour tone and are selling stocks or at least not willing to risk our capital, then there might be real troubles that the investing public is worried about and the market action is sending us a warning sign.

On the other hand, if the new year brings us a healthy rally and a positive outlook on the part of the investors and traders, then the outlook just might be constructive for the year. I have found that most of the power in this barometer is spent by about March or so. But once we get into the trading year, talk of it disappears, especially if it was lower.

Mr. Kenneth Ward was a true pioneer in technical analysis and a good friend to me. When I met him for the first time he was 80 years old and had been on Wall Street for 50 years as a technical analyst. I believe I was about 24 years old, which meant that I hung on every word he said. I remember one time he told me that he kept seasonal factors in the back of his mind, and when the holidays would approach he would dust them off and use them as needed. He was a wise man. These factors never made the market decision but were a part of the background that aided him in reaching an opinion.

FACTOIDS

1. Gaps don't have to be filled. The point is that most gaps on charts are filled rather quickly. But there is no hard-and-fast rule that says all gaps must be filled. Consider what we are looking at when a gap develops on a chart. There has been an event that has caused a gap in price to be created because of fear or high expectations. The sellers or buyers were so motivated as to move a stock or a market beyond a recent high or low. On breakouts or breakdowns or

during a power thrust move at the start of a new intermediate or long-term move, gaps can occur and not be filled. So when we look at a gap, study it from the current vantage point and not by an old-fashioned rule.

2. A very famous technical analyst, Edson Gould, once wrote that every year that ended in 5 since 1885 has shown a gain in the stock market. He wrote that in the 1960s. Since then the record has kept the faith, showing gains in 1965, 1975, 1985, and 1995 respectively. Now as of 2005, I have no idea what will happen because there has never been a reason for the "5" effect in the first place. It's just one of those factoids you should at least be aware of.

3. You will hear a good bit of talk about summer rallies, especially as we go into the summer months. Half the time I think this concept came out of someone's sales office to stimulate business. From time to time you do see a summer rally, but then again you will see rallies in the market in any season of the year. From my vantage point, you can't count on them and they are so much smoke and mirrors. You will be better served by simply using your technical tools to spot rallies, then waiting for a summer rally to begin. This is a part of Wall Street folklore that can be retired as far as I'm concerned.

4. Never believe a rumor but always check it out. How do I check it out, you ask? The one thing I keep coming back to again and again is the idea of the forces of supply and demand. When you get a rumor, and trust me you will, check out the chart. If in fact the chart is showing the correct action given the news you have, then you might be onto something. Please do me a favor. Trust me when I say you are not the *first* person to receive this wonderful rumor. The odds of your picking up something before everyone else are nil. But you can come across a good story, and if it is true you'll see it manifested in the chart

numbers. Prices will be up and volume will be increasing, or a bad-news rumor will yield a bad-news chart.

5. If you elect to purchase your data from a vendor rather than use the standard data from a chart service, then make sure you buy high-quality information. You will have to pay more for the cleaner data, but it is well worth the expense. If you buy inferior data, you will spend most of your time cleaning up errors and not enough time investing.

6. In the beginning of a major up market cycle, it is often wiser for the mutual fund buyers to put their money with an actively managed fund. You want a portfolio manager that can get into the best and fastest-moving areas of the market and keep your money moving aggressively to take advantage of a new bull phase. As the market matures and we see signs of the bull aging, a more conservative approach might be most desired. Therefore, an index fund usually would be a better play. As a rule of thumb, we could look at a normal bull market cycle to be approximately 4 to 4-½ years long. Usually, it will have the shape of 3 years on the upside and 1 year on the downside. From a ballpark standpoint, after about 3 years with an active manager, I'd say thank you very much and move your capital to an index fund for protection.

7. Gold stocks often lead the price action of gold bullion. Now to me this really doesn't make a lot of sense to have the tail wagging the dog, but that's a fact. It might be that the stocks are much easier to influence because of the liquidity factor. The gold bullion market is very large. Perhaps gold stocks are easier to trade and therefore might be more sensitive to the news that affects the bullion market. That you will find is the way of things in the commodity markets. (See Figure 7-2.)

8. Every day you will have the chance to buy anything you want. Stay with the winners and don't try to pick

F I G U R E   1 7 - 2

Bullion versus Gold. Drawn by The Chartstore.com.

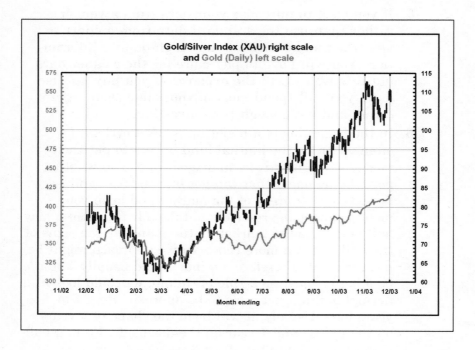

bottoms. If you are going to sell short a stock, look for your selections in the weak names.

Many times a trader will spot a top in the general market and select the most powerful stock in that market because it is up the most. In an attempt to short a high-priced stock in the hopes that it will fall apart in a pullback, you have made your job twice as hard. Not only must you be correct on the market opinion, but also now you want the strength of a powerful stock in the market to fall apart. If the market does decline, then it will be the weak stocks that fall apart, not the good ones.

9. Know where your supports and resistances points are on your chart, and violations of support should be

sold. If an upside resistance is exceeded, raise your stop orders to limit your downside exposure.

10. Many times when you are in the heat of the day, you can find yourself with a mistake on your hands. Sometimes we'll want to buy a stock and hit the sell button in error or perhaps we wanted to buy 1000 shares and managed to put one too many zeros in the order entry machine, and we wind up with 10,000 shares. Cover your mistakes quickly. Do not linger or think they will work themselves out to your favor. I guess they could possibly benefit you, but the odds are against you. Take your lumps and learn to be careful.

11. Stock tips on a free chat boardroom are worth what you paid for them.

12. Dave Steckler, technician and friend, mentioned a very good point to me. That fund manager might have a herd mentality but when they all jump into the pool at the same time, the water really does rise. In other words, sometimes by following the herd you can avoid being trampled.

13. Never meet a margin call. Bottom line is that you're trying to fill up a black hole that might not have a bottom. To paraphrase an old timer from Savannah, Georgia, by meeting a margin call all you wind up doing is making a bigger mess.

I MISS THE NOISE

One of my early jobs on Wall Street was to cut out earning reports from the *Wall Street Journal* for the fundamental analyst. I, along with three other junior analysts, would sit in the tape room with a board on my lap reading the newspapers. At the same time there was a very noisy ticker tape circulating around our long work table. Each of us would listen to the tape for activity, and when the noise increased we would stop what we were doing and start watching the tape for activity. The other part of our job was to circle printed orders on 5000

shares or more on that paper ticker tape. We were all assigned
different-colored pens; blue for glamour stocks, red for drugs,
etc., and different groups to watch. Our markings were distinguished by the color. This paper ticker tape would end up
in the wastepaper can at the end of the table. After some time,
10 minutes or so, our boss would come out, take his glasses
off, (he was blind without them), and read the discarded ticket
tape *by color*, then he would broadcast his intraday stock market report to the salesmen.

Well, all that is long gone, but the idea of following the
action is not. We no longer have the noise to get our attention, but we do have all the activity tools and more to turn
our heads. One of the characteristics of a stock you select
must be that there is sufficient daily volume to allow you an
easy entrance and exit. A classic mistake that many people
make is to buy into a stock with good fundamentals in a solid
group with a great-looking chart pattern, but fail to keep an
eye on the volume. Buying a stock that trades by appoint-
ment only can kill you. The place that we get into trouble the
most is when the secondary issues are in the leadership position in the stock market. The small stocks are running and
the power is across the board because that's how those names
run. They usually run in a herd rather than a small pack. Either the secondary issues are hot or they are not. After the
secondary area has had its advance, we usually will see the
microcaps take the leadership. Here the explanation is a good
deal easier. We have mentioned a number of times that the
market is subject to fear and greed. In this example I have
laid out, the small-cap issues had their normal advance and
investors hopefully made solid gains. Once that run starts to
falter and a normal correction begins, the traders simply will
not stop and take their gains and move to the sidelines. Typically, we see greed take over and common sense goes out the
window. Not only will they beat that horse to death, but they
will pick it up and carry it for a mile or two. When it's over,
we often find traders holding 10,000 shares of a stock when
under normal conditions, traders only trade about 1000
shares a day. This is called a "to whom market," meaning you
ask your broker to sell your stock, and the broker answers:
"To whom?"

Bottom line—stay in the pack. I have heard it said that the most money traders make is found in the outliers, but that's where the biggest mistakes are made also. The point is make sure the stock you are buying has enough liquidity on a daily basis to allow you a fair entry point and a fair exit. In low-volume issues, you can wind up paying much more for your executions.

PRESIDENTIAL CYCLE

We have already covered this point, but I'll repeat the high points. The first and second years of a presidential term usually are less profitable then the last two years. I suspect a skeptic would say that in an attempt to get reelected, policies are more benign going into election time. If you are going to give the voters bad news, do it earlier so they have time to forget. (See Figure 17-3.)

FIGURE 17-3

Presidential Cycles. Drawn by The Chartstore.com.

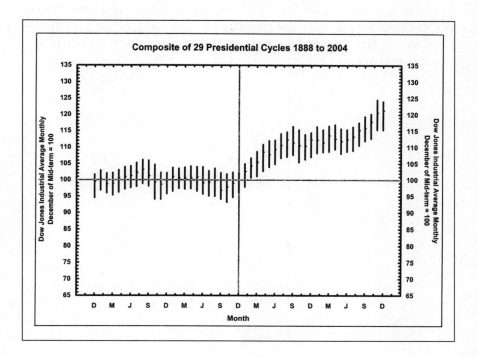

CONCLUSION

I would say that I have only begun to write down all the little sayings that this business has to offer. Many of them I couldn't start to figure out how I could get them past the censors, but you will absorb them as you put time into the field. These signposts are found in the market in a hundred formats. Most of them are common sense. Some have to do with the divergences between what should be happening and what is actually happening. Some are statistical events that have reoccurred over many years. All are part and parcel of our business and belong, if not in the mainstream of technical analysis, then at least as an adjunct to it. The reason is that these forces can and will affect our chart patterns, and we should be prepared to act accordingly. It is also wise to know the past performances in the markets. Try to get a sense of the history of the stock markets and all the other areas. The interrelationship of all the differing facets comes together to make up the financial markets. This is not a static business that you are entering, but one that is always moving, active, and vying for position in order to attract investor's money. The forces of supply and demand are always the bottom line to any chart pattern that we look at and interpret. All of the forces that pull at these charts are a part of the overall picture.

Chapter 18

Conclusion

There is plenty of good advice that I can give you, but none is as valuable as use your common sense. Trust in your data and indicators and never take you eyes off the supply-and-demand equation.

You must determine for yourselves your plan of attack when it comes to investing. When I use the word attack, I do so with the full understanding of the word because many of the tools that we follow have the characteristics of warring armies facing each other. Like a general trying to plan the strategy before the battle, you must answer the question of where you will be most at ease and with what tools you will fight the battle. It is paramount that you understand your own personality to work out what you are suited for in the marketplace. Perhaps you feel most at home as a short-term equity trader, or you might prefer to take an investor's approach to the market. Remember, just because I talk about equities, that is by far not the only arena open to you. The technical concepts we have covered work in all the markets, and they transfer easily between the different areas, which allows you the freedom of choice. The United States and many of the international markets have matured greatly over the last few decades. As a result, opportunities that were never available before to new investors now offer major potential. Due to the accessibility of international data and high-speed computers, markets such as currencies trading and even international index trading can be at your fingertips. The ETF markets and products like the Rydex funds offer easy access to sector and group investing, as well as entry into foreign markets. It was not all that long ago that trying to make a trade in Belgium or Paris would take you most of your day, and you would need to use a very specialized trading firm to get the trade executed. Today it's come down to a few keystrokes. The trading is every bit as difficult as it has ever been, maybe harder, but your entry into other areas is relatively simple. So, my friends, the door is open wide to you, and in order to prosper, the basic rules that I have tried to set down must be learned.

SPREADING YOURSELF TOO THIN

The availability of products can be a double-edged sword, as you can find yourself involved in too many areas that trade differently from one another. Being a Jack-of-all-trades and the master of none might be good for some professions, but in this one you should know your limitations. For a person who is by nature an investor to try to become a day trader is like asking a freshwater fish to swim in the ocean. So take your time in choosing your line of work.

Once you have decided on an area, you will have to select the proper tools to attain your goals. Before you take your first step into the market, you should work with all the technical indicators and techniques with paper trades. Make many of the easy mistakes on paper, but give the tools a chance. The best way to choose your tools is to try all of them, at least in the beginning. There is no substitute for experience, and there is no better way to learn than by "doing."

Trust me when I tell you that once you buy an ETF or a bond or perhaps a currency index and you have your own money at risk, you will pay very close attention to the charts and supply/demand patterns.

HAVE AN OVERVIEW

The next step is to build a scenario for yourself, based on fact and figures that you have gleaned from the indicators and the indexes you are following. Do not start your market outlook based on rumors, hearsay, or some new piece of software you just bought.

I could not operate if I came in the office each day without a general overview. There are plenty of folks who never care about a market opinion or where we are in the grand scheme of things, but frankly I can't work that way. I would strongly suggest that you develop a general market outlook to act as a road map. I am not speaking about some iron-clad, inflexible dogma that must be followed, but rather a general plan of action.

I'll give you an example of what can happen. During a very serious bear trend, it serves little purpose to ignore the falling prices because you would like to be bullish. Many times an investor will hold a falling position in the hope that the next support level will prove to be the bottom. All you wind up doing is pretending to yourself that a bottom is near and you wind up in a deeper hole. The truth is that because of the general market retreat, almost nothing is going to hold, and all you do is continue to let your losses run. You must factor the general market behavior into your daily work. Many short-term traders have been turned into investors because they held on to losing positions too long. This is the time they usually learn the famous trader's prayer, "Lord get me even and I'll never do it again."

Let me commit some blasphemy. Market opinions are a dime a dozen. So be prepared to let them go and change your mind many, many times. The person who has a market opinion that he will not alter is usually called "the victim."

USE ANY AND ALL ADVANTAGES

One great advantage that I have over many investors is that I know lots of very good people in the financial markets. I am lucky to be one of the founders and a member of the International Federation of Technical Analysts and a member of the (STA) Society of Technical Analysts (UK), as well as a founding member of both the Market Technicians Association (MTA) and the American Association of Professional Technical Analysts (AAPTA). I helped start some of those groups and was privileged to be accepted in others, but I had to make the effort to join the flow of information that is out there. I have met and know many technicians around the globe, and a majority of them have no problem speaking to each other and talking about the market and swapping outlooks. As time passes you to will come to trust some other people's opinion and learn how to add and subtract from your own. This comes only with trial and error, but you to should build a cadre of people you can talk to about the business or an idea about an indicator. Take the time to become part of the technical community and become active. In the long run it will all pay off.

In one of the earlier chapters I told you that I am a top-down analyst. I work most comfortably in the equity markets, and I like to have the feeling that I understand a high percentage of forces that are in play in the current market. You will never totally know everything affecting your investments, so don't worry about it. What you have to worry about is changing your mind too many times. You cannot decide to be a long-term investor one day and then become a trader the next. What will happen is that you will wind up accepting short-term profits and missing out on the long-term run, or worse yet you'll trade out at a loss because you were frightened and then watch your stock run. Take a good, hard look at the sudden reaction in the REIT stocks early in 2004 on a hint that interest rates would rise. Many of the holders of those stocks were traditionally long-term investors interested in yield and price appreciation. The way the investing public reacted to news was amazing, especially when in less than one month they were back on track. Nothing is wrong with either approach, but trying to be both is very difficult. (See Figure 18-1.)

My way of drilling down through the mountain of statistics and numbers is to follow from the market overview down to the next level of importance, the sectors. In my case I look at the market as a compilation of 10 sectors. In any given market cycle, these sectors will take on different roles at differing stages of a market move. We sometimes will have the financials leading the rally. This can encompass REITs, major banks, regional banks, finance, brokers, and insurance companies. In later stages of an advance, we might see metals and

FIGURE 18-1

REITs. Courtesy of MetaStock.

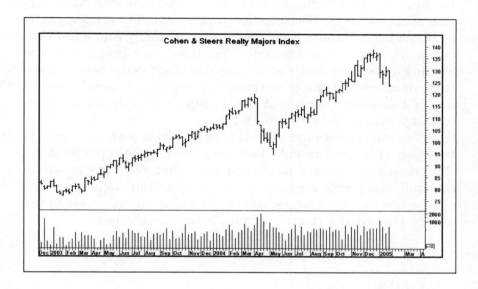

energy issues along with gold and other precious metals taking on the leadership. We can look at all the sectors' rankings
by simply using a relative strength rating for all 10 groups.
You can either rank the sectors against a base like the Standard & Poor's 500, which is the major index that most institutions use as their benchmark, or you can rank the sectors
against themselves.

There is no such thing as a single investment area or stock
that you can rely on forever. I run into people all the time who
will start a conversation with me saying that they only buy—
then they go into a tirade about their approach. I would never
advise someone to find one sector and stay with it alone. Diversification is always the way to go. You can always overweight
a particular idea if you have a mind to, but putting all your eggs
in one basket can turn messy in this business. What we aspire
to, however, is a choice from the top three or four sectors so we
can start to narrow down our search.

Groups

Now that you have three of the top sectors to select from, you might find yourself with as many as 10 groups within those sectors to choose from. The selection process should continue to the next level. From those groups we can most likely find a few that can be removed almost at once: perhaps some group that has already topped out and is on its way down but still strong enough to be in a positive group, perhaps a group that is dominated by one or two large issues and really doesn't give us a true reading for a group. (See Figure 18-2.)

You still might have dozens of names from just a few groups that you still need to cull down to a manageable portfolio. In the process you have a market opinion that you have based on the indicators and analysis of the charts. You then rank and choose the top few sectors, and from there you go down to the groups that fit the relative strength pattern the best.

FIGURE   18 - 2

Semiconductors. Courtesy of MetaStock.

Split Path

At this point you will run into two points of view concerning your next choice. The next step of actually buying an individual issue can start a debate that's worse than politics or religion. There are studies that support both sides of the question, and the people that wrote all the studies are great minds with wonderful credentials that can tell you whatever you want to hear. I believe the old story is that there are three forms of information: lies, damn lies, and statistics. The problem is that on a fundamental or technical basis, a portfolio can underperform for any number of reasons, and it sometimes makes it hard to keep ahead of the stock market. As an example, most institutional accounts fail to keep up with the S&P 500.

In the case of retail accounts, it gets even harder to control performance. Many people will buy a stock, and the minute their money is at risk they forget about every rule they have learned and simply hold a stock until they have a profit. Retail investors will hold onto a declining stock as if it were a life raft in the belief that, like Lazarus, it will return from the dead. In some cases it would take an act of God to get some stocks rising again. Holding on to weak and declining stocks is very seldom a smart idea.

There are many examples of investors taking all the correct steps and coming up short in the profit column. You can call the market correctly and find the correct sector. Then go to the right group and flow down to a stock that fits everything you know and still lose money. This is part of the game and sometimes is simply unavoidable. On this point I am speaking about fundamentals or technical. The news can come in almost any form and can and will catch you flat-footed. The point is you have a choice of either standing there like a deer in the headlights, or you can utilize the tools at your fingertips.

ETFs

Some people prefer buying derivative products instead of stocks. So people have begun looking towards products like ETFs (Exchange Traded Funds) or tradable fund providers like Rydex or

Pro funds that can allow you to purchase a group or an index, either foreign or domestic, just like you would a common stock. Here you have the protection of buying one instrument that incorporates many issues in the one fund. Therefore, you get the protection of diversification. With this product, like most derivatives, all the techniques and rules that we have been talking about still apply.

The other school of thought is that buying a family of related issues in a basket, you will get the bad along with the good, and unless there is a huge move in the market, your performance will be watered down. This is true to a degree, for you will lose a step or two in a strong trending market. In a powerful move, many times the active manager will do quite well compared to an index fund. But as long as you realize that your risk goes up along with your rewards, with an active management approach, things should be all right.

Do I have a preference? Yes, I believe in diversification in my own portfolio. I am spread out in different products and will remain that way as long as I'm satisfied with the results. But I will say I have a majority of my own money in my own hands. I believe that market opinions can be mastered as long as you don't get yourself into the old game of predicting exact numbers and dates. And never fall in love with yours or anyone else's opinion. At best it's a fool's game. You will be able to have an overview based on facts about supply and demand and how that is affecting your indicators. I believe that using your tools that we have laid out, you can reach a sensible conclusion. Discipline is always going to be the key. Here's your last Brooksism: "Knowing a rule and then ignoring it is a waste of time."

Stocks

If you have decided to actively work your own selections, then there are a number of items we should reexamine. The main rule is to be disciplined with what you have learned. So we have a list of issues and the need to whittle the list down.

Use the steps we have covered, and you can quickly weed out the poor stocks. Remove issues that are losing forward momentum and are showing signs of aging. You don't need to be chasing after stocks that are overbought and are forcing you to pay too much to get a position. There is no room in your portfolio for stocks that have violated supports or a trend line. After all that work, to wind up buying a stock that is telling you that the bears are in control does not make any sense at all.

Let's say you have finally narrowed down your stock selection to five issues. You have a few differing groups and after reaching a decision about the market direction, you are ready to go to work.

Run your charts and check where the support and resistances points are found. By using the latest closing price, you will have an idea of your reward/risk ratio. You want to try to buy these stocks near the support zones to get the best reward/risk ratio possible.

Make sure that all of your trend lines are drawn, and preset in your head where you will cut bait and take your loss. You know, it's a funny thing, but nobody has to be told about where you are willing to accept profits, but we all seem to have trouble with those losses. Do not let them get away from you.

I always find it helpful to know where I am in the bigger picture. I want to know about the long-term cycles and the season that I trading. These items might not affect your trading initially, but they could be a factor during the life of the trade.

Remember, if we keep our eyes on financial news and have a general feel for the economy and the overall fundamental background, then our real work boils down to following the supply-and-demand picture. With that information firmly in our grasp, we can successfully prosper in the stock market.

Index

Note: Boldface numbers indicate illustrations.

John C. Brooks is the senior vice president and senior analyst for Lowry's Reports, Inc. During his 40-plus years as a technical analyst, he cofounded the Market Technicians Association and served as one of its past presidents. Brooks was also cofounder of the International Federation of Technical Analysts (IFTA), which today includes 25 nations and 7000 members worldwide. He is currently on the Board of Directors of the American Association of Professional Technical Analysts (AAPTA). He received one of the first Chartered Market Technicians (CMTs) in the United States.